The Imagined Island

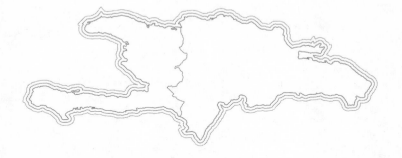

HISTORY, IDENTITY, & UTOPIA IN HISPANIOLA

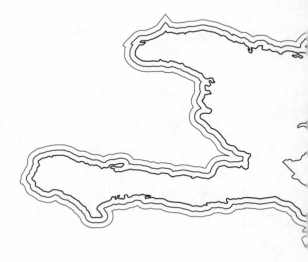

A book in the series

Latin America in Translation /

en Traducción / em Tradução

Sponsored by the Consortium in Latin American Studies

at the University of North Carolina at Chapel Hill and

Duke University

The Imagined Island

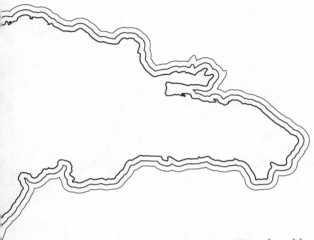

PEDRO L. SAN MIGUEL Translated by Jane Ramírez

The University of North Carolina Press Chapel Hill

Manufactured in the United States of America
Originally published in Spanish with the title
*La isla imaginada: Historia, identidad y utopía en
La Española,* © 1997 Editorial Isla Negra and
Ediciones Librería La Trinitaria.

Set in Scala type by Keystone Typesetting, Inc.

Translation of the books in the series Latin America in Translation /
en Traducción / em Tradução, a collaboration between the Consortium
in Latin American Studies at the University of North Carolina at Chapel Hill
and Duke University and the university presses of the University of North
Carolina and Duke, is supported by a grant from the Andrew W. Mellon
Foundation.

The paper in this book meets the guidelines for permanence and
durability of the Committee on Production Guidelines for Book Longevity
of the Council on Library Resources.

Library of Congress Cataloging-in-Publication Data
San Miguel, Pedro Luis.
[Isla imaginada. English]
The imagined island : history, identity, and utopia in Hispaniola / Pedro L.
San Miguel ; translated by Jane Ramírez.
    p. cm. — (Latin America in translation/en traducción/em tradução)
Includes bibliographical references and index.
ISBN 0-8078-2964-1 (cloth : alk. paper)
ISBN 0-8078-5627-4 (pbk. : alk. paper)
1. Dominican Republic—Historiography. 2. Haiti—Historiography.
3. Haiti—Foreign public opinion, Dominican. 4. Intellectuals—Dominican
Republic—Attitudes. 5. Public opinion—Dominican Republic.
6. Hispaniola—Race relations. 7. Bosch, Juan, 1909– 8. Politics and
literature. 9. Literature and history. I. Title. II. Series.
F1937.5.S2613   2005
972.93′072′2—dc22   2005006283

cloth   09 08 07 06 05   5 4 3 2 1
paper   09 08 07 06 05   5 4 3 2 1

To

Rafael Emilio Yunén,

Roberto Cassá, and

Orlando Inoa,

for many years of

teaching me other

geography and

other history

Identity and utopia are two dimensions of the same problem.

Alberto Flores-Galindo, Buscando un inca *(Mexico City, 1993)*

To respect the wholeness of the past means to leave it open to inquiry, to refuse to neutralize the contingencies of history by transforming them into the safe zone of myth.

David K. Herzberger, Narrating the Past *(Durham, 1995)*

One cannot expect to possess knowledge which does not change one. Once one knows, then one is acting upon that knowledge, whether it is to withhold the knowledge from those who would also be changed, or to give it to them.

Anne Rice, Taltos *(New York, 1995)*

We can only know the actual by contrasting it with or likening it to the imaginable.

Hayden White, Tropics of Discourse *(Baltimore, 1986)*

We look at ourselves in the mirrors of our origins . . . and we understand that every discovery is a desire, and every desire, a need. We invent what we discover; we discover what we imagine.

Carlos Fuentes, Valiente mundo nuevo *(Mexico City, 1992)*

CONTENTS

Preface ix

Introduction: A Kind of Sacred Writing 1

The Imagined Colony:

    Historical Visions of Colonial Santo Domingo 8

Racial Discourse and National Identity:

    Haiti in the Dominican Imaginary 35

The Island of Forking Paths:

    Jean Price-Mars and the History of Hispaniola 67

Storytelling the Nation:

    Memory, History, and Narration in Juan Bosch 98

Notes 133

Index 181

PREFACE

Writing the preface for the English translation of *La isla imaginada: Historia, identidad y utopía en La Española* (San Juan and Santo Domingo: Editorial Isla Negra and Ediciones Librería La Trinitaria, 1997) seems amazing to me. Several years have passed since the University of North Carolina Press decided to include this book in its Latin America in Translation series. On occasion I even thought the publication project was the chimera of a delusional mind—mine, of course. But luckily this was not the case, and after a prolonged wait, *La isla imaginada* has been transformed into *The Imagined Island*. This metamorphosis has been possible thanks to the endeavors of people to whom I would like to express my appreciation.

Above all, I would like to thank Jane Ramírez. I am fully aware of the hard work and determination she put into translating this book. I hope she is aware of my profound gratitude for her outstanding work. Likewise, I would like to thank Elaine Maisner at the University of North Carolina Press for her help during all these years. I am also indebted to Carlos Roberto Gómez of Editorial Isla Negra and to Virtudes Uribe and Juan Báez of Librería La Trinitaria for their endorsement of the publication of the Spanish version of this work.

In the preface to the Spanish edition, I mentioned numerous friends and colleagues who encouraged and benefited me with their knowledge and acumen. To mention them all here would intimidate the reader. But I feel obliged to name those who have continued to support me since the original publication of *La isla imaginada*. In Puerto Rico, Eugenio García-Cuevas, Silvia Álvarez-Curbelo, Carlos Pabón, Humberto García-Muñíz, Fernando Picó, Walter Bonilla, Carlos Altagracia, Jorge Lizardi, Manuel Rodríguez, Alfredo Torres, and the whole gang of Librería La Tertulia—the "cervantinos" and the "serpentinos"—have always encouraged me. In the Dominican Republic, Roberto Cassá, Emilio Cordero-

Michel, Raymundo González, and Mu-Kien A. Sang continue to trust my work—although they sometimes might disagree with it. I likewise cherish their enduring friendship. Elsewhere Félix Matos-Rodríguez, Francisco Scarano, César Salgado, and Jorge Ibarra have been friends and enthusiastic readers of my work. I would like to make special mention of Harry Hoetink, hoping that these words reach him as a deeply felt tribute to his outstanding contribution to Dominican and Caribbean studies.

The preface to the Spanish edition was "signed" in Río Piedras, Puerto Rico, during the Christmas holidays of 1996. Several things have changed in my life since then. Laura Muñoz entered my life from a land far from the Caribbean. Since then, in the Caribbean, Mexico, and elsewhere she has become part of my imaginary geographies, a necessary element of my own personal utopia.

Pedro L. San Miguel
Río Piedras, Puerto Rico/Tepepan, Mexico City
February 2005

The Imagined Island

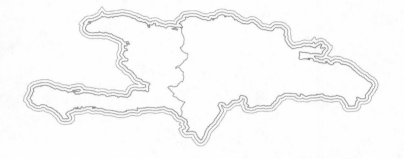

Introduction

A Kind of Sacred Writing

*What we have before us is an attempt to write not a factual history,
but rather a sacred one, a narrative in which life must confirm Scripture.*

   Raúl Dorra, Profeta sin honra *(Mexico City, 1994)*

*History is probably our myth. It combines what can be thought, the
"thinkable," and the origin, in conformity with the way in which a society
can understand its own working.*

   Michel de Certeau, The Writing of History *(New York, 1988)*

The twentieth century was a cornucopia of stories, a kaleido-
scope of interpretations. The very abundance of these narratives
seems to contribute to those "fin de siècle terrors" that today be-
leaguer even the most venerable interpretations.[1] And yet certain
historical narratives continue to permeate our collective life, like
stubborn stains that won't wash out. The trappings may be academic or profane, but the "truths" appear eternal, immune to the
ravages of time. In the Dominican Republic this lore, these narratives, stand majestically in the landscape, as much a part of the
scenery as the Torre del Homenaje, the Cathedral, and the Alcazar
de Colón. Their very antiquity is prestige enough; they need not
demonstrate their validity by modern standards. Lent authority by
the stature of their advocates, they have become dogma. Those who
hold to them, in "holding the threads of the narrative, preserving
the development of the plot," help justify the tradition.[2] Thus can-
onized, the content and discursive structures of these narratives

are exempt from verification. Ensconced in the sphere of myth, they have become a sort of sacred history.

Michel de Certeau has emphasized the great debt that modern historiography owes to religious discourse. Gradually, during the seventeenth and eighteenth centuries, *raison d'état* usurped religion's function of setting standards of behavior. The prince replaced God as the subject of history; profane history, consisting almost exclusively of the chronicles of the powerful, unseated divine history. Lèse-majesté was punished as severely as blasphemy and ultimately replaced it as the unpardonable sin.[3] The Enlightenment marked the culmination of the secularization of learning and saw the emergence of a new paradigm for knowledge, deriving from the growing prestige of the natural sciences. According to the scientific paradigm, it is possible "to know the world as it really is" through the rigorous application of a "method."[4] With "scientific method," the weight of truth rested on "facts": phenomena that could be measured, quantified, verified. Truth would be revealed not by sacred texts or by archangels or prophets but by "facts," carefully sifted through the "method."

Due to the success of the natural sciences—a success rendered palpable by a torrent of amazing discoveries and portentous inventions—scientific precepts colored all disciplines throughout the nineteenth century. History, too, reached for the stars: the new arrival, this dubious Cinderella wanted to go to the ball. History's method, modeled after that of the natural sciences, sought the "facts." As in the scientific paradigm, its ultimate purpose was to establish the "laws" or patterns that governed the evolution of human societies. This was a goal on which authors such as Marx and Comte could agree, despite their enormous differences. Believing blindly and unshakably in the idea of "progress"—although that, of course, meant different things to different people—they sought knowledge that would bring about the culmination of history. Some, like Hegel and Ranke, so dissimilar in other respects, saw this culmination as coming through the nation-State; others, through the universalization of the "positive spirit," the élan vital of the new technological and scientific society; still others, through overcoming the misery and oppression perpetrated by class society and the State.[5]

"The nineteenth century," states Carr ironically, "was a great age for facts." Historical works were evaluated primarily on the basis of "a hard core of facts"; interpretations, in contrast, were just rancid "pulp."[6] In academic circles, any historical interpretation that supposedly lacked this hard core was discredited, whether it called into question the political and social underpinnings of the ruling order or was more compatible with bourgeois society. Historians stigmatized such interpretations as pure ideology or fiction, or as mere "philosophy of history," and scornfully discarded them for failing to support their blind faith in facts. Such was historiography's legacy to the twentieth century.

Ironically, behind an apparently cold and distant—even clinical—relationship to the "facts" was an ardent passion for power, the subject par excellence of history. Historiography's mission was, primarily, to chart the vicissitudes of the nation. However, in most cases, this project amounted to nothing more than a sort of "biography of the State," just one among many historical narratives of the national collective.[7] In societies in which authoritarian or openly dictatorial political regimes emerged, the close relationship between historiography and power was much more obvious.

This relationship climbed to frenzied heights in the Dominican Republic during the dictatorship of Rafael L. Trujillo. The tyrant, hyperbolized, was seen as the very embodiment of the nation. According to Andrés L. Mateo, the Trujillo Era was the only time in Dominican history when power turned to culture to gain legitimacy. In the discourse of that time, history was a deciding factor.[8] Power organized history's memory: it created its archives, founded its libraries, employed its logographers, published its research. Built on an impressive body of documents, publications during the Trujillo Era were massive, majestic. In and of themselves, these features functioned as validators of a memory that presented itself as absolute. The voluminous anthologies of documents and the ponderous histories of the time appeared to encompass everything, say everything, exhaust all possible truths. Because of their (apparent) thoroughness and exactitude, they functioned as the nation's summae of all mysteries and all knowledge. They proclaimed the definitive end of the long cycle of miseries (for such was the view of the country's history prior to Trujillo's ascent to power), the appearance of its messiah, and the beginning of a new "millennium" of stability and progress. The sheer mass of the evidence made this interpretation appear unassailable, a "wholly natural *fact*"; thus was constructed a "truth by assertion."[9] But what made it all coherent was the "pulp" of interpretations surrounding this "truth," for they gave form to the stories that legitimized the power. It was through these stories, with their narrative effects, that the massive documentary evidence that sought to rationalize Trujillo's place in Dominican history was synthesized. Without perceptible dissent, the "facts" in the documents and archives confirmed that "truth."

"THE POETICS OF HISTORY"

But the very notion of "historical fact," so clearly elucidated by Carr, leads us to what White has called "poetic insights" into the construction of historical narratives, and even into the determination of which facts are relevant.[10] It appears not to be the "facts," obtained according to the "scientific method," that determine the story, the nature of the explanation proffered; historical "truth" springs not from them, as the empiricist tradition has claimed, but rather from the narratives—the "poetics of history," to quote White once again—which delimit the "facts" that are to be considered relevant. The criteria for "truth" are based on such narratives. According to White, "a rhetorical analysis of historical discourse would recognize that every history worthy of the name contains not only a certain amount of information and an explanation (or interpretation) of what this information 'means,' but also a more or less overt message about the attitude the reader should assume before *both* the data reported *and* their formal interpretation."[11]

The poetics of history transforms narrated "facts" into "privileged moments whose appearance defines the series."[12] And if they are allowed this defining role, it is because they validate the interpretation or narration into which they are inserted. Through a "process of symbolization," some historiographies—particularly, though not exclusively, those inspired by allegiance to Trujillo—conferred fixed meanings on a series of events and at the same time constructed stories that have acquired "a more or less stable structure."[13] This is the Gordian knot of the relationship between history and power, of writing as a political exercise. Neither the fall of the dictatorship nor the ensuing prolonged political transition has succeeded in eradicating these concepts. Notions of identity have proved particularly resistant to change. Those in power have made the delimitation of identity, codified as "moments" in the essence of the nation and the State, a precondition in constituting *their* utopias.

The historiographies of the Dominican Republic and Haiti have been crucial to the construction of notions of identity. Likewise, they have been problematic spaces in the intersection between writing and power. For these reasons I have concentrated my efforts on studying the historiography of Hispaniola, albeit with a decided emphasis on that of the Dominican Republic. In so doing, I have taken historiography in its broadest sense, not confining myself to works dealing strictly with history. On the contrary, I have been inclusive as to the types of works considered in these essays; I have even used fictional texts, when relevant. This approach seems to me justified on two counts: First, as is becoming ever more evident, the narrative structures of fiction and historiography are not so very dissimilar. Both begin with a reflection on that which is "real" and then translate it into the production of a text with a plot, codified in such a way as to generate and transmit certain meanings.[14] If histories can be cataloged as "persuasive fictions," then fictional works might be called "false chronicles," since they offer powerful interpretations regarding a society's dilemmas.[15] Second, works of fiction may turn out to be "truer" than historical works—not because of their factual content, which may be a complete fabrication, but rather because of the meanings that they evoke. Thus, in Francoist Spain, literature (due to its critical perspective on society during that era) turned out to be "truer" than the regime's historiography, which was committed, despite its factual content, to the justification of the despot and the mythification of Spanish society and its past. "Fiction," says Herzberger, "is superior to history here . . . , not because of the truth value of its discourse but because of its propositions about truth."[16]

Based on his analysis of the texts of the Gospels, Dorra recommends "putting more faith in the [narrative] structures than in the words."[17] Therefore, in the following essays, I have concentrated less on the broad universe of facts or data and more on the smaller sample of the stories. My intention has been to determine how "rhetorical functions" operate to "pre-encode . . . what counts as data"—the "substantive content of the narrative"—in order to provide "a specific explanatory argument."[18] This book, then, is not an exercise in historical criticism as it is usually understood. I have no intention of carrying out any "historical rectifications" or of pointing out factual or conceptual "errors." For my purposes—analyzing historical narratives, their relationship to power, their configuration of identities, their political and cultural designs, the imagining of their utopias—verification of the facts and data subscribed to by the various authors is only a secondary matter. Their data are of interest to me primarily to the extent that they operate as symbols, as "moments" of a particular memory, as instances of a "politics of historical representation" whose purpose is to validate an interpretation and justify a social project.[19] From this point of view, the supposed "errors" in a historical work are a constituent part of its story, of its discourse, and they can be better understood, I believe, if they are examined in the light of the meanings that the author is consciously or unconsciously transmitting. "Errors" are also part of the "rhetorical functions" of a text. If I have paid any attention to the "historical facts" (and, in the end, I have in fact paid a little), it is due to my intention to "better evaluate the workings of the spirit in the interpretation and transformation of the facts."[20]

Nevertheless, the meaning of a text is not exclusively the product of the symbolizing or encoding that arises in the writing. Reading itself assigns meanings, establishes interpretations, fixes definitions. The meaning that we "find" in a text is a product of our attitude toward it and toward the bias we perceive in it, but it is also the product of our own leanings, phobias, and preferences. In the case of historical works, it is the result of our position vis-à-vis its "politics of representation" regarding the present and the past.[21] According to Hutton, "Historical thinking mimics the operations of memory."[22] As with memory, history's choices are not written in stone; that which is to be remembered or forgotten is never permanently established. When we read historical texts—the memory par excellence of modern societies—we are confronted with the *political* meaning of the act of reading: the search for meanings in the way that each text represents society, power, and resistance. The various possible readings of a text form part of what Clifford Geertz has called "the social history of the moral imagination."[23] Therefore, the readings suggested in these essays are not the only possible ones; other, very different ones are to be found. Nor have I tried to make the readings contained in these pages "objective," at least not in the old-fashioned sense. I cannot help their being "subjective"—any such attempt would surely be futile. However, I certainly do hope that they will inspire readers to ponder narratives about the past—to think about their political function and their social and cultural implications, and to consider that they, too, are a part of the struggle between Eros and Thanatos, between life and death.[24] I hope that they may be able to "mediate two worlds"—the past and the present—"through a third":[25] a reader who, like any other, seeks and assigns meanings to what is read.

For Mu-Kien A. Sang, who is also "tragic."

The Imagined Colony
Historical Visions of Colonial Santo Domingo

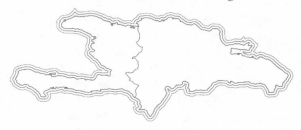

HISTORY, NARRATION, AND FICTION

The story you tell is the story you choose to tell.
   Anne Rice, Taltos *(New York, 1995)*

Power stimulated, as a political act, the enjoyment of the tragic drama.
   Andrés L. Mateo, Al filo de la dominicanidad *(Santo Domingo, 1996)*

What relationship is there between literature and the reconstruction of the past—that is, the writing of history? One of the most persistent among the authors who have addressed this problem recently is the literary critic and theorist Hayden White. According to White, historiographic works, in their "emplotments," reproduce "the archetypes of Romance, Comedy, Tragedy, and Satire." By applying—usually unconsciously—one of these archetypes, the historian confers a particular "meaning" on his or her narration of the past.[1] Using this explanatory model as a base, White takes upon himself the task of reconstructing the "metastories" that dominated the "historical imagination" in Europe during the nineteenth century.

This is not the place to discuss the merits and limitations of White's theories. I do wish to point out, however, that reading White has made me aware of the predominance of certain ways of narrating the Dominican past, in particular the visions that we might call tragic. Tragic visions can be found in many of the major scholars and interpreters of Dominican history; this is true among authors of various periods, authors representing contrasting historiographic schools, and authors from opposing political or ideological camps. It is this recurrence that leads me to suggest some general thoughts on several noted Dominican authors in the field of historiography, taking as my framework White's theories of historical narrative. The following exercise will be somewhat limited and schematic, first, because I am dealing with just the colonial period and, second, because I will examine only a very few works (although these include some of the classic and even "foundational" works in Dominican historiography) and even fewer authors. These authors are Antonio Sánchez-Valverde, an eighteenth-century chronicler; Pedro Francisco Bonó, a very well known nineteenth-century man of letters; José Gabriel García, known as one of the founders of Dominican historiography; and three of the most important cultural and political figures of the twentieth century: Manuel Arturo Peña-Batlle, Joaquín Balaguer, and Juan Bosch. I hope to provide a critical analysis of the historiography of the Dominican Republic that will allow us to place that writing within the framework of the great debates of the country's cultural, social, and political history.

THE BEGINNINGS OF TRAGIC NARRATION

One of the earliest interpretations of the colonial past is found in Antonio Sánchez-Valverde's *Idea del valor de la Isla Española y utilidades que de ella puede sacar su monarquía* (Idea of the Value of the Island of Hispaniola and the Benefits That Its Monarchy Can Draw from It, 1785), unquestionably one of the foundational works of Dominican historiography. Sánchez-Valverde's purpose in writing this work was to demonstrate to the Spanish Crown the possibilities for economic growth in Santo Domingo.[2] In keeping with that purpose, he drew a comparison with the French colony of Saint-Domingue, "that smaller, inferior portion of the land."[3] According to Sánchez-Valverde, the key to the differences between the two colonies was the French colony's slaves, who were themselves a "key" that could unlock the "hidden treasure of the bowels of the earth." The colonists in Santo Domingo lacked this "key" due to the country's relative neglect by the metropolis. Therefore,

Sánchez-Valverde proposed that the Crown foster slave trade to Santo Domingo so that the colony might, following the example of Saint-Domingue, develop a lucrative economy based on agricultural exportation.[4]

In support of this economic and social project, Sánchez-Valverde ventures into the Dominican past. He offers his interpretation of the mother country's policy toward its colony and of Hispaniola's role in the emergence and growth of Spain's power in the Americas.[5] Sánchez-Valverde highlights Hispaniola's role in the conquest of the rest of the Caribbean and the continent. Many expeditions by the conquistadors, he writes, departed from Hispaniola, and the riches of Santo Domingo financed a good number of them. In other words, Sánchez-Valverde is reminding the Spanish monarch to whom his appeal is addressed of the favors and benefits that the Crown had received from Hispaniola, emphasizing the services rendered during the Conquest by the colonial elite, from whom Sánchez-Valverde claims descent. By citing a putative heroic genealogy dating back to the Conquest, Sánchez-Valverde validates his claims before the Spanish Crown.[6] In keeping with this vision of the colonial past, he refers to the "aire of greatness and splendour" of Santo Domingo (the capital city) in the sixteenth century.[7] Contributing to this "aire," according to Sánchez-Valverde, were the structures built in the city thanks to the wealth obtained from mining, raising livestock, and trade with the metropolis. The growth of the island's population—particularly Spaniards, who are to him the essential element of criollo identity—contributed in turn to the founding of many settlements. In his euphoria, the author is guilty of a number of exaggerations and mythifications, as others before me have pointed out.[8]

In the eyes of Sánchez-Valverde, the sixteenth century was truly a golden age, to which he traces the foundations of the community he would like to portray—a community in which peninsular Spanish ethnic and cultural elements are predominant. Consequently, other ethnocultural elements—particularly Afro-Dominican elements—are played down, marginalized, or totally ignored.[9] In Sánchez-Valverde's reconstruction of colonial history, the sixteenth century constitutes a founding, a veritable Eden, "a mythical age, happy if not perfect, at the beginning of the universe," to quote Jacques Le Goff.[10]

In Sánchez-Valverde's narrative, the fall began as early as the sixteenth century, but it became fully evident in the seventeenth, when the colony entered a period of economic depression and neglect. In his view of the causes of this decline, Sánchez-Valverde attributes fundamental importance to the extinction of the native population. He vehemently denounces Francisco de Bobadilla and Nicolás de Ovando for this, blaming them for the *repartimientos*[11] that resulted in the decline in the indigenous population. Without the natives, "the Mines, which had been and will be always the essential and swiftest source of riches, no longer prospered." As the island's economy weakened, a process of "transmigration" began: Spanish settlers left Santo Domingo for more attractive colonial areas. "The wealthiest Residents were the first to leave her," says Sánchez-Valverde resentfully.[12] Coming on top of the loss of the native population were the "Devastations" of 1605–6, when the colonial authorities destroyed settlements along the northern and western coasts of Hispaniola in order to deter smuggling. This policy contributed to a further diminution of the population, as many Spaniards living on the island chose to move to the American continents, and new settlers departing from the Peninsula, lured by the fabled indigenous kingdoms of Terra Firma and by the greater interest shown by the Crown in its mainland colonies, found little to attract them to the Caribbean.

A major consequence of the colony's decline was the impoverishment of the Hispano-Dominican elite, whose origins Sánchez-Valverde traces back to the "dynasty of the conquistadors."[13] Thus he complains bitterly that, in his own times, even the highest-ranking dignitaries of Church and State found it necessary to manage their haciendas, lands, and holdings personally. He also bemoans the fact that they had so few slaves, in contrast to the landowners of Saint-Domingue, the French colony that had emerged in the western part of the large island of Hispaniola and that was, in the eighteenth century, the flower of the colonies, the most lucrative European possession in the Americas, perhaps in the world. One of the consequences of the economic prostration in which

Spain's "abandonment" of its colony left Santo Domingo was racial mixing among the elite. This spurred Sánchez-Valverde to write a defense of the Hispano-Dominican elite, claiming for them a greater degree of racial purity than that which existed in the elite classes of any other European colony in the Caribbean. In these other colonies, he claimed, there had been much more mixing with the black races than had occurred among the Dominican elite.[14]

Sánchez-Valverde's narration of the colonial past focuses first of all on the "tragedies" Santo Domingo experienced beginning in the late sixteenth century, when the long-term effects of the diminution of the native population began to become evident. In contrast to other colonies such as Mexico and Peru, in Santo Domingo it became necessary to import slave labor from Africa, and this had unwelcome ethnic and racial consequences. The decrease in the indigenous population also led to deterioration in the economic position of the conquistadors, from whom Sánchez-Valverde considered himself to have descended. Their situation grew even worse with the Devastations, the transmigrations to the American mainland, and the economic neglect of the seventeenth and eighteenth centuries. For all these reasons, the "criollo homeland" to which Sánchez-Valverde aspired took as its model the neighboring colony of Saint-Domingue, which was growing prosperous thanks to slavery and an economy based on agricultural exportation.[15] Consequently, although Sánchez-Valverde's debates with European intellectuals who denigrated all things American were a defining moment in the groundswell of criollo patriotism, his political stance was reformist, channeled toward working out a compromise between the criollos and the colonial regime.[16] Like others of his class on the neighboring islands of Cuba and Puerto Rico, Sánchez-Valverde was betting on the promised splendor of cane fields and slave labor to make his homeland thrive.[17]

HISTORY AS A SAGA OF THE PEOPLE?

While Sánchez-Valverde initiated the narration of colonial history as tragedy, Pedro Francisco Bonó (1828–1906) shifted the focus away from the elite and inaugurated a history qua "saga of the people."[18] Bonó's historical and sociological thinking is, then, related to progressive romanticism, best represented in nineteenth-century Europe by the French writer Jules Michelet (1798–1874).[19] Like Michelet, Bonó "combined his desire to break with Enlightenment thought with political ideas of a progressive populist nature."[20] Goaded by the many problems of the young Dominican Republic, Bonó threw himself into the task of diagnosing the impediments to its consolidation as a political organism, giving special attention to the factors that were working against the development of a vigorous nation-State. Unlike other Dominican intellectuals, however, whose analyses of the Republic's fragility focused almost exclusively on the weaknesses in the structure of the State, Bonó emphasized the social substratum of political processes and institutional life. In his writings, as in Michelet's, the people are "an image of the collective memory's inspiring power."[21]

Although Bonó's writings are actually more sociological than historical in nature, one can discern in them his vision of the Dominican past.[22] What strikes one immediately is his attention to the material foundations and economic processes that contributed to the development of Dominican society: for example, his writings on the structure of agriculture in the nineteenth century, the origins of which he finds in the colonial period.[23] Bonó deplores the consequences of the reduction in numbers of the native people: to halt the total depopulation of the island, the Crown issued Cédulas or Amparos Reales (royal letters patent) that distributed land in plots measuring "many square leagues," or it condoned the emergence of large properties granted in perpetuity "in secular and ecclesiastical entailments." As a consequence, a good part of the colonial territory was held in mortmain; this circumstance, along with the use of the land for cattle raising, impeded the development of agriculture.[24]

The second consequence that Bonó blames on the horrific extermination of the indigenous population is the importation of slaves from Africa, which he calls "a second murder."[25] Nevertheless, Bonó makes a distinction between the system of slavery in the Spanish colony and that of the French colony of Saint-Domingue. In the former, unlike the latter, "the Spaniard displayed supreme benevolence, great charity, and much tenderness, within the social inequalities that such a system [that is, slavery] required," so that between masters and slaves there was "relative equality, without the unthinkable suffering borne by the slave race in the French colony."[26] This view of slavery in the Spanish colonies, as opposed to that of other European colonies, has found adherents among modern scholars studying systems of slavery. It is sufficient to recall the famous debate over Frank Tannenbaum's theories on slavery in the Americas.[27] Certainly, Bonó paints an extremely simplified picture of slavery and race relations in colonial Santo Domingo. One can understand, however, why he offers this type of interpretation. His purpose is to put forth one of his principal theses: the existence of relative racial harmony as one of the original elements of the Dominican people. This would give the Dominican Republic "moral superiority," along with the potential for adapting to "any civilization," "since its affinities are manifold in race and tradition."[28] Unlike other writers of the nineteenth century, who deplored the mixing of the races as a debilitating factor in the national collective, Bonó saw this mixing as one of the positive elements of the Dominican people.

Bonó's dissenting view of Dominican history and society manifested itself in other ways. For example, when the intelligentsia and the ruling class advocated the expansion of the large exporting latifundios, Bonó preferred to defend those agricultural activities that had contributed to the vigor of the collective—above all, those with a campesino base. We need to bear in mind his well-known view of tobacco, which he called the "true Father of the Fatherland."[29] The economic activities that grew up around the cultivation, transport, and marketing of tobacco were the motive force that drove the Cibao, a region that Bonó viewed as having played a major role in the development of Dominican society since the colonial period, even despite the restrictions on Dominican trade imposed by the metropolis. Following an explanatory paradigm that is common in his writings, Bonó's observations suggest that the tobacco industry developed in the colonial period in spite of a system of institutions that limited economic initiatives and, as a result, shackled Dominican society. The tobacco economy was, nevertheless, an achievement attributable to the positive energy of colonial society, seen especially in the hardworking Cibao campesinos. Bonó contrasts the ineffectual colonial institutions with the vigor of the working classes; in view of the inadequacy of the first, he emphasizes the initiative of the second, particularly of the large numbers of campesinos who had sustained the economy of Santo Domingo since colonial days. In various passages that foreshadow the French historian Fernand Braudel's analysis of historical times,[30] Bonó stresses the consequences in the *longue durée* of the social processes that had shaped Dominican society from colonial times. Referring to that period and the early days of the republic, he writes, "I saw, in the course of times past, entire generations groveling wretchedly in despair and pain. I saw Spanish colonialism, with its terrible errors. I saw the slave, full of suffering, nearly naked. . . . I saw the master, . . . broken, barefoot, pale, haggard, stupid. . . . I saw, in the intermediate times, . . . those classes continue to thrash about, mired in the bog of their prolonged process of organizing themselves, in the same ignorance and with the same savage, pain-filled life."[31] Bonó is far from looking at the colonial past as a golden age, full of splendor; in this passage there is none of that sense of a paradise lost that can be seen in other authors.

Transcending the merely episodic, the "historical chaff" of events, Bonó perceives a social sedimentation—to use the sort of geological metaphor that Braudel likes so much—a kind of organic layer pointing up the limitations of the ruling classes and highlighting the ability and the creativity of the "working classes." Paradoxically, Bonó sees this social sedimentation, achieved with such effort by the working classes, as threatened "at present" by "pressures that are different, yet all senseless."[32] Thus Bonó situates "the fall" not in the past but in his present, a present dominated by the destructive power of economic growth that is unjust and ever more lacking in that quality that to him defines true progress: "wealth with justice."[33]

THE COLONY: A MIRROR OF VICES AND VIRTUES

If Bonó corresponds to Michelet, so might José Gabriel García (1834–1910) be compared to the German historian Leopold von Ranke. García's work, like Ranke's, is based on extensive documentary evidence—a notable feat, given the lack of any organized archives, as Cassá has noted.[34] For this reason, García may be considered to be the founder of a documentalist tradition that was continued on into the twentieth century by such figures as Emilio Rodríguez-Demorizi and Vetilio Alfau-Durán. But the parallels with Ranke do not end with this fervor for documentation. Of greater significance is the two authors' shared sense that history par excellence is that which centers on the formation and vicissitudes of a nation-State, whether those vicissitudes are caused by strictly internal processes or relations with other States. Of García it may be said, as it was of Ranke, that the "idea of the nation" was not just a "datum" but rather, first and foremost, a "value."[35] In García that nationalism, and its concomitant worship of the State, is nuanced by his refined liberal credo, which leads him to take critical positions in regard to certain powerful figures of his time and, more generally, in regard to the debilitation of the State that he saw as a consequence of the absence of any institutional structure that might put his liberal principles into practice.[36] As it happens, his *Compendio de la historia de Santo Domingo* (Compendium of the History of Santo Domingo, 1878) is fundamentally "contemporary history"; of its four volumes, only the first is devoted to the colonial period.[37]

García's judgments regarding colonial history clearly evince the nationalism and liberalism that inspired his historiographic work. In his eagerness to show the depth of the formative currents that shaped Dominican nationality, García is not infrequently anachronistic. For example, in speaking of the indigenous inhabitants of the island of Haiti—their name for the place that would come after the Conquest to be called Hispaniola—García reproaches them for their total lack of "notions of progress, or ideas of greater glory, . . . or interest in international relations."[38] Nevertheless, the Taínos' resistance to the Conquest is seen by García as evidence of their "patriotism." Cacique Caonabo's call to rebellion initiated his "heroic war of independence, . . . [his] eloquent protest against the atrocity of the extermination of a noble and generous race."[39] It is precisely the Taínos' rebellion against Spanish oppression, which García perceives as a sort of national struggle, that wins for them his admiration.

As he goes more deeply into the indigenous wars against the Spaniards, evidence of another feature of García's narrative style emerges: his propensity for categorically pronouncing moral judgments on historical figures. Obviously, one of his criteria would be their loyalty to—or treason against—"the national cause." By letting down that cause, García states, Cacique Guacanagarí earned for himself "the contempt of his fellow citizens."[40] In contrast, García comments that when Cacique Enriquillo surrendered to the Spaniards and settled with his "subjects" in Boyá, they were "condemned by fate to lose, in time, the few prerogatives that they still possessed, and utterly to disappear as a race, . . . leaving to those who would inherit the land that had been theirs no other reminder than the torment of their glorious martyrdom and the example of their love of liberty and independence."[41]

For García, the Spanish Conquest was a highly contradictory phenomenon. As a doctrinaire liberal, García was a firm believer in the idea of progress. We have already seen his lament over the living conditions of the inhabitants of Hispaniola before the Conquest: stateless, responding only to the need of the moment. Their situation was that of a "people without history," isolated even from the passage of time; García described the early state of the island of Haiti not as "empty" but rather as oblivious, encapsulated in its own time and space.[42] Contained in time and space, rather than acting upon them, these aboriginal people were unable to overcome their "backward state" and their "scant culture," according to his vision. Thus, although the Conquest turned "the New World into a theater of crimes and scandals . . . which helped create in the discovered lands . . . a radically flawed and corrupt society,"[43] it also made it possible for precolonial Haiti and its inhabitants to enter the stream of history. Because of the Conquest, pre-historic Haiti, now transformed by the very act of being renamed "La Española" (Spanish island; Hispaniola), became part of the structure of the great civilizing project that was sponsored by the Spanish Crown and of which Columbus was the spokesman.

Nevertheless, this civilizing project was distorted from the outset owing to the propensity of the historical actors to allow themselves to be carried away by the "passions" that extinguish "reason."[44] Indeed, García narrates the period of the Conquest as a drama, in the most literal sense of the term, in which the principal "actors"—conquistadors, rulers, and those who opposed them—struggle and contend among themselves. In this drama, some represent the forces of good; others, evil. Some seek peace, the material progress of the colony, and the establishment of order; others promote war, contribute to economic underdevelopment, and obstruct the civilizing rule of law. And this pattern repeats itself, from the beginning of the Conquest throughout the colonial period. There are even those who, spurred by personal ambition, exceed their rightful powers. Such was the case, according to García, of Francisco de Bobadilla, who took command "violently" and, as "usurpers commonly did," made "ill use" of his power.[45]

It can be said that for García, history was a "teacher of life" or, better yet, a "teacher of politics."[46] Given his understandable emphasis on political events, he pays considerable attention in his history to the behavior of rulers, those who were able by their acts to define the community's welfare. His history is a moralistic narrative, whose purpose is to show the disastrous results obtained by governments who fail to lead their countries in accordance with liberal principles. Thus, Bobadilla cleared the way for the relaxation of "discipline and demoralized the society" since he "committed every imaginable abuse, trampled the most sacred rights, and profaned in various ways the majesty of the laws."[47] As might be expected, García's judgment of Bobadilla's successor is much more favorable, since Nicolás de Ovando righted many of his predecessor's wrongs. Nonetheless, García's assessment of Ovando reflects the tension between the author's liberalism and his unadulterated nationalism. To the extent to which Ovando acted lawfully, reestablished order, and ruled honestly, he receives García's praise. On the other hand, García condemns "the reenactment on a grander scale of the painful scenes . . . [of] the bloody drama of the Conquest" that occurred under Ovando's administration.[48] The repression of the native inhabitants, parallel in García's narration to the Dominican people and their struggle for sovereignty, is presented in his work as the most objectionable aspect of Ovando's governance. In other words, though from the liberal point of view Ovando may well be vindicated, the nationalist stance taken by García—expressed in the nineteenth century by means of literary "indigenism"—leads him to adopt a more critical attitude toward the governor.[49] In a final, impassioned reflection on Ovando's "pacification" of the island, García pours out his indignation: "In order [to accomplish this pacification], he had to authorize the very abuses that he had been charged with remedying and, even more painful [to us today], to become a vengeful oppressor of the helpless people that he had been called upon to civilize and to protect, molding innocent savages into useful members of society and loyal subjects of the State, but by acting as he did, he did no better than follow the current of the times, obeying the corrosive principles that Spain concealed in her bosom beneath the splendour of her national glories."[50]

In his *Compendio*, García assigned positive or negative marks to subsequent governors of the colony, all in unfailing accordance with his own ideology. Also included in these judgments were the prelates of the Catholic Church, the only other institution whose imprint was felt on the society, consequently becoming a proper object of García's attention. Thus, Sebastián Ramírez y Fuenleal, who was both governor and bishop, "showed signs of good judgment and wisdom," particularly in that his actions demonstrated "that the colony's interests should be above one's passions."[51] In contrast, other historical figures are roundly condemned for actions contrary to the general good, for having served their own "passions" or private interests.

García's historical assessments are not exhausted, however, with mere applause or censure for certain individuals. Throughout his work, whenever he refers to the state of the economy, he condemns what he considers misguided government policies, which were largely a product of the socioeconomic burdens that he avers were weighing down Spain itself. In a passage that foreshadows twentieth-century writers (including Juan Bosch), García emphasizes that the colony's depressed economy had its origins in the fact that in Spain "the ill effects of feudal traditions were still being felt." In order to escape this lamentable situation, he argues, it would be necessary to apply "liberal and equitable policies" that could hardly be expected from the metropolis.[52] García, a believer in economic liberalism, condemns the Spanish rulers for failing to recognize the beneficial role played by smuggling in the economy of Santo Domingo and, in consequence, for having carried out the Devastations of 1605–6. The Devastations were an example of "what usually happens when government officials allow opposition to blind their reason; irritated when they see that they cannot triumph lawfully, they resort to violence in order to impose, in a most authoritarian manner, the triumph of error." In a fit of doctrinaire liberalism, García concludes that the Devastations were "in open contradiction to the most trivial of economic principles and the most basic of political theories." To top it all off, he adds later, the depopulation of the northern and western coasts opened the door, in time, to French colonizers in the western part of the island. Thus García links Santo Domingo's future ills to the impolitic practices of the metropolis. The application of liberal economic measures—for example, a more open trade policy—would in his view have prevented the emergence of a French colony on Hispaniola.[53]

The Devastations, the appearance of the French colony of Saint-Domingue, and the attacks from the sea that Santo Domingo suffered in the late sixteenth century signaled the commencement of a slow process of economic, territorial, and political disintegration for Hispaniola. These pages of García's narration are marked by constant lamentations. The above-mentioned events bore "sad fruit," produced a "cumulation of difficulties," as well as "atrocious penury," not to mention "the proximity of [an] antagonistic people" that "has caused so many tears to be shed by the Dominican family"; piracy, for its part, filled the Caribbean Sea with "dread."[54] Meanwhile, on the island of Tortuga the buccaneers lived in disorder, "without wives and without family," with all their goods "in common," since "socialism reigned among them." In fact, life on that small island was lived in a "state of anarchy."[55] The buccaneer society of Tortuga was emblematic of all that was opposed to the liberal dogmas of law, order, and property in which García so firmly believed. His reasons for condemning that society were both deeply rooted in his nationalism and also sustained by the grand myths of liberal philosophy.

The rise of Saint-Domingue in the seventeenth century altered the destiny of Santo Domingo, which from that time forward came "to serve as a theater for the playing out of exceedingly bloody dramas." If Spain retained her dominion over the colony, it was primarily because the "Dominicans" defended "their fatherland gallantly."[56] Going against the grain of the colonists, who were trying to defend their land against the encroaching French, Spain was legitimizing French claims to territory on the island by entering into treaties with France. Nor was animosity between the two colonies alleviated, according to García, with the development of trade relations between them.[57] And even the slight progress that Santo Domingo experienced as a result of these relations was limited by Spain's "protectionist" (read: mercantilist) measures, which tended "to impede the growth of business dealings."[58] Not until Charles III ascended to the Spanish throne and liberalized colonial trade did Santo Domingo's economy begin to take off to a degree, in dealings not only with the French colony but also with traders from other nations who found their way to its coasts. It is with great pleasure that García reports that the 1770s, under Brigadier José Solano, "was the happiest and most fortunate period . . . of the age that we are discussing."[59]

However, this good fortune was to be short lived. The Haitian Revolution, which indiscriminately jumbled "treasures and traditions into one great heap of rubble," infected Santo Domingo with "the poison of its ruin" and "misfortune."[60] With the revolution began what García calls the "period of border troubles," when "the Haitian territory" became a "dangerous neighbour to the Spanish part." Thereafter, the major concern of the authorities in Santo Domingo would no longer be controlling smuggling but rather halting the "revolutionary contagion."[61] At this point, García's narration becomes more hostile toward all things Haitian, despite the fact that according to historian Emilio Cordero-Michel, Toussaint L'Ouverture succeeded in stirring various sectors of the Dominican population to support him.[62] But García paints L'Ouverture (as he does Dessalines) virtually as a predator, whose actions in Santo Domingo were utterly lacking in any praiseworthy end or purpose. He expresses equally unfavorable opinions of those Dominicans who collaborated with the Haitian forces.[63] On the other hand, Ferrand, the military officer in charge of reestablishing French colonial dominion over Santo Domingo, is described as "an honourable and a valiant officer."[64]

These stances assumed by García bring us to the problem of the multiple evocations that the Haitian Revolution, its leaders, and its effects on Santo Domingo inspired in him—particularly in view of the fact that the Haitian presence called into question some of the great myths upon which the identity of the dominant sectors of colonial society had been erected.[65] Above all, the revolution was an offense against the dominant notions of relations between the "races"—notions based on the premise of a "natural order" in which whites commanded and blacks obeyed. The Haitian Revolution represented an "upside-down world" in which those who were *supposed* to obey—because they were black, slaves, and African—had taken over the world, disrupting the order of those who were *supposed* to command, direct, and govern because they were white (or so, at least, many claimed to be) and European.[66]

Though expressed in the language of nation and national identity, García's position vis-à-vis the Haitian Revolution is basically that of the Latin American/Caribbean *letrado*, or "man of letters," in the face of the dilemma between "civilization and barbarism." Thus, García may be considered one of the founders of the tradition that, as Laënnec Hurbon has pointed out, "read[s] the history of Haiti as one long night of barbarism." According to Hurbon, in the eighteenth century a new dimension, originating in the ideas of the Enlightenment, was added to the Christian tradition, which dealt with the dilemma of civilization and barbarism in religious terms. For the elite of the Caribbean, including Haiti, part of the dilemma had to do with their relationship with the masses of former slaves. After all, according to the logic both of slave-owning societies and of their successors, the "former slave has no legitimacy, no right at all to power." Therefore, "the discourse of the freedman," often himself a mulatto, is "to pass himself off as a cousin of the (white) master and as his legitimate successor to power."[67]

Attempting to satisfy his twofold purpose of constituting a nation-State and of validating "civilization" in the face of a "barbarism" (both internal and external) that seemed to corrode the essence of the nation, García tried to establish the boundaries, the borders by which it could be defined. To quote Hurbon once again, "Where the State or 'reason' (of State) wishes to establish itself, it commences by indicating where its margins lie." It should not surprise us, then, that in his reconstruction of colonial history, García emphasizes those elements which, in his view, represent the borders of the liberal, national State to which he aspired: "the borders of irrationality, of the imaginary, of barbarism."[68]

Far from continuing in the intellectual tradition represented by Bonó, in which Dominican history is narrated as an epiphany of ordinary men and women, Dominican letrados of the early twentieth century returned to the principal lines of interpretation that Sánchez-Valverde had laid down in the eighteenth century. First of all, the history of the sixteenth century began once again to be seen as a "fall," that is, as the loss of "paradise" or the decline of a "golden age." This tragic vision was common in the late nineteenth and early twentieth centuries; a "pessimistic" attitude prevailed that originated (in the words of Andrés L. Mateo) in "infinite frustrations of the plans and projects for social regeneration, in their links to political power."[69] For this reason, these "men of letters" proposed the emergence of a strong central State that would be able to validate national sovereignty, foster economic progress, and make of their country a "civilized" nation. This civilizing project, constructed on the idea of the market and the nation-State, was to find its chief expression in the "domestication" of the rural masses, which were seen by the intelligentsia of the time as a threat to social and political stability and, in consequence, as a hindrance to the consolidation of the nation.[70]

The very racial composition of the country was seen as a factor limiting material progress and the advancement of "civilization"—civilization, naturally, of European origin. This racist interpretation was common among the social and intellectual elite throughout Latin America and the Caribbean, who believed that the presence of large sectors of inhabitants of indigenous or African origin constituted an impediment to the "progress" of the region's countries. "To govern is to populate" was proclaimed throughout the length and breadth of Latin America and the Caribbean, but "to populate" was, more than anything, an appeal to "whiten" the population by means of increased migration from Europe and the marginalization, in some cases even extermination, of population groups that were undesirable in the eyes of the elite and the letrados, their partners in the great "civilizing" project.[71] In the Dominican Republic, these racist interpretations led to an anti-Haitian discourse, with many Dominican intellectuals ready to denounce Haiti as "the enemy" and to blame it for most of the "misfortunes" that they claimed the country had suffered.[72]

In addition to the "misfortune" of living on a shared island, on an "island in reverse,"[73] other misfortunes stand out in the tragically tangled narration of Dominican history. Indeed, "Dominican pessimism" was full of "revolutions," ragtag *montonera* militias, and clashes among caudillos; these "ills" resulted from the struggle for power and the insurrectionary proclivities of the rural masses and from the worrisome encroachment of foreigners from the North American mainland into the Caribbean, which grew ever more problematic near the end of the nineteenth century and culminated in the U.S. occupation of the Dominican Republic (1916–24). It should be noted that this pessimism was that of the elite letrados, frustrated in their efforts to mold the nation into the image and likeness of their utopias. Looking upon such a panorama, how could people of this class not feel they were living out a tragedy?

Manuel Arturo Peña-Batlle (1902–54) is one of the principal exponents of this tragic vision of Dominican history.[74] To his mind, one of the greatest disasters to befall Santo Domingo was the emergence of the neighboring colony of Saint-Domingue, resulting eventually in the establishment of the Republic of Haiti. Peña-Batlle saw in these events the summa of all the tragic ills that had afflicted his country throughout its history: first, because the creation of that neighboring nation had truncated the island territory and, second, because Haiti's Afro-Antillean population was a perennial threat to the racial and ethnic composition of the Dominican Republic, which Peña-Batlle considered to be of fundamentally Spanish stock.

The very chronological divisions that Peña-Batlle distinguishes in Dominican history hinge on what he calls the four "social vicissitudes" that the country had gone through, each lasting for a century. In the sixteenth century, the vicissitude that the colony had to face was the Protestant Reformation, of which smuggling was merely a secular, material expression. In the seventeenth, it was the buccaneers and the freebooters, representatives of the crass individualism spawned by nascent capitalism. The eighteenth century was the period of territorial encroachment by the French colony that had sprung up in the western part of Hispaniola. And finally, in the nineteenth century, Santo Domingo had to validate its existence in the face of the influx of refugees from the slave revolt that had broken out in Haiti, the positivism and materialism that had come from France, and the Haitian Domination.[75] Given such onslaughts, according to Peña-Batlle, the Dominican community had to struggle mightily to maintain its Hispanic identity.

To support his hypothesis, Peña-Batlle creates an idealized version of Spain's rule over the island. In his estimation, there were no marked social inequities during the colonial period, despite the existence of slavery. "There were no problems of caste," he avers, "nor was life based upon inhumane formulas of exploitation."[76] The colony's characteristic social structure, a product of the Spanish genius, clearly differentiated it from its French counterpart, in which slaves lived under an unspeakable regime of exploitation. Even more important, the French colonial system precluded the development of an integrated society that would allow a healthy national entity to emerge. The existence of large slave contingents, impervious, according to Peña-Batlle, to "any cultural influence," was the greatest obstacle to the formation of a society with the potential to become a modern nation.[77] Thus, while the French colony at the time of its independence lacked a unifying culture that could serve as the basis for creating a nation, in Santo Domingo there had occurred "a process of cultural and institutional sedimentation, thanks to the imprint left by Spain."[78] And this sediment was what Peña-Batlle saw as endangered in the nineteenth century by the revolution in Haiti and the Domination of 1822–44. In his eyes, Haiti represented the total negation of Spanish values. Therefore, it is not surprising that in his complaint against all things Haitian, Peña-Batlle, in the twentieth century, should resort to the idealization of the colonial past. In doing so, he creates a positive counterpart to Haiti's "black past"; in doing so, he founds a new promised land, the golden age of the origins. This is his political dream, and he sees it coming true during the dictatorship of Rafael L. Trujillo, for Peña-Batlle sees in the Trujillo regime a sort of "postapocalyptic paradise" that reclaims the essence of Dominican nationality, which was negated or diminished by the dismal events of the period of the "fall."[79]

Parallel to this view is Joaquín Balaguer's reconstruction of the Dominican past, although Balaguer employs a more biologically oriented anthropology, in which "biology begets society."[80] This metaphor is evident in his use of the term *raza* (race), which he takes as synonymous with "nation."[81] Reconstructing the history of the Dominican population is central to his argument; his purpose is to reveal "the fundamental whiteness of the Dominican people and the Haitian influence on its 'ethnic corruption.' "[82] This corruption indeed began with the decline of the Spanish colony after its brief period of splendor in the sixteenth century. Santo Domingo's prolonged decline translated into a corresponding decline in population, which continued until the nineteenth century, when the fragility of Santo Domingo's meager population opened the colony to Haitian penetration.[83] Concomitant to his peculiar reconstruction of Dominican demographic history is the "mythification of the country's racial composition."[84] Balaguer attempts to show that once the indigenous population had been eliminated, Santo Domingo became the seat of the "most *spiritually* select and *physically* homogeneous race of the American continent."[85] His hypothesis regarding the fundamental whiteness of the Dominican population leads him to minimize the importance of the slave trade, which, he argues, left no significant mark on the racial composition of Santo Domingo until the late eighteenth century, after cession of the Spanish colony to France. Thus, for Balaguer, the national prototype is the white campesino.

In comparison with Peña-Batlle's narrative, Balaguer's reconstruction of the colonial past is astonishingly schematic. Nevertheless, his ideas about the colonial period agree fundamentally with those of Peña-Batlle. Each man views that period—and Dominican history in general—through a filter of robust elitism. Both lament the transmigration of wealthy, "pure-blooded Spanish" families as a result of Hispaniola's economic, social, and political difficulties in the late sixteenth and early seventeenth centuries. Families of Spanish background who chose to remain on the island are highly commended on two counts: first, for avoiding racial mixing and thus maintaining the "ethnic" nucleus that Peña-Batlle and Balaguer consider fundamental for a true Dominican nationality to eventually emerge; second, for becoming bastions in the conservation of Spanish culture and values. These families (including, according to Balaguer, important campesino nuclei, particularly in zones such as Baní and the upper regions of the Cibao)[86] produced the heroes of the cultural and demographic resistance in the face of "Haitian imperialism." It fell to these families to preserve immaculate the traditions, language (Spanish), religion (Catholic), virtues, and morals that had been brought over from the Peninsula. It was they who kept alive the memory of a pure past, when Santo Domingo had not yet been sullied by the Haitian—that is, black—presence: This is the supreme good for those who, like Peña-Batlle and Balaguer, revile the vigorous Afro-Dominican component in the ethnic and cultural formation of the Dominican nation.

TRAGIC VISIONS RIGHT AND LEFT?

Tragic narration, however, has not been the exclusive property of those intellectuals most closely identified with the Trujillo dictatorship and its model of society. We find a marked tendency toward tragic historiography among those of the democratic tradition as well, despite their ideological and political differences with the traditional authoritarian intelligentsia who advocated that "reactionary nationalism" to which Roberto Cassá refers.[87] The similarities and parallels bespeak a common diagnosis of the country's "ills." Both presuppose a truncated modernity that hinders the full expression of the civilizing project of the educated elite, a project based on the nation-State and a well-developed market economy.[88] Consequently we find that both democratic and reactionary authors, in their reconstructions of the past (particularly the colonial period), highlight the factors that worked against the emergence of a modern society in the Dominican Republic. Two authors of the democratic persuasion were Juan Isidro Jimenes-Grullón and Juan Bosch. I hope to write about Jimenes-Grullón on some other occasion; for now, I will focus on Bosch.[89]

It is common knowledge that Juan Bosch began his career by writing short stories and a novel with rural themes.[90] Near the end of the 1930s, however, he became active in the anti-Trujillo movement that had been coalescing among Dominican exiles. This affiliation led to a tendency in Bosch toward politically and socially oriented essays, as can be seen in his prologue to Jimenes-

Grullón's book *La República Dominicana: Análisis de su pasado y su presente*. This essay, dated 1940, was Bosch's first effort at producing a coherent and comprehensive interpretation of Dominican society.[91] As a prologue to another author's book, however, it only sketched a number of sociological ideas. Not until the 1950s would Bosch make an attempt at a global view of the Dominican past: his *Trujillo, causas de una tiranía sin ejemplo*, published in 1959.[92] As the title indicates, Bosch's main purpose in this work is to interpret the historical and social circumstances that led to the dictatorship of Rafael L. Trujillo. To this purpose, he examines the colonial period, which is, he argues, where the deepest roots of the dictatorship can be found. Since my own purpose is to analyze historical visions of the colonial period, I will focus on that era, setting aside other aspects of Bosch's arguments. Above all, I wish to point out how his interpretations of the colony parallel the tragic narratives of the other authors I have mentioned, such as Peña-Batlle and Balaguer, despite obvious political and ideological differences.[93]

In the first place, Bosch refers to the "distortions" that Dominican society had suffered throughout its history as a result of foreign invasions and occupations. The first of these invasions was the Spanish Conquest, which established a caste system that forever marked the course of Santo Domingo's history. This teleological vision, locating in the remote colonial past the origin of the Dominican Republic's twentieth-century troubles, is the first point of contact between Bosch, on the one hand, and Peña-Batlle and Balaguer on the other. Of course, there are differences. In Bosch's view, colonial society was distorted from the very beginning, since Spain itself was distorted in comparison with other countries of western Europe. That is, while Europe was moving toward the modernization, in the capitalist sense, of its economic, social, and political structures, Spain clung to a feudal structure that generated a caste system which would, in turn, be transferred to Santo Domingo. According to this interpretation, social rivalries between "first- and second-class people" would be a constant throughout colonial history; this was "the evil introduced at the very root of the birth of the Dominican people."[94]

To this underlying cause of the distortion of Dominican society during colonial times were added other elements, all of them tragic in nature, which contributed to the "petrification" of this social division: that is, the caste system "written in stone." Santo Domingo's economic decline in the late sixteenth century and throughout the seventeenth decimated its population. The lines between the castes were not blurred, however; on the contrary, Bosch alleges that "State dignitaries . . . kept alive the sense of the importance of certain persons in the midst of an impoverished population."[95] In the face of the obvious lowering of social barriers defined by clear economic indicators, the upper class defended itself by becoming more "recalcitrant" to social contact and to the penetration of its exclusive circle by second-class people.[96] Ironically, argues Bosch, the social position of first-class families was not supported by any clear economic preeminence. Unlike other Spanish colonies, Santo Domingo had no "oligarchy of landowners," since "practically all of the families had descended into poverty." The first-class people, therefore, "were sustained in their circle by family tradition."[97] Not even the "racial" factor carried much weight where social divisions were concerned, "given that the races were mixing with each other in the context of the general poverty." Bosch concludes, "The only thing that endured was the division into castes."[98]

In his work on Trujillo, Bosch concentrates on two principal aspects of the colonial period. The first, as we have seen, refers to the social structure, which Bosch examines in light of his peculiar theory of "castes" and of the "petrification" of the caste system that he sees as having taken place during the colonial era. The second aspect has reference to the origin of the French colony of Saint-Domingue in western Hispaniola, the "direct consequence of Spain's prolonged neglect, century after century, of what had been the first of its innumerable colonies."[99] Bosch's interpretation of the origin of Haiti resembles that of Peña-Batlle, who built a full-scale historical conception of France's penetration of Hispaniola on his studies of the island of Tortuga.[100] In a passage that sums up his view of the subject, Bosch says of the small but historically significant island of Tortuga: "It became the platform of the smuggling trade . . . , then pirate headquarters, then the point of entry into the Caribbean for the French empire, and finally the *egg* from which Haiti was hatched, a country whose existence changed the course of Santo Domingo's history."[101] Due to the emergence of Saint-

Domingue, the "principal concern" of Santo Domingo, its own formation still in process, was "to struggle against the French."[102] Bosch approaches a theory of permanent rivalry between the inhabitants of the two colonies, despite the fact that intra-Caribbean relations during the colonial period were marked by the existence of widespread trade networks, both legal and contraband.[103]

Bosch also subscribes to the theory that the Haitian Revolution affected Santo Domingo negatively in a number of ways, contributing to the decline in population, to the paralysis of "active trade," and to a halt in the expansion of productive activity—all this as a result of "the exodus of the wealthy, cultured families." To summarize, Bosch argues that "history snatched the Dominican fruit from its tree before the sap of life could ripen it as Nature intended."[104] To Bosch, one of the ills that has afflicted Dominican society throughout its history has been the absence (or weakness) of governing groups, of sources of "social authority" able to steer the country toward modernization; thus, the blow supposedly dealt by the Haitian Revolution to the incipient nucleus of leaders in Santo Domingo is yet another sign of the misfortune of having "the French colony of Haiti on one side of its island."[105]

Trujillo was the first of many works in which Bosch would set out to interpret the Dominican past.[106] In later writings he modified some of these historical interpretations, both in general and in particular. Many of the changes no doubt correlate with transformations in his own political and ideological perspectives. This is evident in the late 1960s and throughout the 1970s when, after the bitter experiences of first being toppled from the constitutional presidency (1963), then witnessing a foreign military occupation in the Dominican Republic (1965), and finally suffering electoral defeat (1966), his views approached Marxism. In those disastrous years, Bosch produced some of his best-known political and historical texts, achieving international renown with such works as *Pentagonism* and *De Cristóbal Colón a Fidel Castro* (From Christopher Columbus to Fidel Castro).[107] Palpable in these books are interpretations, conceptions, theories, and discursive forms approaching those of third-world Marxism, which was in vogue during those years because of the worldwide ripple effect of the Cuban Revolution, anti-imperialist defiance of U.S. aggression in Vietnam, and the flowering of national liberation movements in the third world. During those same years Bosch would also write what is undoubtedly his most important work of historical interpretation about the Dominican Republic: *Composición social dominicana*.[108]

In spite of unquestionable differences between these later texts and the work on Trujillo, which was written in the late 1950s, it is revealing that certain lines of reasoning carry over, albeit with new shadings. Both *Pentagonism* and *De Cristóbal Colón a Fidel Castro* may be seen as a further development of one of the central theses in his *Trujillo*: the determining role played by foreign occupations in the history of the Dominican Republic and the Caribbean in general. Both works conceive Caribbean history from an essentially geopolitical standpoint, viewing societies of the region as little more than inert victims of great imperialistic "designs." Caribbean history has been molded by external forces, by a sort of Moira or cruel Fate that defines the region's evolution in fundamentally tragic terms. In *Composición social dominicana*, this fatalism is expressed in other ways, some of which we can find inchoate in *Trujillo*. There Bosch mourned the destruction of the nucleus of "wealthy, cultured families" as a result of the Haitian Revolution; in *Composición* he makes the absence of a ruling class a constant in his country's history. This lack, or absence, distinguishes Santo Domingo from other Latin American countries, where governing classes did emerge that were capable of developing the productive forces of their respective nations and of taking up the reins of the State.[109]

Independent of the ideological stances Bosch assumed in different periods and in varied political circumstances, we certainly see in his historical works a propensity for narrating history as tragedy. In this he shows undeniable similarities to other Dominican authors whose ideologies and politics are far from totally compatible with his. Naturally, there are important differences in the meanings assigned to specific historical processes. For example, the notion of a "golden age" is not as patent in Bosch's *Trujillo* as in Peña-Batlle and Balaguer, who quite explicitly so describe the beginning of the colonial period before it degenerated, producing a tragic "fall." Bosch is closer to García in seeing the Conquest as tragedy from the very beginning, because Spain brought into Santo

Domingo archaic social structures that were alien to the capitalist modernization that was in evidence in the late fifteenth and early sixteenth centuries in several countries of western Europe, although not in Spain. In another example, while Peña-Batlle and Balaguer emphasize the supposed racial purity maintained by "select" families during the colonial period, Bosch suggests that what really occurred at that time was a general blending of races, which tended to blur racial lines between social groups; in this interpretation Bosch is more like Bonó. Yet we find also in Bosch a tragic conception of colonial history that, he avers, has marked Dominican society for centuries yet to come.

PARADISE LOST OR UNFINISHED STORY?

Criticism makes no sense unless it is made from a social place and with a defined horizon—a horizon that must of necessity be utopian. Without a horizon there can be no criticism.

   Raymundo González, Bonó, un intelectual de los pobres
   (Santo Domingo, 1994)

Acknowledging a past does not mean accepting it. Seeking its lessons and trying to use it to interrogate the future does not mean prolonging it.

   Alberto Flores-Galindo, Buscando un inca (Mexico City, 1993)

Michel de Certeau writes: "Historiography (that is, 'history' and 'writing') bears within its own name the paradox—almost an oxymoron—of a relation established between two antinomic terms, between the real and the discourse. Its task is one of connecting them and, at the point where this link cannot be imagined, of working *as if* the two were being joined."[110] In historiography, discourses on what is "real" are joined to the practices of fiction in a hidden and surreptitious way rather than openly and obviously. It is privileged territory for the formation and canonizing of discourses that claim (unlike fictional discourse) to be based on "knowledge" and to be validated by "scientific objectivity." The very act of enunciation is an attempt to transform particular, partial, limited, contingent, and biased knowledge into *the* truth, the only truth that is legitimate and valid. Historiography is, then, a practice, an exercise, in power; it is an attempt to impose a consensus about the "past," its particular field of action. Historiography calls upon ancestors, genealogies, "patriarchal" figures (usually male), seminal "facts," foundational acts, and germinal processes in an effort to generate strong identities, anchored in origins. A "history" is a totem: the historiographer attempts to take disparate and conflicting fragments and bring them together around that totem in order to construct an "imagined community," to "invent a tradition."[111] One of historiography's mechanisms of authority is to canonize works and authors, with the "goal of imposing a consensus, a cohesion."[112] This cohesion implies closing off certain spaces, as if the "authorized (and authoritarian) voices" had said all that needed to be said. These voices set the subject's limits, determine factual content, and provide all possible interpretations—that is, all interpretations legitimized and permitted by the canon.

Associated from the beginning with the emergence of the modern State, historiography has guarded it like Cerberus. As Gelpí suggests, reading a classic critically, not as a devotee, implies a recognition of its strategies in the face of power. Such a reading implies recognizing that its "alibis"—like those of any other text, including this one—are built on ethical considerations, that is, on *political* considerations, in the deepest sense of the term. It implies recognizing that the putative "truth" of a text is also a construction, aimed at validating or questioning a given order of things; that the study of the past, far from being a peaceful, erudite activity, is a passionate battle to control the words, metaphors, narratives, and knowledge of *the present and the future*. In the case of "nationalist discourses," the intention is "to counteract every sort of dispersion, dislocation, or disintegration . . . by invoking . . . a common, nostalgic, utopian origin or space."[113] "Imagining the past" as a lost paradise may imply a nostalgic vision of the classes and social sectors that have lost their ancient privileges. On the other hand, it may serve as a powerful instrument of struggle and resistance for subaltern sectors, which are increasingly marginalized by the social and political projects of the dominant groups.[114]

Losing a paradise may be a tragedy. It will always be a tragedy for those in positions of authority, whose reputed "heirs" will lament the absence of that safe, enclosed space over which they held dominion—or at least exercised usufruct. In their "memoirs" (their historiography), they will tell us of those intruders who undermined their inheritance or who seduced the weak in order to sow dissension and internal disaffection. They will write of their evil "brothers" and "cousins"—such narratives often employ the rhetoric of kinship—who squandered the family's patrimony. What they will not tell, or will mention only as an insignificant sidelight, will be the struggles and the resistance of those who did not partake of the joys of paradise, for whom that "paradise" was, perhaps, an inferno. Nor will they speak of how the other paradises—alien utopias, founded on transgression, self-deification, or even deicide—have been forgotten or silenced by the narrators.

Racial Discourse and National Identity
Haiti in the Dominican Imaginary

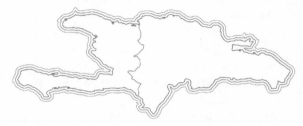

ON IDENTITY IN THE CARIBBEAN

History should be able to free us from the past, not to leave us . . .
confined in those longue durée *prisons of ideas.*
      Alberto Flores-Galindo, Buscando un inca *(Mexico City, 1993)*

From the eighteenth-century criollos to contemporary authors, the problem of identity has tortured the intelligentsia of the Caribbean. The complex historical evolution of the region, which has been molded by its particular place in colonialism and in the Atlantic economy, has made it difficult to reach a consensus on identity. Many factors have marked the discourse on this subject, including the large number of European countries that colonized the region; an outward-oriented economy usually dominated by plantations and slavery; and a new breed of humankind formed by immigrants from many parts of the world, whose place in the social hierarchy was influenced by both their national and ethnic backgrounds and their economic status.[1]

For some, identity was defined through their ties—economic, political, and cultural—with the metropolis; a larger but less powerful group construed themselves in other ways. The local elite, made up of foreigners and criollos, trusted in their ancestry to distinguish them from the masses of slaves, who were the human hub of the region's economies. Skin color defined not only one's social condition but also one's ethnic and cultural identity—in addition, of course, to one's position in the structure of production. In the face of the "other"—generally African, slave, and black—the hacendado, the merchant, and the bureaucrat affirmed their much-vaunted whiteness and their European roots.

In time, the descendants of the slaves would undergo demographic, cultural, and social changes. In the beginning, slaves were of African origin (those newly arrived from Africa were known as *bozales*), but ever larger pockets of criollo slaves would later appear. Moreover, many who were descended from slaves imported into the Americas would later become freedmen and freedwomen. Then sexual relations between whites and blacks—usually extramarital and often a reflection of the superior rank of white men vis-à-vis black women—increased the racial mixing (*mestizaje*) of the populace. Mestizaje, however, was an extremely complex process, involving much more than just the "mixing of races."[2] Racial mestizaje was accompanied, in varying degrees, by cultural mestizaje. As a result, there arose Afro-American communities that were not as simple and homogeneous as the dominant sectors allowed themselves to believe; the equation of black = slave = African was breaking down. The slaves were adapting and resisting, creating an Afro-American world with fluid boundaries and no absolute dichotomies. The varied rhythms of the economy and the slave trade combined with these demographic changes to create this fluidity; no less important were metropolitan policies, interactions between the diverse social groups, the slaves' resistance, and cultural exchanges and adaptations.[3]

In the end, the economically and culturally hegemonic sectors had to face the truth: blacks and mulattoes in Caribbean societies were no longer simply slaves, nor were they exclusively African. Many of them even clamored for a greater "space" within the slavery-based society. For example, freedmen would demand the right to own property, participate in trade, and broaden their social, cultural, and political horizons.[4] For their part, most of the slaves tried to adapt to the system, seeking ways to temper the rigors of their lot. They had a number of means at their disposal in their attempts to at least alter, if not demolish, the terms under which they were to be exploited: Slaves participated in the internal market, cultivated small plots of land, became involved in urban life, wrested small but significant concessions from their masters, and managed to achieve a degree of autonomy.[5] Meanwhile, a minority group among the slaves struggled to escape the system by rebelling or running away; these fugitive slaves were the *cimarrones*, or Maroons.[6]

In very specific circumstances, when solidarity among dominant groups became strained or when relations between the colonial State and the hegemonic sectors broke down, slaves contributed en masse to the destruction of the system, or at least accelerated its fall. The epic struggle of the slaves of Haiti illustrates the first of these circumstances; less conspicuous but equally tenacious endeavors in Brazil and Cuba are examples of the second.[7]

Through means both circuitous and contradictory, Afro-Americans overcame the "natal alienation" originally imposed by slavery—that is, being cut off from all social and family ties and uprooted from their autonomous cultural heritage.[8] Their claims of rights and spaces that had traditionally been denied them were then more legitimate (from the point of view of the dominant culture). The specific moments and circumstances when this transition took place would have to be pinpointed according to the particular rhythm of each society. What must be emphasized is that in various historical contexts there were large Afro-Caribbean sectors within the Antillean societies that did not conform to the prevailing economic and cultural model (black = slave = African). This fact presented a formidable dilemma to groups interested in reconceptualizing the emerging criollo societies, whether by redefining the "colonial compact" in search of greater autonomy or by breaking altogether with the metropolis. Rethinking criollo societies came to involve articulating a new ideology vis-à-vis both the metropolis and the other ethnic and cultural traditions which had shaped those societies and which could no longer be ignored.

Responses were varied. In Cuba, José Antonio Saco, determined to define and affirm "Cubanness," saw the black presence as a threat to his project. Thus he took an early antislavery, though nonetheless conservative, stance. (To Saco, as to others, "Cubanness" was incompatible with blackness.)[9] Others, generally bureaucrats, saw slavery and the slave trade as a threat to the colonial system, in the long run at least. In Puerto Rico, for example, Pedro

Irizarri, magistrate (*alcalde ordinario*, or "ordinary mayor") in San Juan in the early nineteenth century, made clear his preference for free labor over slave labor. This stance might appear, upon uninformed reading, to be based on abolitionist convictions, but it actually originated in his obvious fear of a "Haitian solution" to the contradictions arising from slavery.[10] Irizarri's position, by the way, was shared by other important leaders in the colonial State. In the 1840s Governor Juan de la Pezuela took steps toward eradicating the slave trade. His purpose, of course, was that of any colonialist: He hoped to guarantee Spanish dominion over the island, and to do this he had to counter the dual dangers of the "Haitian specter" and a possible invasion from England.[11] In contrast, there were criollos (although their cases were not typical) who advocated including blacks and mulattoes in their social reforms and even, on occasion, in their affirmations of nationality; examples from the "long nineteenth century" range from Toussaint L'Ouverture to José Martí.[12]

ON DOMINICAN IDENTITY AND THE HAITIAN "OTHER"

The Dominican Republic presents a very unusual situation with respect to the problem of identity and ethnoracial discourse. Two colonies were established on the island of Hispaniola, one Spanish and one French. This situation would give rise, in the Dominican Republic, to a national discourse of opposition to Haiti. This is not the place for long and complicated historical narrations; suffice it to say that from the time the French first entered the island as a colonial power in the seventeenth century, their relations with the Spanish colonists were characterized by more-or-less peaceful trade as well as by conflict. Unable to deter the Spanish colonists and the criollos from their participation in illegal trade, the Spanish Crown opted in 1605–6 to depopulate the northern and western coasts of the island, in what would become known as the Devastations. These expulsions were counterproductive, however, in that they opened the door to French occupation.[13] From that time on, Dominican relations with the French would be generally characterized (officially, at least) by attempts to keep the French from penetrating to the interior of the island. Even so, the French succeeded in occupying the western part of Hispaniola and in eventually developing there one of the most lucrative colonial possessions of the eighteenth century.

Thus, two colonial societies coexisted on the island by the mid-1700s, each with its own economic, social, cultural, and political characteristics. The plantation economy of Saint-Domingue (the French possession that for the sake of convenience I will call Haiti) was exceedingly well developed. The colony's social structure was highly stratified, with a white minority of French origin dominating an enormous mass of slaves—more than four hundred thousand, by some accounts.[14] Santo Domingo, on the other hand, did not have a strong plantation sector. Its economy was based chiefly on small campesino farms and cattle ranches. The social structure of the Spanish colony, despite existing divisions, lacked the rigidity of its French counterpart.[15] This was a result of the very mediocrity of its exporting sector: for example, due to the poorly commercialized Dominican economy, many slaves were able to develop what Sidney Mintz has called "peasant adaptations," comprising more or less autonomous activities; small cattle ranches, the basis of the Spanish colony at that time, were another response to the same situation.[16]

New historical processes helped reconfigure relations between these two colonies sharing one island. The slave revolution in Saint-Domingue, the emergence of the Republic of Haiti in 1804, the eventual occupation of Santo Domingo by Haiti (1822–44), the series of attempted invasions and conflicts between the two countries (1844–60), border disputes, and the waves of migration from Haiti to the Dominican Republic in the twentieth century have marked the Dominican Republic's national, criollo discourse. And to the dominant racist discourse inherited from colonial times, anti-Haitianism must also be added. The definition of "Dominican" became "not Haitian."[17] This dichotomy could be seen in nearly every sphere: Haitians practiced voodoo, Dominicans Catholicism; Haitians spoke Creole, Dominicans Spanish; Haitians were black, Dominicans were of mixed race or white. More than this, Haitian culture and society were seen as an extension of Africa, whereas Santo Domingo clung to its pure Spanish origins. In short, the ideology of Dominican nationality has been markedly influenced by a sense of contrast, of "otherness": Haiti.[18]

This racist, anti-Haitian discourse reached the apex of its ideological and political expression during the long dictatorship of Rafael L. Trujillo (1930–61).[19] In its crudest expressions, the anti-Haitian discourse represents a struggle for geographic space fought between two absolutely incompatible national entities. This view, patent in a variety of authors, was emphatically formulated by two outstanding figures of Dominican political and intellectual life in particular: Manuel Arturo Peña-Batlle and Joaquín Balaguer.[20] But the Haiti discourse, like any ideological construct, has not been uniform; variations on the theme have been many from the eighteenth century to the present. These diverse perceptions of Haiti have been marked not only by the fluctuating relations between the two countries but also by very real cultural and social differences. But prejudice and the political projects of the powerful have also helped mold Dominican views of its neighbor. Examining these variations, beginning with the eighteenth century, may help clarify the constituent elements of the anti-Haitian discourse.[21] This is essential in identifying the various stages or phases in the construction of a national discourse in the Dominican Republic.

THE SLAVEHOLDERS' UTOPIA

One of the most detailed eighteenth-century pictures of what Haiti signified to the Dominican people (or at least to the Dominican elite) is found in Antonio Sánchez-Valverde's *Idea del valor de la Isla Española y utilidades que de ella puede sacar su monarquía* (Idea of the Value of the Island of Hispaniola and the Benefits That Its Monarchy Can Draw from It), originally published in Madrid in 1785. This work is a lengthy report addressed to the Spanish authorities and designed to alert them to the colony's economic potential.[22] To that end, Sánchez-Valverde contrasts the bleak state of Santo Domingo with the economic expansion enjoyed by its French counterpart, Haiti. He emphasizes the fabulous wealth produced by "that smaller, inferior portion of the land occupied by the *French* colony."[23] After detailing the profits realized by the French State, Haiti's trade volume, and its agricultural production, he states with a hint of sadness, "From all of which it may be concluded without exaggeration that the *French* Nation makes more use of its Colonies on that *Island* than does ours [Spain] of the entire *Continent.*"[24]

What factors contributed to the development of this lucrative enterprise in the French portion of Hispaniola? Sánchez-Valverde's answer is categorical: The "most principal cause" that made the difference was "the *Negroes*, whose arms are the prime movers of so much productivity."[25] Black slaves were the "key" that could unlock the "hidden treasure of the bowels of the earth," to use Sánchez-Valverde's graphic metaphor. The "Spanish or Criollo Colonists" were not ignorant of this "key," yet Sánchez-Valverde asks, "Do they have it, or is it within their discretion to have it? Neither one nor the other. . . . Give them this key, as it has been given to the *French*: and if they fail to do as much or more than they, it may be said that they are inept and do not know how to use it."[26]

In these passages, Sánchez-Valverde's purpose becomes completely transparent. His project, following the French model in Haiti, is to foster the importation of slaves into Spanish Santo Domingo in order to develop an economy of exportation. In justifying his plan, Sánchez-Valverde does not hesitate to invoke geographic determinism, arguing that Negroes "are the only ones purposefully fitted to the cultivation of the *Torrid Zone* and its production." Criollos, "habituated by the heat of their *Zone* . . . , are indefatigable in the most arduous tasks." But since both were in short supply, increasing the slave population was essential in order to achieve economic parity with the French.[27]

In the late seventeenth century, Santo Domingo began to fall into a state of neglect and poverty. The Devastations of 1605–6, "transmigrations" to other parts of the empire, and epidemics had taken their toll on the colony's Spanish population. Santo Domingo's fortunes sank even deeper as Spain turned its eyes to its colonies on the mainland. The eighteenth-century Dominican elite gloried in their descent from the conquistadors, who had given such valuable service to the Crown, but they found themselves in a lamentable state not at all in keeping with their lineage. According to Sánchez-Valverde, the "*Regidores*" (aldermen or magistrates), "Captains," and "Canons and Ecclesiastics"—all members of the colony's elite—were obliged to manage their haciendas personally and sometimes even to do manual labor alongside their slaves, all because they lacked the means to hire overseers. Meanwhile, the hacendados of Haiti were living ostentatiously, in idleness, "gluttony, and other vices."[28]

Despite his tone, bordering on moral condemnation, Sánchez-Valverde saw in Saint-Domingue the utopia of his social class. He was a true representative of the Dominican elite—a "dark-skinned" criollo, priest, and hacendado[29]—and as such he considered the French colony a model worthy of emulation. If it were possible to reproduce in Santo Domingo what the French had done in Saint-Domingue, then the cycle of poverty, isolation, and neglect could be broken, and in the process, the Spanish colony could recover its lost luster. To do so would simply require more "Negroes"—that is, more slaves. This is the linchpin of Sánchez-Valverde's economic and social proposal.

He puts forth several measures by which the number of available workers might be increased. For example, he advocates putting to work "free *Negroes* and *Mulattoes* of both sexes and . . . poor white persons." Once again following the French model, Sánchez-Valverde insists on the need to call a halt to the manumission of slaves, a practice that he says results in "freedmen and freedwomen who are idle and unkempt and who must, of necessity, subsist by iniquitous means."[30] The measures he suggests are particularly hostile toward female slaves, claiming that their "sinful familiarity" with their owners was the chief cause of the proliferation of freedmen. Slave women acquiesced in these relations "not by the command or violence of the Master, but rather by the lure of his promises of freedom." In other words, Sánchez-Valverde (dubiously) absolves slave owners of the violent acts they committed against their female slaves.[31] At most, he considers relations between a female slave and her master to be a trade-off: freedom in exchange for sexual favors. But in his view, the degradation of the female slaves was not the worst aspect of these relations. What he truly condemns is that this "concubinage" rendered useless "to the State the hands of these [female] Slaves and their descendants."[32] Sánchez-Valverde wanted, in fact, to establish a rigid economic and racial system similar to that of the French in Haiti, in which slaves "apply themselves to tilling the earth" instead of uselessly filling up the masters' houses.[33]

Although Sánchez-Valverde saw the element of race as subsumed within the economic project, he could not ignore the ethnoracial consequences of his proposal. In one of the few passages of the book in which he comments directly on the racial question, he takes offense with several "Forayne" authors who had dared "to open our veins and stain our blood, the blood of both the *Indo-Hispanics* and their *European* Progenitors," by accusing them of mixing with Negroes. Sánchez-Valverde is particularly offended with a certain "Mr. Weuves," who praised the French, Swiss, and Germans while reviling the Spanish and Portuguese for their lack of "a single drop of pure blood, having taken this mixture either from the *Negroes* or from the ancient *Moors*."[34] At the discursive level, Sánchez-Valverde's reply to this attack is based first of all on the use of the term "Indo-Hispanic" as an ethnic definition of the Dominican population. This term allows him to distinguish that population from white Europeans and, at the same time, Negroes. Calling the colonial inhabitants "Indo-Hispanic" is an admission that they are racially mixed, but it ascribes their origins to two and only two sources: they are a combination of the indigenous people and the Spanish. His apologia of the racial composition of the Dominican population leads him to employ a second argument that could even be seen initially as puerile: he accuses the French colonists of more intense racial mixing than their Spanish counterparts.[35]

In Sánchez-Valverde's argument there is an early use of indigenism as a means of explaining Santo Domingo's ethnic formation. This solution obviously distorts the colony's ethnoracial composition, for it utterly denies the existence of a large black and mulatto population. Sánchez-Valverde's racial rhetoric would later become a recurrent theme in Dominican literature. Faced with clear evidence of mestizaje in their country, many authors from the eighteenth century onward have explained that mixing as a racial synthesis between the Spanish and the indigenous population. Thus the true origin of mestizaje in Santo Domingo is concealed, and the demographically dominant black presence is ignored. By using his double argument that the Dominican people are "Indo-Hispanics" and that Spanish colonials had engaged in less racial mixing than had other Europeans, Sánchez-Valverde is able to explain away the evident contradiction of an overwhelmingly mixed population.

Above all, this double argument allows him to sustain the myth of his own class, an elite whose whiteness is at best questionable, as one sees in the case of Sánchez-Valverde himself. He openly acknowledges the apologetic character of his work. His defense is presented on various planes; racial definition is merely one of them. On one level Sánchez-Valverde also makes a claim regarding the historical role played by the colonial elite in the expansion of Spain's empire: he constructs a historical genealogy that traces the origins of his own social sector back to the conquistadors.[36] By this means he hopes to legitimize his demands that the metropolis develop a new colonial policy that will foster its economic recovery and, in consequence, strengthen the material foundations of its dominant groups. Sánchez-Valverde states in the very preface to his book that "the Apologia of the *Criollos* of [Santo Domingo] with respect to activity and genius, is an essential article without which the *Island* could not be encouraged to develop."[37]

Sánchez-Valverde also attempts to exonerate the Spanish-Dominican elite for the colony's economic prostration. He strikes the chord of a theme that will recur in modern Dominican literature: the historical tragedy of emigration. He particularly bemoans the emigration of wealthier families that began in the sixteenth century as a result of the decaying economy.[38] Although Sánchez-Valverde tries to conceal it, one of the consequences of that emigration was the "mulattoization" of the colonial elite. Since it is impossible to represent that elite as pure-blooded Spaniards, he employs the subterfuge of reminding his readers that the French were themselves racially mixed and of underscoring the efforts of the Spanish-Dominicans to avoid mestizaje, despite the colony's decline and isolation. In any case, the Dominican elite defined itself as "Indo-Hispanic" or as "criollo Spanish." The exoneration of the elite is thus given on two planes: the economic and the ethnosocial.

But Sánchez-Valverde's ultimate goal is the colony's economic recovery. That is why he emphasizes the resources that might be tapped in Santo Domingo and demands more slaves; that is why his model society is Haiti. He even argues that if the Spanish colony were strengthened economically, the French might eventually be evicted from the western part of the island. Determined to see his colony regain its lost splendor, Sánchez-Valverde sees slaves as the "key" to raising Santo Domingo to Haiti's level. He does not, however, address the racial and cultural consequences of bringing thousands of slaves into Santo Domingo. He does not even mention the potential danger of slave uprisings. How are we to interpret this silence? Is it a deliberate attempt to forestall possible opposition to his project? Or is it a reflection of a particular viewpoint of the masters: Negroes have no culture; they are a tabula rasa with nothing to contribute save the strength of their arms? Whatever the case, everything tends to indicate that Sánchez-Valverde's fundamental desire is for the Dominican elite to retain its Spanish roots. We may infer that this was guaranteed because the Spanish-Dominican elite did not share the "vices" of other groups of European extraction—that is, the propensity for sexual mixing with the Negroes.

Sánchez-Valverde constructs an apologia of the criollo elite, of his own class, as the future leaders of a new society. In defending the glory of their sixteenth-century ancestors, he aligns himself with that "we" which contributed to the efforts of the empire. His fundamental "other" is the French colonist occupying the western part of the island. Even though Haiti was a potential geopolitical threat and even though its dominant groups displayed—in Sánchez-Valverde's analysis—great moral weakness, the incipient Dominican elite of the eighteenth century saw in the French colony the most advanced model for a criollo utopia. In this new utopia, lost fortunes could be recovered and old hierarchies restored.

BONÓ: "MULATTOISM" AND NATIONAL PROJECT

But Sánchez-Valverde's utopia was only a chimera: the Haitian Revolution of 1791 did away with his dream.[39] Echoes of the revolution were heard clearly in Santo Domingo. The slaves in Haiti had actually rebelled against their masters: in Dominican eyes, this transformed the Negro from slave to bloodthirsty menace. The slave, once merely a means of getting work done, was now an arsonist, rapist, and murderer; his machete, once an agricultural tool, was now a weapon for chopping masters to bits. Likewise, the Haitian armies that occupied Santo Domingo during their struggles with the French, the Spanish, and the English were seen as sheer "hordes of savages."[40]

Later events tended to reinforce this image of the Haitians. In 1822, following a principle laid down by Toussaint L'Ouverture (whose purpose had been to defend the freedom of the Haitian masses), Haitian troops occupied Santo Domingo, thus initiating the period known as the Haitian Domination (1822–44). During these years the Haitian government and its president, Jean-Pierre Boyer, introduced various measures that negatively affected the interests of the dominant sectors. For example, Boyer's first official act after taking over the government of Santo Domingo was to abolish slavery. He next launched a program to distribute small-holdings among the freedmen and campesinos and then challenged the interests of the cattle ranchers and the Catholic Church. As a result, hundreds of Dominicans fled the country.[41]

In 1844 a clandestine organization of Dominican rebels wrested their independence from Haiti. From then until the late 1860s, the fate of the Dominican Republic depended on its ability to stave off Haitian attempts to reoccupy the eastern part of the island. In the midst of this uncertainty (characterized additionally by caudillismo and internal power struggles) a new alternative emerged: annexation. Diverse Dominican factions, fearing the "Haitian peril," advocated annexation to some large State that could protect them from absorption into Haiti. Some preferred the United States, while others looked toward Europe. Finally, in 1861, thanks to the efforts of its then president, General Pedro Santana, Santo Domingo was annexed to Spain. But the people revolted, in what became known as the War of Restoration, and national sovereignty was reestablished.[42]

This is the context in which Pedro Francisco Bonó (1828–1906) worked and wrote. His generation saw the birth of the Republic following the Haitian Domination; came of age during the postindependence period with all its conflicts, when the Republic had to validate its existence in defiance of Haiti; and finally played a significant role in the War of Restoration against Spain (1863–65).[43] Bonó's writings deal to a great extent with economic questions, yet his economic project appears to be subordinated to an affirmation of nationality. In other words, Bonó is trying to strengthen the foundations of a young nation whose framework is still shaky.

Bonó belongs to what we might call, for lack of a more precise term, the middle sector of Dominican society. His native Cibao was a region of small and medium landholdings; Bonó himself was a lawyer and a public official. Above all, however, he made his name as an economic and political commentator; thanks to this body of writings, Bonó is considered one of the founders of Dominican sociology.[44] He certainly belongs to the world of letters; although immersed in the political struggles of his day, he keeps a prudent distance from strident partisanship. It may be this relative withdrawal from power and the struggle to obtain it that allows him to take a critical stance vis-à-vis events, public figures, and processes.[45] Unlike Sánchez-Valverde's proposal, which attempts to reestablish the material bases of a social class by means of a project founded on discrimination and on clearly defined hierarchies, Bonó's project is integrative. He advocates equality under the law, a typical nineteenth-century liberal demand, but he also underlines the role of the subaltern classes in the formation of nationality.

Bonó traces the origins of Dominican society to the Spanish Conquest. It was Spanish domination, he claims, "that left the deepest mark" on Dominican society, "because it was the longest."[46] Above all, the long Spanish intervention left its stamp on Santo Domingo's institutions, which, having held sway for "twenty generations in succession," had become firmly entrenched "beliefs." This stamp was imprinted on a population fundamentally composed of Spanish and African elements, since the "indigenous race" had been swiftly wiped out.[47] This interpretation clearly contrasts with Sánchez-Valverde's with respect to the country's ethnoracial composition. Bonó, however, is less interested in human sedimentation than in the institutional substratum that accumulated over the centuries.

Bonó indicates that the Haitian Domination, while in many ways opprobrious, was "a transitional period that equipped the Dominican Republic to experience liberty." Thus, after the separa-

tion from Haiti, "the Dominican people displayed a new counte-
nance, [different] from that assumed under Spain's regime." Bonó
particularly emphasizes advances in "the rights of man" and the
abolition of slavery as positive elements of the Domination.[48] Indeed, Bonó believes that President Boyer, the Haitian governor of
the island during the Domination, had the opportunity "to have
founded the union of the two peoples on a more equitable and
advantageous basis[:] . . . confederation."[49] Haitian policy, however,
was based on the principle of the "indivisibility of the island,"
which in practice translated into attempts to subjugate the Dominican Republic. This principle was in direct conflict with attempts to
affirm a Dominican nationality. As a result, once independence
from Haiti was achieved, there emerged a "fundamental, inde-
structible antagonism between the two peoples."[50]

This antagonism between Haiti and the Dominican Republic
was marked by obvious differences in language and customs; it
also included a racial element. According to Bonó, the creation of
the Haitian State was based on exterminating "two races from its
soil, the white and the mixed."[51] This principle, while perhaps
"justified by previous events" and by "the barrier to slavery that
they [the Haitians] wished to erect," served to alienate the Dominican people. Thus Bonó writes that while Haiti developed a policy
based on "the exclusivity of a single race," the black race, the Dominican Republic was guided by "cosmopolitanism, the expansion
of all the races on its soil, although," he adds, "with a preference for
the white race."[52]

In Bonó's view, the origin of this difference between the two
countries is found in their respective colonial pasts. When Haiti was
a French colony, a deep-seated rancor developed between blacks and
whites, a product of the "hateful regimen of slavery of the former."
In contrast, in post-Conquest colonial Santo Domingo, "the Spaniard displayed supreme benevolence, great charity, and much tenderness, within the social inequalities." As a result, slaves in the
Spanish colony were not subjected to the "unthinkable suffering
borne by the slave race in the French colony." This moderate form of
slavery "made the mixing of the races easier" and precluded the
racial hatred seen in Haiti. Santo Domingo's colonial past made it
not only "morally superior" but also more open to other civiliza-

tions, "races and traditions" than Haiti. Moreover, that colonial legacy "has made and will make social or racial wars impossible in the Dominican Republic."[53]

Bonó's argument rests on an idealized view of slavery and race relations in the Dominican Republic. In the first place, we must remember that Hispaniola was actually the site of the first Caribbean ventures into slavery. The Spanish colonists began to import slaves from Africa as a substitute for indigenous workers when the demographic crisis of the sixteenth century brought on a labor shortage.[54] In other words, Africans were introduced into colonial Santo Domingo primarily for economic reasons. And while detailed studies of the subject are lacking, we must assume that master-slave relations in the predominantly plantation economy of the sixteenth century differed little from what would later be observed in other regions of the Americas. The plantation, slavery's birthplace in the Caribbean, was characterized by a rigid social structure; the proper places of masters and workers were clearly delimited.[55] At most, it might be argued that the decline of Santo Domingo's sugar economy led to somewhat more relaxed racial relations and, perhaps, some flexibility within the system of slavery.[56]

In the second place, Bonó fails to mention the numerous instances of Dominican life that contradict his claims of racial harmony, in the colonial period as well as the Republic. For example, when slaves fled or rebelled against their masters, that would have to be classified as episodes in that "social war" that Bonó claims was impossible in Santo Domingo.[57] The differences Bonó points out were more likely due to the dissimilar rates of economic development in Haiti and Santo Domingo, rather than to the "moral superiority" of Spanish colonialism, as he suggests. Dominican society's greater racial porosity compared with Haiti, as reflected in its more mulatto population, was primarily the result of the economic and demographic forces that molded Caribbean societies in general.

In short, Bonó believed that it was Haiti's particular colonial experience versus the Dominican Republic's that defined racial relations in each country. When colonialism ended in both, there emerged the opportunity to achieve a degree of harmony between the two nations. Haiti, however, chose the wrong path (according to

Bonó). First, Haiti chose racial "exclusivism"; second, it rejected confederation and attempted to impose its own political views on Santo Domingo. Had President Boyer followed the path of confederation, Bonó writes, "the diverse elements of the two peoples, which today have no center of balance, isolated as they are, would have combined to maintain an equilibrium between the black and white races."[58] But Boyer chose otherwise, and in consequence he closed the door to a confederation between the two nations and allowed them to follow conflicting racial policies.

In terms of racial policy, Bonó favors what we might call "mulattoism." This ideology of mulattoism is typical of his thought; he consistently shuns extremes. Thus, in response to the vast latifundios, Bonó champions the smallholding; in response to social polarization, he advocates strengthening the middle class; in response to proposals of centralization, Bonó defends federalism and local autonomy.[59] Nevertheless, his racial centrism has very specific implications. One of the detrimental effects of Haiti's racial exclusivism, according to Bonó, is that it isolates that society from European immigration and civilization. By separating from Haiti, the Dominican Republic broke away from that country's "exclusivist path" and took steps toward "attract[ing] the constant emigration that Europe casts from its soil for lack of space." This influx of immigrants would allow the formation of "a Dominican mass molded from all the foreign intelligences and forms of industry."[60] From that point of view, Bonó's defense of mulattoism may be seen as a means of diluting Dominican blackness. His mulattoism also implies a "modernizing" project: By distancing itself racially from its neighbor, Santo Domingo moves closer to Europe. Dominican mulattoism, or "cosmopolitanism" as Bonó calls it, would help to spur national regeneration through contact with Europe.[61]

In Bonó's view, the Dominican national character was founded on a Spanish substratum, yet it cannot in any way be defined as merely an extension of Spanishness. Furthermore, his view of Haiti includes some positive elements. As we have seen, for Bonó the contradiction between Haiti and the Dominican Republic has a racial overtone. Although he insists, sometimes emphatically, that the two countries are separated by historical, cultural, and political elements, he also acknowledges that common interests might arise that could lead Haiti and the Dominican Republic to overcome those differences. Above all, Bonó stresses the necessity of abandoning Haiti's racial exclusivism, in keeping "with the gradual disappearance . . . [of] concerns about color and origins." Due to its greater openness to the various races, the Dominican Republic would then have a "greater aptitude than its neighbor for producing the nucleus of a powerful confederation that would contribute in a worthy manner to the mission of the inhabitants of the Americas on the planet."[62] In fact, he does not see the racial element as an immutable factor, destined to be a permanent impediment to relations between the two nations.

But how representative is Bonó's way of thinking? Is it consistent with the predominant views of nineteenth-century Dominicans? To answer these questions adequately would require entering into a number of considerations, including hermeneutical questions, that are beyond the scope of this essay. At this point the best one can do is to place Bonó in the context of the *letrados* (men of letters) of his time, who are more or less representative of the perceptions of the hegemonic sectors. How, then, does Bonó compare with them? Briefly, he is at variance with predominant nineteenth-century opinions regarding Haiti. As I have indicated, his interpretation of Haiti's stamp on Santo Domingo is far from being completely negative. Moreover, he highlights a number of favorable results of the Haitian Domination, an event that is vilified by a good part of the Dominican intelligentsia, past and present.[63] By their very acts, dominant political figures of the nineteenth century reveal their aversion to Haiti: for example, Pedro Santana pushed for annexation to Spain mainly as a safeguard against Haiti; Buenaventura Báez, another important caudillo (who opposed Santana), was also known for his ardent anti-Haitianism.[64]

Where did Bonó's relatively favorable perceptions of Haiti come from, then? Were they simply the product of his intellectual ponderings, or did they stem, rather, from another type of reasoning? Indeed, it should be noted that not all sectors of Santo Domingo considered themselves to have been injured by Haitian rule. Freedmen and freedwomen, many of them blacks or mulattoes, along with more or less significant campesino groups, had reasons to identify themselves with the regime.[65] I have already mentioned

Bonó's opinions on the abolition of slavery. The Haitian government's policy of land distribution in Santo Domingo should also be considered. Bonó assigned a major role to smallholdings and campesinos in the emergence and survival of the republic. He called tobacco, which was grown on these small campesino plots, "the true *Father of the Fatherland.*"[66] Thus Bonó, who was sincerely democratic as well as liberal, must have seen the measures favorable to those sectors for what they were: progressive elements of the Haitian regime.[67] Finally, with respect to the racial question, substantial differences can be seen between Bonó's thought and that of politicians and letrados of his time. Far from lamenting mestizaje, Bonó came to think of it as an original element, not only of Dominican society but also of all of Hispanic America. Thus he hailed the coming of a sense of identity based not on Spanish origins but on the new realities of the New World.

New elements emerging in the late nineteenth and early twentieth centuries rerouted the Dominican discourse on Haiti and the racial question. Taken together, these factors widened the gap between the two countries and made Bonó's hope of confederation even less likely, albeit for new and different reasons. Special mention must be made of the development of the labor-intensive sugar industry. At first, the industry hired Dominican day workers, but it later turned increasingly to migrant workers. By the 1920s, braceros from Jamaica, Puerto Rico, and other Caribbean islands played a central role in the Dominican Republic's sugar production.[68]

Dominican and migrant workers were soon joined by ever larger contingents of Haitians. During the U.S. occupation of 1916–24, Haitians became the largest labor sector in the Dominican sugar industry.[69] Although these workers were basically foreigners, the sugar industry was reprising Sánchez-Valverde's dream. Haitians now wore a new mask.[70] No longer were they insurrectionist slaves or bloody invaders but rather "hands," a workforce. But in the imaginary, whether poetical, mythical, or political, masks are superimposed: one mask does not cancel out another. On the contrary, in the case of Haitians in the Dominican Republic, one mask reinforced the other: the image of the twentieth-century bracero confirmed the image of the eighteenth-century slave. But this image, grounded in the economy and production, reinforced previous images related to a very different reality.

The border dispute between Haiti and the Dominican Republic, still unresolved in the early twentieth century, heightened the perception of the Haitian as an invader. The border zone was rough and unprofitable terrain, but it became the site of a vigorous commercial, human, and cultural exchange between Dominicans and Haitians. Life in the border zone was often characterized by more or less peaceful coexistence, but just as often by a sense of competition that occasionally broke out into open hostility. To the Haitians, "crossing over" provided alternatives that were in short supply in their own country. Above all, it was easier to obtain land, pasture, and a water supply, assets that were highly valued by the inhabitants, most of them campesinos.[71] But for many Dominicans, Haitians settling in Dominican territory were evidence of an "imperialist" policy that was a continuation of the principle of the "indivisibility of the island" promulgated by Toussaint in the late eighteenth century and carried on by the "invading hordes" in the nineteenth. Dominican perceptions of the Haitians came together in a mutually reinforcing stream of images. Haitians were "thieves" and "usurpers," and they were "bloodthirsty." Unable to progress beyond the most rudimentary levels of social life, Haitians were, in short, "primitive": a hard mask, reinforced by those in power.

Anti-Haitian sentiment in the Dominican Republic was exacerbated during the dictatorship of Rafael L. Trujillo (1930–61).[72] The racial question and Haitian relations became the hubs—or effigies—of a nationalist discourse that was expressed on various planes. At the diplomatic level, attempts were made to resolve the border dispute once and for all. On the intellectual plane, intensive efforts were set in motion to reinforce anti-Haitianism. Manuel Arturo Peña-Batlle (1902–54) and Joaquín Balaguer (1906–2002), two of the most relevant intellectuals and public figures during the Trujillo regime, excelled in that respect. In the works of these two authors, the racial problem and anti-Haitianism are of central importance. In their view, Dominican nationality is defined, basically, in contrast to Haiti. Both assume that this contradiction had its origin in the very moment when the French began their contraband incursions onto the island of Hispaniola. In addition, they consider the coexistence of two nationalities on one island to be a contradiction in terms, an almost unnatural phenomenon, which translates into an ongoing struggle for space.

Naturally, proving this thesis would require a rewriting of Dominican history. According to Peña-Batlle, throughout its history Santo Domingo has suffered from a series of "social vicissitudes . . . , that may be classified in four periods, each one lasting a century": (1) During the sixteenth century, "we struggled against the [Protestant] Reformation," with contraband being "an agent in Calvinism's struggle against the powers of Catholicism"; (2) in the seventeenth century, there was a "state of war" against French buccaneers and freebooters, a confrontation with the "crass individualism that gave birth to the entire modern capitalist system"; (3) the following century was the setting for a long and sustained effort to "obtain a firm border that would save us from French penetration"; and (4) nineteenth-century Santo Domingo had to confront the "predominance of the slaves and the influence of the ideas and systems of French materialism and positivism," which translated into the Haitian Domination and the "turbulences" deriving from it.[73] The constant in each of these moments is the image of one (Dominican) community struggling against outside forces that threaten to distort or destroy its Spanishness.

In the opinion of Peña-Batlle, when the Treaty of Basilea (1795) gave France dominion over the former Spanish colony, Santo Domingo was already "a fully evolved country in accordance with the social order created by three elements: a civil and military government, an ecclesiastical government . . . , and a culture guided by classicism." Idealization of the colonial past is carried to the extreme in Peña-Batlle's writings. Like Bonó, he acknowledges social inequalities in the colony, but unlike Bonó, Peña-Batlle claims that in the evolved society, there were no elements of social inequity. By then, "a strict accommodation of classes and hierarchies" prevailed. Even the existence of slavery did not interfere with the "calm" rhythm of collective life: "There were no problems of caste, nor was life based upon inhumane formulas of exploitation." The slaves were in "a de facto state of manumission"; they did not try to gain their freedom because "they had no need for it."[74]

Haiti, in contrast, organized around the "infamous black slave trade . . . , did not evolve toward any form of culture." Above all, the absence of "religious influences" and an "organized political" system hampered the "process of national integration."[75] The "mass of slaves . . . was impervious to any cultural influence"; the freedmen were "persons [only] semi-incorporated into civilization." Bereft of any religious training, the slaves clung to animistic practices brought over from Africa. They did not even rise to the level of "a language that would serve as an instrument to express their ideas": the patois that developed from mixing different African languages was unable to "support cultural formation." In other words, Haiti had developed "below even the most elementary strata of a true culture."[76] As a result of such divergent colonial experiences, Santo Domingo and Haiti went through utterly dissimilar processes of national formation. The French colony lacked a "unifying culture": "Theirs is a society with nothing that one could properly call 'history,' with no traditional antecedents, with no starting point and with no spiritual roots. The history of Haiti as a nation begins with the slave uprising and has no past upon which to establish itself."[77]

With the slave revolution, the lack of this unifying element was even more sharply felt. After all, it was a rebellion of "the oppressed classes, with no historical tradition, with no cultural formation, with no spiritual structure, with no judicial structure, . . . with no established family order, with no organization of property."[78] Due to the extermination or emigration of "the white social class," the former slaves became the human foundation of the new social and political regime—a totally disastrous situation, from Peña-Batlle's racist and elitist perspective. Moreover, the Haitian Revolution was not organized from the beginning around any clear principle of human freedom or political independence; it was, rather, the actions of "dispersed and inorganic" groups with no ruling ideal to guide them. The revolution originated in hatred and a "hunger for vengeance"; it was "the negation of any rule." From such a revolution "no truly constructive result" could be expected.[79]

Meanwhile, in Santo Domingo there had occurred a process of cultural and institutional sedimentation, thanks to the imprint left by Spain. This three-hundred-year process had produced on Dominican soil a community that was *Spanish* (at least culturally); in

Peña-Batlle's words, there was a "consubstantiation of our social forms with those of Spain."[80] In a passage worthy of inclusion in an anthology of the mind-set of the colonized, Peña-Batlle says, "The Santo Domingo of 1795 and of 1809 was more Spanish than Godoy and Ferdinand VII and represented the values of tradition with greater purity and meaning than did they."[81] Haiti, according to Peña-Batlle, was the negation of that "world of values and social hierarchies of a truly Spanish character."[82] Thus the Haitian Revolution and its aftermath represented a threat to "the oldest Christian country in America."[83] From the Treaty of Basilea until the Haitian Domination ended in 1844, Santo Domingo lived under "a denationalizing regime" that tended to force "the roots of our spirit" underground; Peña-Batlle stresses that during that period "we suffered the domination of the horde."[84]

That is why, according to Peña-Batlle, Santo Domingo's independence in 1844 had a "conservative conformation."[85] The Dominican Republic was created in response to a "definite sense of culture"[86]—that is, the separation from Haiti was a reactionary movement in defense of Spanish culture, which had been threatened by the measures imposed by the occupiers. Had that regime continued, Dominicans would have lost "the very essence of nationality . . . which is founded on the language that we speak, the religion that we profess, the habits and customs that make us a society; on the way in which we build our towns, use our wealth [of resources], comply with the principle of authority . . . , all direct results of the civilization and culture that Spain brought to the island."[87] The struggle against Haiti was the crucible in which the Dominican nation was formed. In 1844, the year of the separation from Haiti, "we had no definite national consciousness";[88] the hostile period against Haiti was a catalyst to that end.

From that time on, the center of gravity for the Dominican people would be the defense of their judicial, territorial, social (that is, racial), and cultural personality vis-à-vis Haiti. To Peña-Batlle, the country's noblest figures on both the intellectual and political planes are those who strive to validate the Dominican "personality" in the face of the Haitian "menace." He justifies the actions of the previous century's annexationists to the extent that they "attempted to ensure the cultural conquest implicit in a separation from Haiti by means of effective contact between our culture and that of another European nation, preferably Spain."[89]

Even Trujillo won Peña-Batlle's admiration and support, thanks to Trujillo's policy of "Dominicanization," which was manifested in the dictator's efforts to set definitive boundaries between his country and Haiti. In fact, Peña-Batlle played a major role in the border negotiations, and the border issue is prominent in his writings.[90] "Under the Trujillo regime," stated Peña-Batlle in 1945, "we have won unimaginable victories," particularly in conserving "the Spanish character of our nationality."[91] In his opinion, the "misfortunes" that Dominicans had suffered throughout their history and that had hampered the country's definitive conformation had disappeared under Trujillo. It was during his regime of force that the Dominican Republic was able to confront the State of Haiti effectively.

Two of the ideological mainstays of the regime were anti-Haitianism and a refined Hispanophilia. This "reactionary and aggressive nationalism," to quote the historian Roberto Cassá,[92] was accompanied by messianic propaganda that presented Trujillo as the protector of Dominican nationality from Haiti's expansionist pretensions. Peña-Batlle's obsession with the "Haitian problem" leads him in his apologia to Trujillo to justify even the most ominous elements of the dictator's policies. Thus, the heinous massacre of Haitians that took place in the border zone in 1937 is presented as an event of primary importance in the defense of Dominican nationality. This was one of the "unimaginable victories" of the Trujillo government. It happened the way it did because Trujillo understood that the "mathematical calculation" of the boundary line was only one (and according to Peña-Batlle, the least complex) aspect of the border issue. What he considered to be the fundamental aspect, Haitians' settling in Dominican territory, was handled by means of "the pruning" (*poda*),[93] the popular designation for the Massacre of 1937.

Let us remember: this incident occurred during the rise of fascism in Europe and the maelstrom of the Spanish Civil War. In other words, these were the years when the most atrocious crimes were committed in the name of the purity of the "nation"—as defined by those in power and based on a set of fixed and exclusive characteristics. In the Dominican Republic, as in other countries of the Americas, certain influences were becoming palpable: the influence of fascism and of doctrines in Europe that were promulgating the "cleansing" of one's nation of all those elements which were considered alien to the national "essence" and which were thought to somehow weaken that nation.[94]

Although Peña-Batlle's nationalist discourse is clearly racist, it does include a culturalist and historicist element: the cultural and historical divergences between Haiti and Santo Domingo and the way these differences molded the Dominican national spirit. His vision of the nation is idealistic, even mystical; we should recall his use of "consubstantiation," a term with obvious religious roots. Whereas Sánchez-Valverde's project is based on a clearly defined economic program and whereas Bonó is as concerned with the nation's political and administrative foundation as he is with its material bases, Peña-Batlle views nationality primarily as defined by its cultural, religious, and institutional substrata. To Peña-Batlle, strengthening the Dominican State (achieved in particular during the Trujillo regime) and broadening the Republic's material bases were the means by which that legacy could be preserved.

ANTHROPOLOGY, DEMOGRAPHISM, AND RACIAL DISCOURSE

Although Peña-Batlle's vision was very influential, it was not the only interpretation of the formation of the Dominican nation to flourish during the Trujillo dictatorship. Among the more widespread discourses is one that has obvious Malthusian roots and is based on the most reactionary modalities of physical anthropology and demography: the kernels of this discourse are "race" and color. Among the works of this order, I will especially note *La isla al revés*, by Joaquín Balaguer.[95] As Meindert Fennema and Troetje Loewenthal have pointed out, for Balaguer "race" (defined phenotypically) and "nation" are synonymous.[96] Thus, what makes Dominican nationality distinctive is its "Spanish physiognomy"; Haiti, on the other hand, is distinguished by its black population (which is seen in the final analysis as an element of "Africanization").

In keeping with this view, Balaguer sees culture as a derivative of race. For example, the predominance in Haiti of voodoo and magico-religious practices is "a product of race": biology begets society. Likewise, he explains the "underlying superstitiousness" among Dominicans by alluding to "the presence in our blood of features characteristic of the primitivism of the African race." Fortunately, Balaguer declares, the "African influence" in Dominican culture "has been almost imperceptible" in comparison with that in Haiti. Therefore, "our cultural tradition preserves the stamp of our Spanish origin."[97]

In any case, the "African" influence (by way of Haiti) on Dominican culture and society is totally pernicious. Therefore, Balaguer concludes, "the [Dominican] Republic, in order to subsist as a Spanish nation, must safeguard the *somatic* differences that distinguish it from Haiti."[98] This goal, however, has been hampered by the supposedly "peaceful invasion" of Dominican territory by Haitians. According to Balaguer, the Haitian government, having failed in its attempt to regain total control over the island, opted for "gradually taking over entire zones of the border region." This strategy was implemented by establishing "large family nuclei from the neighboring country" in Dominican territory. Balaguer sees the fact that these families are from "the classes in the lowest social conditions" as further aggravating the situation.[99]

Balaguer goes on to note that "Haitian imperialism" is a greater danger in the present than in the past "for reasons of a biological nature." The density of Haiti's population, since Haitians multiply "almost as fast as the vegetable species," tends to lead to emigration. To Balaguer, that is the root of the Haitian migrations into the Dominican Republic. He does indeed mention other factors, such as the sugar industry's demand for a labor force and even Haiti's declining economy, but beneath it all, his interpretation is biologistic.[100] This argument reinforces the perception that the Haitian people are utterly primitive. Even their reproductive patterns, similar to those of plants, fall outside the realm of humankind! These immigrants cause an increase in the black population of the Dominican Republic and "corrupt its ethnic physiognomy."[101] Given Balaguer's identification of race and nation, this is a sign of a process of "denationalization." Contact with Haitians brings "ethnic decay" (which to Balaguer signifies physical degradation) and coupled with that a relaxing of "our public customs," which in turn produces a number of national ills.[102]

The Balaguerist interpretation of Haiti's population growth and of migrations to the Dominican Republic wraps itself in the mantle of science.[103] Balaguer bases his argument on what Arcadio Díaz-Quiñones (referring to Puerto Rican writer Tomás Blanco) has called "statistical language."[104] His purpose is to demonstrate the "torrential" population growth that must occur in Haiti, since in that country "the biological act of procreation" does not meet with the "restraints to be found in a state of advanced civilization."[105] In several passages of his work, Balaguer links Haiti's high birth rate to its economic, social, and cultural "primitivism"—a term he considers synonymous with "barbaric customs," "sexual promiscuity," and "incestuous unions," practices that are in opposition to the "family of the Christian variety."[106]

In keeping with the preeminence that he assigns to the racial factor in the formation of the two countries, Balaguer attempts to reconstruct the history of the Dominican population in furtherance of his principal thesis: the fundamental whiteness of the Dominican people and the Haitian influence on its "ethnic corruption."[107] In his view, once the brief period of splendor in the sixteenth century had passed, the colonial era was characterized by a long process of depopulation. According to his figures, that tendency began to change in the second half of the eighteenth century. But as a result of Santo Domingo's cession to France at the end of that century and of the Haitian Revolution and its aftermath, the Dominican population dropped dramatically.[108] Balaguer argues that this fragile demographic base was an advantage to "Haitian imperialism." The nineteenth century, he claims, was the nadir of the Dominican population.[109] But this opinion contradicts his own figures, which show a recovery beginning at that very time, in spite of invasions, wars, and the Haitian Domination.[110]

The reconstruction of Dominican demographic history in *La isla al revés* involves, above all, a mythification of the country's racial composition. Balaguer is determined to show that Santo Domingo, following the extermination of the "indigenous race," became the seat of the "*spiritually* most select and *physically* most homogeneous race of the American continent." Balaguer evidently equates "spiritual" with "physical" excellence, both of which are represented, according to his criteria, by the white "race." He writes,

"The population of the colony consists of the flower of the families that had emigrated to America." Ignoring a lengthy record of slave trade beginning in the sixteenth century, he opines that it was the cession of Santo Domingo to France at the end of the eighteenth century that opened the floodgates and allowed the Spanish part of the island to fill up with African slaves. Subsequently, the emigration en masse of the "most select nucleus of the Dominican population," Spain's lack of interest in its colony's affairs, and the ineptitude of various republican governments all contributed to the increase in the "African penetration."[111]

In this mythification of the past, Balaguer employs a method that is common in other regions of the Caribbean, particularly Puerto Rico: he erects a myth of the white campesino.[112] Based on a rudimentary, ideologically charged anthropology, Balaguer points with simultaneous pride and longing to the existence of campesino communities "that preserve all their primitive [that is, white] ethnic features, owing to the fact that for entire centuries they had no contact with descendants of the African race." Such was the case, according to Balaguer, of numerous communities in the Cordillera Central.[113] It is, however, the municipality of Baní that best represents the "Dominican spirit," "the flower of the Republic." Baní is "the least [racially] mixed area of the country," where "the virtues of the [white] race" are preserved and "the simplicity of patriarchal customs" is maintained. For these reasons, Balaguer wishes to make "of the entire Dominican population a community like that of Baní."[114]

Balaguer's rejection of the black element in the Dominican Republic leads him to revile even mestizaje. Here, once again, he attempts to validate his arguments "scientifically." Citing various anthropologists in extenso, Balaguer argues that "crossing . . . two diametrically opposed races" produces harmful results.[115] Although he cannot avoid acknowledging the extent of mestizaje in the Dominican Republic—for the census data is against him this time[116]—he believes that it is truly a threat to the nation. At best, mestizaje is only a palliative in the process by which the "white race" is being absorbed by the "Ethiopian race."[117]

In Balaguer's work, national identity is defined in terms of a physical anthropology that dovetails with nineteenth-century racist thought. His statements, then, are clearly anachronistic,[118] although the anachronisms were not as obvious when his stances were first published. Balaguer's line of reasoning in *La isla al revés* revolves around a recovery of a lost paradise: a return to the Spanish past.[119] This past, as in the writings of Peña-Batlle, is defined in cultural and spiritual terms; in Balaguer, the two categories converge in the trope of "race."[120] Balaguer's national project, then, is aimed at making the Dominican Republic "a clean nation," at recovering its "original features,"[121] purportedly Spanish. In his view, racial homogeneity is a necessary condition for the nation's existence.

EPILOGUE

The Dominican Republic is an island surrounded by water and Haitians on every side.

   Dominican student's answer on a geography test,
   cited by Rafael E. Yunén, La isla como es *(Santiago, 1985)*

Deep within us all are the seeds of hate for what is different. We do not have to be taught these things. We have to be taught not to give in to them!

   Anne Rice, Taltos *(New York, 1995)*

It takes a variety of elements, we are told by a wide range of authors, to bring about the emergence of a nation. Although some emphasize one factor and others another, scholars who have studied the phenomenon of nationhood have stressed, above all, the existence of a common territory; a shared history; the development of original cultural forms—products of community life and interaction with other societies—one of the most important of these forms being language; and the existence of material bases that provide for the survival of the group and ensure the integration of its diverse social components. The interaction of these factors, with all their historical peculiarities, usually results in the creation of an autonomous nation-State. In the case of a subject nationality, movements often arise whose goal is the constitution of their own State.[122]

Traditionally, Marxism has considered the emergence of an integrated internal market to be indispensable in the formation of a nation. According to this view, a nation is the result, first and foremost, of the development of its productive forces. Generally speaking, this process began in Western Europe in the sixteenth century.[123] However, valid though this view may be for Europe, it is insufficient to explain the complex historico-cultural entities found in other parts of the planet. What are we to say, for example, about modern States—such as countries in the Andes region—where diverse cultural formations coexist? Is the nation, as a historical category, the exclusive economic, political, and ideological creation of the bourgeoisie? Or is the nation not so much a set of "objective" characteristics as it is a cultural construct, an "imaginary community" as Benedict Anderson suggests?[124] How are we to evaluate the perceptions of nationhood that arise from sectors that are subordinated, sometimes distanced from official structures and disconnected from the dominant economic and cultural currents?[125] What relationship exists between the perceptions of the national collective that develop among economically and culturally hegemonic sectors, on the one hand, and subordinate sectors, on the other?

Of course, almost all societies are culturally and ethnically heterogeneous; after all, nationality is not monolithic. But despite this diversity (sometimes openly acknowledged, in some rare cases even encouraged), there is usually some implicit consensus on what "belongs" in the nation and what does not. Consequently, the nation as a specific entity tends to be defined by contrasting it with an "other." That "other"—whether near or far, known or unknown, as Todorov explains—delimits the "we" of "we the people."[126] The images that are created and re-created of that "other" will depend on a number of factors. Thus, for eighteenth-century Dominicans (especially those of the dominant groups), the black population of Haiti, far from presenting a threat, represented the possibilities of a new economic order. But the Haitian Revolution showed these sectors the other side of the coin, and the occupation of Santo Domingo by armies of freedmen and the Haitian Domination reinforced the image of a "bloodthirsty," "invading," and "primitive" Haitian. In short, from the eighteenth century to the nineteenth, the image of the "other" was inverted; in fact, the Haitian then became the "other" par excellence.

But how widespread was this perception in the nineteenth century? The question is not easy to answer satisfactorily, let alone fully. Still, some signs indicate that certain sectors of the Dominican population held a less ferocious image of Haiti. Bonó's vision indeed suggests this, even though he is critical of Haiti's government and State policies. Did this vision of Bonó's spring from his ideological affinity to the popular sectors of the Dominican Republic? If so, then his writings are part of the "heterogeneous literary currents" in the Americas, texts which though immersed in the dominant culture express alternative views of the world and society. According to Martin Lienhard, one source of these alternative views is popular culture, especially that of groups marginalized for ethnoracial reasons.[127] Thus, while the actions of the hegemonic groups demonstrated their anti-Haitian xenophobia, Bonó pointed out features of the relationship with Haiti that had contributed to the emergence of the Dominican nationality.

But Bonó's words of moderation were drowned out by events of the twentieth century, when the "border problem" and the importation en masse of Haitian braceros for the sugar industry became the relevant constituents of the "Haitian image." Although these events were a reflection of extremely complex historical processes and sociocultural realities, a number of authors interpret the two phenomena on the theory of a "peaceful invasion." The authors used this term to evoke the conflict-filled relations between Santo Domingo and Haiti during the colonial period and also to establish a link between migratory processes and the politically determined occupations of the nineteenth century. Consequently, they interpret the Haitian presence without taking into account new historical conditions that motivated the massive twentieth-century immigration into Dominican territory. In addition, the Haitian presence is seen as a denationalizing element; the Haitian is the "other" who is establishing himself, threateningly, in the nation. Once the nation is identified with "Spanishness," a term that carries all sorts of cultural and racial baggage, then by extension everything that is "black" and identified with Haiti becomes antinational. Those who begin by merely detailing differences soon "turn [the Haitian] into 'the enemy,'" to use Zaglul's appropriate conceptualization.[128] During the Trujillo dictatorship, which coincided with the rise of fascism in Europe, anti-Haitianism took on the rank of reasons of

State. Thus, as part of the policy of "Dominicanizing the border," in 1937 thousands of Haitians were murdered in a Dante-esque massacre.

National constructs in Peña-Batlle and Balaguer are in keeping with these perceptions. In each, there is a conception of the nation based on a number of fixed attributes; thus the Dominican nation becomes characterized by a putative Spanish cultural and ethno-racial legacy. Their projects of national affirmation are defined by a need to rescue that past, which has become contaminated by the black presence. By despising that black presence, they indirectly reject the decisive contribution of the popular sectors in the formation of the nation. After all, the basis of the nation should be the families that were "spiritually select and physically homogeneous," to use Balaguer's terminology. Their national utopia is not only openly racist but also frankly elitist.

But what is the relationship between the interpretations of letra-dos in service to the State—what Gramsci called "organic intellectuals"[129]—and popular perceptions? In particular, is anti-Haitian prejudice among the popular sectors simply a reflection of the ideology of the dominant classes, instilled in the masses from above, by the State? There is no doubt that anti-Haitianism and racism increased during the Trujillo regime because they were the "official" policy. The popular sectors, however, have also developed their own vision of the Haitian "other."[130] This version, less articulated than the "lettered" edition, constitutes a formidable obstacle to the emergence of any national project contemplating a qualitatively different relationship with the Haitian nation. And this is without taking into consideration the anti-Dominican prejudice that exists in Haiti.

For the two peoples, this is a major dilemma. The facts of the present situation indicate that the "national problem" and the question of identity in Hispaniola will soon be even more acute. First, the stream of immigration is not drying up; on the contrary, it has been swelling since the 1960s. Today, more than ever before, the Dominican Republic seems to be "surrounded by Haitians on every side." Their presence has not been confined to the *batey* of the sugar industry but rather has extended to a variety of economic activities, in the cities as well as the country. Furthermore, the social, economic, political, and cultural situation has become much more complex in both countries. Economic instability; the obvious ecological crisis on the island (more patent in Haiti, although with direct effects on the Dominican side); the vigorous demographic growth on both sides of the border, typical in underdeveloped countries; the migration of Haitians and Dominicans in search of better opportunities in life (Haitians move primarily toward the Dominican Republic, while Dominicans move especially to the United States and Puerto Rico); and the search for more representative and democratic political systems are but some of the factors that currently have a bearing on relations between the two countries.

New visions of the Haitian "other" will have to take into account not just the old "masks" but also these current realities. What, specifically, will be the content of these visions? Will they lean, as Bonó desired to some extent, toward cooperation or perhaps even some sort of integration? Or will they tend toward the intensification of old phobias and rivalries? This latter impulse would seem to be more likely, given the current international situation in which long-dormant national claims have reawakened. Eastern Europe and the former Soviet Union are only the most conspicuous examples of this phenomenon. The socialist regimes of Europe were unable to adequately resolve their "national problem": all too often, the alternatives that were implemented were mere formalities, "patches," unable to satisfy each national group's legitimate longings for autonomy. On the other hand, in highly developed capitalist countries, the very prosperity of their economies has incited migration from the less developed periphery. In Western Europe and in the United States, the growing presence of "others," mainly from the third world, has already provoked defensive reactions and even, in some sectors at least, a return to xenophobia.

The national utopias at the end of the twentieth century certainly seemed to privilege homogeneity over diversity. But is another type of utopia possible? According to Todorov, it is possible to "discover the other in ourselves."[131] He indicates that it is also possible to discover ourselves in others. Can we find in this double recognition the possibility of constructing new utopias and new identities?

To Emilio Cordero-Michel and Américo Badillo:
for them, there are no forks in the path to being Antillean.

The Island of Forking Paths

Jean Price-Mars and the History of Hispaniola

A BOOK AND A LABYRINTH

A labyrinth of symbols. . . . An invisible labyrinth of time.
   Jorge Luis Borges

Argentinean writer Jorge Luis Borges tells of an imaginary novel that is "a huge riddle, or parable, whose subject is time." In this novel, the fictitious author casts off the linear concept of time, constructing instead "an infinite series of times," like a maze—a "fabric of times that approach one another, fork, are snipped off, or are simply unknown for centuries."[1] Borges's story is an appropriate metaphor for the writing of history, for any perusal of the past—be it mythological or historiographic—is a reflection about time, a poetics of time, an attempt to gain mastery over time "in order to satisfy one's own aspirations for happiness and justice or one's fears in the face of the deceptive and disturbing concatenation of events."[2] As they do in Borges's labyrinth, times in history may intersect or run parallel to each other; they may converge or diverge, merge or split, confirm or negate one another. The same image may be used to describe the coexistence in one space of multiple time streams—for example, one island with two histories. Thus *La República de Haití y la República Dominicana*,[3] like the novel in the Borges story, is a book and a labyrinth. Its author journeys down different paths—history, ethnology, sociology, literature—in his attempt to trace Hispaniola's evolution from the colonial period onward, highlighting factors that led to the emergence of two distinct nations. In so doing, he treads the tortuous routes to national identity.

Jean Price-Mars (1876–1969), the author of this monumental work, is to Haiti what Fernando Ortiz, Gilberto Freyre, and José Carlos Mariátegui are to Cuba, Brazil, and Peru, respectively.[4] In the early twentieth century these intellectuals set out to define and reevaluate their national identities, often based on approaches— problematical and contradictory, of course—to the popular cultures. Like Ortiz and Freyre, Price-Mars joins ethnology to history in order to "uncover" the African roots of Haitian society and culture; *So Spoke the Uncle* (*Ainsi parla l'Oncle* [1928]), a collection of lectures delivered in the 1920s, is a pioneer work in the study of Haitian popular culture.[5] Included in this text is Price-Mars's study of the magico-religious beliefs of Haiti's great campesino population. His intention here is to show that despite current prejudices, voodoo is a religion in the full sense of the word, equipped with deities, a priesthood, a theology, and a morality.[6] But his contributions to the study of Afro-Antillean culture go beyond the borders of the Republic of Haiti, which is why Price-Mars is considered a precursor of the Negritude movement in the Caribbean.[7]

Price-Mars's interest in the subaltern sectors of Haitian society is not surprising; "men of letters" (*letrados*) in most Latin America and Caribbean countries shared this interest, especially during the critical decades of the 1920s and 1930s. At that time reevaluations were being made of the contributions of the popular sectors— particularly those of African or indigenous origins—in the formation of the various societies of the Americas. While some conceptualizations arose that rejected all nonwhite, non-Western elements in the cultures of the Americas, other intellectual currents emerged that championed indigenous and African roots. This type of vindication would culminate in the cultural and political movements known as Negritude and Indigenism.[8] In the case of Haiti in particular, this approach was determined by the active resistance of the popular sectors (especially the campesinos) to the U.S. occupation of 1915–34. In reaction to what the young Price-Mars saw as the elite's virtual abandonment of the revolutionary tradition that had put an end to the colonial regime, he raised to the level of national heroes those Haitian campesinos, known as *cacos*, who defied the U.S. forces.[9] It was at this juncture, so crucial for the Republic of Haiti, that Price-Mars wrote his essay "La vocation de l'elite" (1917) in which, according to Jacques Antoine, he denounces the elite for its inability to promote the welfare of the Haitian masses.[10] Price-Mars takes Haiti's elite to task for rejecting its African heritage wherein lay, he claims, the nation's true ethnic foundations. After independence, the elite sectors—particularly the mulattoes—had adhered to a "Gallo-Latin" cultural tradition, whence originated a "moral disequilibrium resulting tragically in the American Occupation." The "harmful gap between the elite and the masses" was such that there were "two nations within the Nation."[11]

Based on these reflections, Price-Mars coined the term "collective Bovarism" to describe the propensity of the lettered and dominant sectors in Haiti for identifying themselves culturally with Europe while denying or ignoring their African legacy. In the view of the intellectual and social elite, the black masses "had no history, no religion, no morals," and "their only hope was to acquire these things from Europe."[12] Price-Mars's conception of the distant, isolated life of the elite was a key element of his thought. (Among his contemporaries, it was Dantès Bellegarde, one of the principal intellectuals of his time, who was best known for defending the Western cultural tradition that was the goal of the elite's civilizing project.)[13] To Price-Mars, "Bovarism" was a state of virtual cultural alienation, with obvious psychological connotations; he also used it to explain the stormy relations between Haiti and the Dominican Republic. Also noteworthy is his attempt to link questions of identity and national formation to the social problems of the great masses, above all to those of the campesino sectors in Haiti. As was common among the Latin American and Caribbean intelligentsia of the time, Price-Mars found in the overwhelmingly black campesino masses the essence of Haitian nationality. In this there were clearly points of contact between Price-Mars and those who saw in the rural masses (be they Afro-American, Native American, or white) the basis for the societies of the New World. In the words of Ángel Rama, "rural cultures" had a "long history and conservatism" that "provided a broad legitimating foundation for conceptions of nationality."[14] Therefore Price-Mars did not simply ponder the cultural and political implications of the conduct of the elite vis-à-vis the Haitian masses; in addition, he denounced the economic exploitation to which these masses were subjected.

These two closely entwined threads—defense and vindication of the African heritage and condemnation of the economic exploitation of the masses—were meant to buttress a new ethnic, social, and cultural identity, thus clearing the way for a redefining of the nation. These threads also lent an ethical component to the project of national regeneration. It was not a new strategy. Latin American and Caribbean elites had adopted similar political and discursive practices in diverse historical circumstances. "We the Indians" was the cry of the elite in Cuzco, an appeal to an "imaginary community" forged by the upper class of the Peruvian sierra for the purpose of validating before the national government their proposals for greater regional autonomy.[15] The same pretext was used in Puerto Rico by the nineteenth-century criollo elite, who would (when it suited their purpose) put on a "jíbaro (campesino) mask" before the Spanish colonial rulers in the hopes of justifying their demands for co-government.[16]

To Price-Mars, the concept of "elite" has specific dimensions. First of all, it includes economic and political connotations, patent in the existence of a state system that depended to a great degree on the taxation of crops. That is why Price-Mars denounces the levies imposed on coffee—the country's chief export, produced by the campesinos.[17] The privileged position of the elite is also manifest in regard to access to the machinery of State and the political system in general. A second determinant in the makeup of the elite is its ethnoracial composition. Although the rule is not absolute, the elite tended to be of mixed blood, unlike the bulk of the population; this difference translated into disdain for the black components of Haitian society. It is for this reason that racial questions—the so-called caste problem—occupy such a prominent place in the writings of Price-Mars. Moreover, these topics were among the first that he dealt with publicly, as evidenced by his essays on "Haiti and the Racial Problem," which he delivered as two lectures in 1906 and 1907.[18] His concept of the elite, however, also carries with it a moral dimension, requiring a leadership role in the material, political, and cultural progress of the nation. Consequently, Price-Mars gives considerable attention to educational themes: schools, literacy programs, and the dissemination of the written word are all part of his civilizing program. This concern resulted in his surveys of the "intellectual tools" available in Haiti (in which he takes stock of printing presses, newspapers, magazines, libraries), of the population's "taste for reading," and of the "formation [or education] of the elite" (in which he inventories elementary and secondary schools, students, and graduates).[19] It was the responsibility of the elite, by virtue of their position in society and their cultural formation (in the Western mold), to promote the progress of the masses. To educate was to civilize.

As an outgrowth of his educational project, so intimately linked to his political concerns, Price-Mars arrives at the systematic study of "folklore"—that is, of popular culture. By way of ethnology and sociology—due above all to his concerns regarding the racial question—he comes to history, although there is no clear-cut separation in his work between the various disciplines. His focus is, after all, on the formation of the Haitian nation, in the interests of which Price-Mars develops a number of different perceptions, hoping to shed light on its mysteries and discover the way out of the intricate maze. Several corridors of the labyrinth lead him directly to a scrutiny of Haiti's relations with the Dominican Republic, a subject that, by his own testimony, he had been studying since the 1930s.[20] History, geography, anthropology, and politics were all to intersect in this new terrain.

A LABYRINTH THAT IMPLIED THE STARS

I imagined a labyrinth of labyrinths, a maze of mazes, a twisting, turning, ever-widening labyrinth that contained both past and future and somehow implied the stars.

Jorge Luis Borges

Price-Mars is an author of categorical interpretations. His book on Haiti and the Dominican Republic is marked by a number of theses that organize his arguments and his narrative. The "great tragedy" of the "Negro" is the connecting thread running through his work, which is conceived as a drama with obvious epic connotations. The Haitian epic dates back to the country's origins. It was the demographic differences between Haiti and Santo Domingo that gave rise to the subsequent "problems" between the two countries, despite the fact that Price-Mars considered those differences to be matters "of degree, not of kind" (a point that would be disputed by several Dominican authors). From those differences erupted conflicts between the Spanish and French regions of the island during the colonial period, in spite of "centuries of contacts" and "the indeterminate jumble of hues," a phrase that evokes the ethnic and cultural *mestizaje* that began with the European conquest. A crucial aspect of the historical drama of the "Negro" in Hispaniola is "the cruelty of slavery," especially in the French colony of Saint-Domingue. From the oppression and suffering of the slaves sprang resistance in various expressions, including the slave rebellion of 1791, and the slaves' "tenacious will to constitute a nationhood." Erected upon this foundation of will was the desire to unify Hispaniola under a single government, an idea that was demolished by the Dominican "lack of comprehension." From that time onward, the Republic of Haiti (virtually synonymous in Price-Mars's narrative with "the Negro," the black people) would struggle to keep Hispaniola from falling prey to "imperialists in disguise." Ironically, Price-Mars concludes, these historical processes would lead to a "perspective of destruction of one or the other of these nationalities."[21]

Having outlined the historical processes involved, Price-Mars concludes that Haiti's nation building has significance that transcends its borders. Haiti's hallmark is a pure "vocation for liberty"[22] that can be seen throughout its history, and it is in this light that Price-Mars perceives historical processes as having profound significance, transcending the strictly episodic and/or any immediate implications or consequences. The events of the history of Haiti and of its relations with Santo Domingo are interpreted, in Kahler's words, as "part of something larger, or superior"; each event is "a link, or a function within a comprehensive whole, that . . . points to something beyond."[23] In addition to their immediate significance in the formation of a new nationality, the historical processes that took place in Hispaniola from 1492 forward are a part (in Price-

Mars's conception) of world history. The struggles of the slaves, the processes that defined Haiti's nationality, and even the conflicts between Haiti and Santo Domingo are all merely tributaries feeding the wondrous current of the struggle for "human freedom." Paraphrasing Benedetto Croce, we might say that Price-Mars conceived of history as a saga, a story, an adventure in the search for liberty.[24] His nationalism is thus interwoven with an enlightened humanism that sees the nation as part of a greater whole. On one level, Price-Mars perceives his nation in the context of American societies striving for identity and autonomy; on a second level, he relates it to humanity's struggle for liberty.

Price-Mars's notes on the history of Haiti from the colonial period until independence (1804) clearly show his emphasis on Haiti's "vocation" for liberty. Forming the cornerstone of this vocation were *cimarronaje*[25] and rebellions "against the regime of slavery." Price-Mars argues that the punitive measures utilized by colonial authorities were all in vain, since in this epic struggle, "like Hydra in the legend, the resistance of the Negroes would cease only to arise once more, and more menacingly, decades later, no longer incited and organized by the same individuals . . . but rather preserved in the workshops as a gratifying memory and passed down from father to son, like the most glorious of traditions, through many successive generations."[26]

Price-Mars affirms that the slaves were "a gregarious multitude whose only homogeneity lay in their common suffering,"[27] yet in his emphasis on their tradition of passionate resistance, he implies that the Haitian masses were far from being the "bland, amorphous society" with "an almost total lack of any unifying culture" described by Dominican writer Manuel A. Peña-Batlle.[28] That tradition of struggle provided the slaves of Saint-Domingue with a collective memory and a sense of unity; it created a sense of belonging among successive generations of enslaved Africans and enabled them to "invent" or "imagine" a community unified by its resistance to slavery.[29] This collective memory was passed along as oral tradition and included a body of syncretic religious beliefs from which developed voodoo.[30] The memory of great rebel slaves—Michel, Polydor, Macandal, and other noted *cimarrones*—

and of mulattoes such as Vincent Ogé (tortured to death for organizing a rebellion against white colonial leaders in the hopes of obtaining for the freedmen the civil rights of the French Revolution) was part of that common memory of resistance.[31] The "uprising of the slaves in the north" in 1791 was simply the culmination of that glorious tradition of rebellion. Thus, though they may have lacked other unifying elements because of their varied African ethnic backgrounds, the slave masses in Saint-Domingue took action in accordance with their century-old tradition of resistance. Though disconcerted by the labyrinth of cultural, linguistic, and ethnic differences, the slaves managed to forge solidarity out of common sufferings and, above all, the struggle against slavery. Therein lay their "center of gravity in the past" that Peña-Batlle tried to deny them.[32] Price-Mars seems to be telling us that shared sufferings and struggles can also forge communities; these sufferings and struggles were the "thread running through the labyrinth" that enabled the slaves to solve the riddle of their identity.

The slave rebellion of 1791 was no less significant because the rebel masses were unaware of the higher implications of their acts—although Peña-Batlle advanced that argument in an attempt to minimize its importance. In his view, Haiti did not gain its independence due to any "higher conception" (social, cultural, or political) but rather by means of unorganized masses whose actions reflected no lofty purpose beyond their immediate manumission and revenge for the offenses they had suffered at the hands of the whites. Peña-Batlle ruthlessly scourges even the leadership of the revolution. Toussaint L'Ouverture was merely a "feeble figure," noteworthy chiefly as the embodiment of the "spirit of his class [slaves] and of his race [black]." He then reduces L'Ouverture's role in attaining independence to simple political opportunism, aimed at "securing and consolidating his personal influence over the Haitian masses"; actual independence is thus seen as a consequence of "forces, interests, and pressing needs of an international nature." What Price-Mars views as an epic struggle for freedom, far transcending Haiti's borders, Peña-Batlle interprets as a series of acts "without moderation or restraint" in which the enslaved masses indulged in "the appalling satisfaction of their hatred and their thirst for vengeance." Referring to dark motives as well as dark skin, Peña-Batlle dismisses the uprising as the "black revolution."[33]

In contrast to Peña-Batlle, Price-Mars believes that although few among the rebels in 1791 "could imagine that they had just set off a great revolution," the result of their actions was a "social revolution" that involved not only the abolition of slavery but also "the rehabilitation of the Negro."[34] In other words, the importance of the revolution sprang not from any awareness among the rebels of the ultimate implications of their acts but from the very transcendence of that revolution—transcendence achieved through its contribution to the history of human liberty. Therefore, even though the rebellion was "a dreadful war," "unrestrained and lawless," and the "black multitude" acted fanatically, "galvanized by the righteousness of their cause," still the revolution and its aftermath, the emergence of the Republic of Haiti, had "intrinsic" virtue.[35] The slave rebellion of 1791 may well have been the result of countless acts, both individual and collective, with no definite conscious end beyond emancipation from slavery; in Price-Mars's view, that does not disqualify it as a landmark in modern freedom fights. The effects of the revolution grew when independence was declared in 1804. Those effects were felt first and foremost in the region of the Caribbean. To the colonial powers of the Caribbean, the Republic of Haiti was "an example as disturbing as it was dangerous," for it well might be the focal point of revolutionary "contagion."[36] To the evidence of a slaveholding system destroyed as a result of the rebellion of subaltern sectors were added the equally threatening examples of a colonial regime smashed by "the wretched of the earth"[37] and the emergence of a new black State.[38] In the final analysis, as Barrington Moore has argued, social actors do not customarily foresee the historical effects of their deeds.[39]

In the eyes of the world, Haiti was the supreme abomination. It would have to defend its right to exist as an independent nation. It is little wonder that, quoting Marx, revolution was like trying to tear a star out of the sky; Price-Mars would agree with that. But if that is true, then we can at least say that despite its being an intricate labyrinth, made up of a multiplicity of wills, of individual, concrete acts, of advances and retreats, of heroic acts small and large as well as treacherous and cowardly acts ranging from the minuscule to the colossal, the Haitian Revolution was a labyrinth that implied the stars.

A FORKING ROAD

The road dropped and forked as it cut through the now-formless meadows.
Jorge Luis Borges

With Haiti in the maelstrom of a revolution, its nearest neighbor was caught up in the turbulence. A Spanish colony until transferred to France by the Treaty of Basilea in 1795,[40] Santo Domingo was at the mercy of the revolutionary turmoil in the western part of Hispaniola. In the opinion of nineteenth-century historian José Gabriel García, the revolution indiscriminately jumbled "treasures and traditions into one great heap of rubble" and made of Haiti a "dangerous neighbour" for Santo Domingo.[41] The Haitian revolutionaries' ambitions of extending their power into the eastern part of Hispaniola (a project that would necessitate expelling the remnants of French troops that were still in Santo Domingo) initiated a new era of conflict between Haiti and Santo Domingo. Yet according to Price-Mars, it was not these conflicts that created strife between the two countries; the dispute was grounded in the very ethnosocial formation of the two peoples. In support of this opinion, Price-Mars delves into comparative history.

It has been said that Price-Mars investigates history by means of ethnology.[42] And it is true that his examination of the history of the island of Hispaniola is greatly concerned with determining the ethnoracial composition of the two colonies and the effect of that composition on relations between them. In fact, that is one of the major premises of his interpretation of relations between Santo Domingo and Haiti. His evidence is taken from economic and social history. Price-Mars finds that the central difference between the two colonies was the prominence of slavery in Saint-Domingue: "A distinction of this nature left its mark . . . [on] usages, customs and aspirations" in both peoples. Those differences, however, go back to the settling of the colonies and to geographic factors. Thus, while the eastern part of the island was distinguished by "greater valleys and broader plains," the distinctive feature of the west was its "mountainous development." Consequently, when colonization began, the Spaniards tended to congregate in the east, finding it more attractive than the mountainous west. To this factor of geographic determination, another was added in the process of establishing settlements: the Spaniards' frenzy for gold. The precious metal was abundant in the eastern part of Hispaniola, scarce in the west. One effect of all this was that "the colonizing efforts became ever more accentuated in the eastern side," while the west was losing settlers and so became the target of raids by Spain's enemies.[43] This was the first fork in the road in Hispaniola's history, coming even before the existence of two colonies on its soil.

The second fork: The French occupied the west, thus initiating border disputes between Spain and France. Though these disputes are a central theme in Dominican history, Price-Mars merely sketches the agreements and treaties that established, in different periods, the boundaries of the two colonies.[44] Fundamental in his view were the processes that defined, during the seventeenth and eighteenth centuries, the economic, demographic, social, and ethnic physiognomy of the colonies that shared the territory of Hispaniola. The decline of the gold economy in Santo Domingo brought about the emergence of other economic activities, a reduction in the colony's population, and the transformation of the "racial substratum of the eastern community." In spite of the importation of several thousand slaves to Santo Domingo, in the end its "ethnographic description" differed from that of the French sector due to the "crossing of races." In conjunction with low population density in the east (Price-Mars calculates that the number of inhabitants between 1795 and 1822 did not exceed 153,000), this mestizaje was the predominant feature of the population of Santo Domingo during the colonial period.[45] In these "two facts" Price-Mars finds the fundamental fork in the road in Dominican/Haitian history: the "psychological drama that brought about the separation of the eastern part from the Republic of Haiti."[46]

Despite the fact that Price-Mars saw the differences between Haiti and Santo Domingo as differences "of degree, not of kind," in the matter of ethnic makeup the inhabitants of the eastern part "have always believed and still believe themselves to be full-blooded white Spaniards." In other words, the Dominicans took what Price-Mars believed to be the true ethnic makeup of Santo Domingo and superimposed on it a racial imaginary that disdained the African roots common to the two countries. This disparity, already present in the colonial period, intensified with the slave rebellion and with the emergence of Haiti as an independent nation—especially in light of the fact that the revolt of the slaves against an oppressive regime was also a confrontation between black masses of African origin and white oppressors of European origin. "Whiteness" became identified with the oppressive slave system and with the French colonial regime. Consequently, the leaders of the new Haitian nation were "obsessed with the idea of having the whole island under their control in order to defend or safeguard their independence," all the more since slavery was still "on the increase" in the Caribbean in general and in particular only "a few hours from their borders, in that eastern territory." Yet blinded by their own racial perceptions, the inhabitants of Santo Domingo saw themselves as the heirs of the whites, of the "conquering race that took control of the planet." The "irreducible" conflict between the two peoples stems from ardor in the defense of hard-won freedom (the central drama of Haitian history, according to Price-Mars) and the incompatibility that he saw between this principle and the unification of the island. Due to the racial perceptions prevalent in Santo Domingo, its inhabitants found it unacceptable that they be "incorporated into a nationality and a community that they consider infinitely inferior to their own condition as whites."[47]

Haiti having been born, in a sense, in bastardy, Price-Mars writes that his people have been discriminated against and rejected by the Dominicans from the very beginning. It is perhaps for this reason that he is so determined to show that what he calls the "eastern campaign"—a multistage military campaign initiated in the times of Jean-Jacques Dessalines—had as its aim the upholding of those principles of liberty that, in his view, were the lifeblood of the Haitian State. In 1805, for example, Dessalines occupied Santo Domingo for the purpose of expelling General Ferrand's French troops from the island. Price-Mars emphasizes two aspects of Ferrand's presence in the east. First, he avers, the sovereignty of the Haitian State was endangered, since Ferrand could very well launch an incursion against western Hispaniola from his position in Santo Domingo. Second, Price-Mars protests that Ferrand had set in motion a campaign to press citizens of the new State back into slavery.[48] In Price-Mars's narration, Ferrand comes to symbolize the antithesis of the principles on which Haiti had been founded, whereas Dessalines, on the other hand, evokes not only those principles but also those universal values that, in the eyes of Price-Mars, were the emblems of Haiti's struggle for freedom. The "question of the East" was not simply a battle between Haitians and the French or between Haitians and Dominicans. It was, to Price-Mars, a conflagration of epic—almost millennial—proportions, proclaiming the highest libertarian ideals of the modern bourgeoisie, as sustained by the revolutions in France and the United States. The universal significance of Haiti's struggle justified the call to unify the island of Hispaniola under the banner of Haiti.

The principles embodied by the Haitian State were defined by the solemn commitments made by the liberators, the founders of the Haitian nationality, whom Price-Mars presents in the likeness of biblical figures on a Mosaic mission. Toussaint L'Ouverture had "apostolic aspirations." The words attributed to him upon being taken prisoner by the French—"They have only felled the trunk of the tree (of the freedom of the blacks); branches will sprout, for the roots are numerous and deep"[49]—are called a "prophecy" by Price-Mars. At his death Toussaint displayed "the courage of a martyr."[50] If Toussaint figures in Price-Mars's text as some sort of prophet or messiah, Dessalines is an avenging angel, poised to unleash his divine wrath on those who abjure his creed of liberty. Thus, the proclamation of independence that Dessalines signed along with his generals contains an oath "to renounce France forever, to die rather than live under its dominion, and to fight for independence until the last breath"—an oath taken on "sacred principles," of supreme importance, sworn "before posterity and the universe." Later, consumed by a kind of divine rage when he saw that his military campaign had failed and motivated by the collaboration of sectors of the Dominican population with the French, Dessalines embarked on a wave of "reprisals" against the inhabitants of Santo Domingo. Avenging angel or god of war, Dessalines symbolized heavenly vengeance against the apostates of liberty. He wreaked his apocalyptic vengeance on behalf of "a series of mute victims [slaves], over whom the barbarism of the times had erected [the idea of] the superiority of a category of men [whites]." He was the "apostle of extermination," who devoured "the oppressors and even the sons of the oppressors," by which act he vindicated the blacks, oppressed for centuries, and purified the promised land. "Drunkenness on blood" was the price to be paid for the "liberation of the oppressed," the symbol of the "mission of salvation that Destiny had assigned to Haiti and to its leaders."[51]

Yet Price-Mars stops short of deifying Haiti's foundational figures, of setting them above reproach, in some mythical dimension beyond good and evil. On the contrary, he criticizes the actions of Haiti's rulers and liberators, including their conduct during the "eastern campaign." For example, he denounces the tax of one hundred thousand pesos that Dessalines levied on the inhabitants of the city of Santiago de los Caballeros after its surrender to the Haitian caudillo. But Price-Mars saves his most caustic criticism for the acts of violence committed by Haitian troops during their retreat after the fruitless attempt to take over Dominican territory. This withdrawal from Santo Domingo "was one of the most dramatic and bloody episodes of a dramatic and bloody history," because Dessalines ordered his soldiers to "lay waste all of the enemy territory as you pass through it again." Every sort of violence was committed at that time; "nothing was omitted from that scene of pointless horrors." Nevertheless, Price-Mars continues to see the actions of the Haitian troops through the alembic of the central postulate of his book: that Haiti symbolized the struggle for freedom. In the eyes of Dessalines, "the people of the eastern territory" had to be punished for their complicity with the French, who were the "most ferocious adversaries" of the nation of Haiti.[52]

Jean-Pierre Boyer, the president of Haiti who initiated what Dominican historiography refers to as the Haitian Domination (1822–44), receives his share of Price-Mars's disapproval for a number of measures that he implanted in Santo Domingo. Confiscation of properties, application of the "rural code," and the effects of the onerous economic compensation that France imposed in return for recognizing Haiti's sovereignty—these were some of the factors that won for Boyer, according to Price-Mars, the "growing antipathy of the people." To these were added other measures (abolition of slavery, advancement of the black sectors, land distribution) that, while essential features of the Haitian revolutionary tradition, were damaging to the social and economic interests of important sectors in Santo Domingo. Crowning all the rest were the autocratic policies prevailing among Haitian government leaders, "imbued with the customs and traditions of the old regime." As a result, the "Boyer regime" was discredited, and with that loss of faith was lost any possibility of achieving real unification of the two countries: "The twenty-two years of union had produced nothing but resentment, misunderstandings, and a sullen hostility between Haitians and Dominicans."[53] This was a period when the Haitian and Dominican peoples might have converged in the labyrinth that has been their shared history; Price-Mars sees 1822–44 as a lost opportunity to achieve harmonious relations (an opinion put forward in the nineteenth century by Dominican writer Pedro Francisco Bonó).[54] The moment for conciliation was lost; the paths of the two countries diverged forever as a result of the Haitian regime's insensitivity and inadequacy. This forking was further induced by "the systematic attempt to impose uniformity on the two parts of the territory," a policy that "had cast aside perfectly respectable traditions."[55] If to Price-Mars the period of the revolution and independence was a heroic era, and the illustrious figures of the fight against slavery and the colonial regime were the heroes of that epic—with mere mortals becoming the torchbearers of the Promethean flame of freedom—then the failure of the "union" brought on a period of decline that split the destinies of Santo Domingo and Haiti further and further apart.

ENEMY OF A COUNTRY?

I was struck by the thought that a man may be the enemy of other men, the enemy of other men's other moments, yet not be the enemy of a country.
    Jorge Luis Borges

This decline was not "a static continuum but rather a continuum that is intersected by *transformations*, by changes, by crises,"[56] springing in part from the "interests" and "prejudices" of Dominicans who clashed with the Haitian regime in 1822–44. Price-Mars highlights the "prejudices" associated with the ethnic composition of the two societies and with their respective racial perceptions. For Dominicans, he argues, it was unacceptable to maintain such close ties with an overwhelmingly black society, since in Santo Domingo the prevalent racial ideology emphasized the essential "Spanishness" of its society.[57] This Spanishness was cultural, according to various Dominican authors, but Price-Mars disagrees, insisting on the racial character of Santo Domingo's "Hispanicism." We should not forget, however, that in the nineteenth century, ethnicity, culture, and "race" were virtually equivalent terms: one's "race" included and determined one's culture. Race opened or blocked access to what were (in the eyes of the dominant sectors) the higher forms of culture. Western civilization—which, of course, viewed itself as *the* civilization, civilization per se—was a privilege to which one gained access by approximating the white or Caucasian "race." In Latin America and the Caribbean, "white" was synonymous with European; that is, to be white was to be identified with Western culture, the culture of the "civilized" world. As distance from this ideal increased, culture began to "die." Being "Indian" (*indio*) or "black" signified barbarism, the antithesis of civilization. The ideal of "whitening" society was, therefore, a civilizing project.[58]

Santo Domingo's rejection of Haiti was, in part, a response to the dilemma of civilization versus barbarism, culture versus savagery; this perception can be found not only in the letrados of the nineteenth century but also in many of the twentieth.[59] As Hayden White points out, the concept of savagery, or "wildness," is a discursive construct used by some "to designate an area of subhumanity that was characterized by everything they hoped they were not." It is one of those concepts whose "general cultural function" is "to dignify" the "specific mode of existence" of a given society or of certain groups by contrasting it with the mode of existence of other humans, "real or imagined, who merely differ from themselves."[60] Haiti represented barbarism par excellence. Its Creole tongue was completely foreign to European languages, the vehicles by which civilization was transmitted. Voodoo was further evidence that (to paraphrase Peña-Batlle) Haitians were impervious to culture; at the opposite end of the spectrum was Christianity, the religion that was brought from Europe and was consequently the ultimate ethical expression of the civilized world. Economic patterns and family organization were also circumscribed by an African heritage that assumed, per se, a position of absolute cultural inferiority to all other countries on the planet. Even in Haiti the social elite, infatuated with their French lineage, disdained the overwhelmingly black campesino masses with their "African" culture and way of life. If to the rest of the Western world Haiti contained all possible "faces of the barbarian," to its own elite it was the campesinos who wore that face. Their blackness was merely its most obvious sign. The ideological substratum of the elite vis-à-vis the Haitian masses is similar to that of European nations regarding those of the "third world." As Hurbon has said, both cases presuppose a Eurocentric worldview in which Europe is "the only possible place" where "the humanity of man" can develop and flourish, with the rest of the world condemned to a state of barbarism.[61]

Haiti represented another threat: a "race war," implying (in the political imaginary of the times) total chaos, the "world turned upside down." A principal concern of the nineteenth-century elite, it was one of the criteria for passing judgment on the Haitian Revolution and its sequel in Santo Domingo. José Gabriel García claims, for example, that Boyer found it difficult to stir up "racial hatred" in Santo Domingo because "social [that is, racial] concerns . . . were not very deeply rooted in the Spanish part," thus depriving Boyer of a solid foundation for his "iniquitous work."[62] The "race war" or "caste war," however, was a perennial preoccupation of the Latin American and Caribbean elite, a concern that reached the level of paranoia in the late eighteenth century, a period during which various societies in the Americas were convulsed by great "nonwhite" rebellions. That which Magnus Mörner calls "the revolt of the man with dark skin" developed into an endless nightmare, subjecting colonial societies (and, later, newly independent nations) from Patagonia to the Caribbean, by way of the Andes, Venezuela, Mexico, and Brazil, to unprecedented social and political pressures.[63] Túpac Amaru, leading an indigenous rebellion as the incarnation of the "return of the Inca"; Macandal, poisoning whites while protected by his lycanthropic powers; the "Comegente" (people eater), a mythical figure of colonial Santo

Domingo calling up blood-curdling visions of the black cannibal—all of these are simply regional variations of the terror inspired by the threatening "other" who seemed to be closing in on the "white" world.[64] This siege was a danger to "civilization" as well; defeat would send it toppling into the abyss.

And it was not just the popular imaginary that was marked by these figures. Martínez-Fernández tells us that in Cuba, "the fear of a massive slave insurrection stimulated and molded political thought"; in Santo Domingo, the "aggressive presence of neighboring Haiti played a similar role."[65] The notion of civilization versus barbarism was inseparable from race relations in nineteenth-century debates; it was to remain inseparable in the twentieth century. These concerns defined the limits for discussions of the "protonational" question; they set the parameters for conceptions of the nation in Santo Domingo as well as in other regions of the Caribbean.[66] Culture was merely a sort of "dependent variable" of the racial question. Therefore, the contradictory terms "civilization" and "barbarism" were defined racially. And political projects were consistent with this conception. One of the political consequences of the civilization/barbarism dichotomy was the emergence of annexationist projects in nineteenth-century Santo Domingo. Frequently seen in the light of the immediate political or economic interests of the caudillos, the diverse annexationist projects should be placed within the framework of contemporary notions on progress, civilization, and order. Their standards were Europe and—though to a lesser degree—the United States. On the edge of the abyss of chaos, the "patricians" developed a powerful "will for order," hoping to establish an order that would be guaranteed by the State. (Such a will for order was already patent in Bolívar, who was appalled by the consequences of the "caste war.") The dominant discourses sought to reject popular culture, which they saw as a strickle leveling off society at the stage of barbarism, savagery, chaos, and disorder. It was, Julio Ramos tells us, "a period traversed by the circulation and prevalence of representations of Latin America as a sick body, *contaminated* by racial impurity and the survival of traditional cultures and ethnicities presumably destined to disappear in the unfolding of progress and modernity."[67] Some letrados did attempt to formulate alternative discourses: for example, the Cuban thinker José Martí. According to Ramos, Martí considered such conceptions "colonizing discourses"—the "tiger within," in Martí's words. Martí believed that the lack of integration in Latin American countries was the result, rather, of "the exclusion of traditional cultures from the space of modern political representation."[68] In nineteenth-century Santo Domingo, Bonó could be placed within a similar tradition, as Raymundo González has shown.[69]

Price-Mars's writings also fall into this category of thought. Viewed through this lens, the sections of his book dedicated to examining the great powers' designs regarding Hispaniola take on a new dimension. This assessment differs, in the first place, from the express intent of the author, who above all is trying to show how the larger nations attempted to manipulate the conflicts between Haiti and Santo Domingo in order to take over the island, or at least to appropriate part of its territory so as to strengthen their strategic military presence in the Caribbean. It also differs from the interpretations offered by a number of Dominican intellectuals in both the nineteenth and twentieth centuries, who see in these extensive sections of Price-Mars's work merely a poorly disguised justification of Haitian "imperialism." But is Price-Mars really a defender of "Haitian expansionism"?

Certainly, Price-Mars would have preferred the emergence of a true union of the two countries. For this reason he laments the "Dominican prejudice" that made that union impossible; for this reason he also criticizes the measures taken by Boyer, who failed to respect the peculiarities of Dominican society and attempted to alter its way of life to fit into Haiti's. Various factors contributed to the "separation" of the two peoples, but once they were separated, "nothing would have been more in keeping with international brotherhood than for Haitians and Dominicans to be able to live in peace," says Price-Mars. What is more, he considers that in his present, "the unification of the two countries cannot be accomplished"; therein lies the true "sense" of "the History that we are writing." What Price-Mars does refute, and with passion, is that "the unification of the two countries, in 1822, was accomplished entirely by violence." He also rejects the argument that the occupation of the east by Haitians was an act of pure pillage.[70] It is true that in Price-Mars's opinion, with the independence of Santo Domingo in 1844, unification of the two countries became impossible. But that does not deter him from trying to demonstrate that in the attempts made in the 1850s and 1860s to occupy Santo Domingo, there were higher motives, transcending the Haitian will for dominion over the entire island. He argues that there was in these attempts the intention to prevent Santo Domingo's being absorbed by a foreign power, which would have endangered Haiti's own sovereignty and could even have cleared the way for the reestablishment of slavery in Hispaniola. The political project and the social project reinforced each other.

Consonant with this assessment, Price-Mars sets out to demonstrate the interference of the great powers—sometimes France, sometimes England, the United States, or Spain—in the island's affairs. This interference is seen even in the "Dominico-Haitian wars," which Price-Mars analyzes in the light of two principles that eventually are shown to be incompatible. The first principle is "the right and will of the Dominicans to form an independent nation," and the second is the "necessity of keeping the entire island under the protection of the government of the Republic of Haiti" for the purpose of preventing European or U.S. rule.[71] In such circumstances, Dominican calls for foreign mediation could not help but facilitate foreign interference. This was too high a price, he says, for it opened the doors to reestablishing the dominion of the great empires over Hispaniola.[72] In these sections—a substantial part—of his work, Price-Mars changes his narrative strategy. In this new tactic, the author brings in as players a number of political forces and characters who seem to operate behind the scenes to direct the destinies of the two countries, working against one another in their imperial plan to "divide and conquer." Unlike other parts of Price-Mars's work, in which he writes with power and intensity, even passion, in these sections "the presence of a character who is organizing, arranging, and presenting is supposedly concealed behind the documents that appear to speak spontaneously."[73] And, in truth, it is the documents that seem to be "speaking" in these sections; the author's voice is secondary, limiting itself to drawing together the general lines of the content of his sources. Let there be no doubt: This discursive tactic is a political strategy to the extent that Price-Mars hopes to confer authority on his own postulates by means of the supposedly neutral voices he cites. This is an example of the "politics of historical representation" that gives preference to the supposed "objectivity" of the source in contrast to the subjectivity, the passion, the desire, or the imagination of the author.[74]

For the purpose of exposing European and U.S. maneuvers to gain an advantage in Hispaniola (sometimes in Haiti, sometimes in the young Dominican Republic), Price-Mars reproduces a great number of original documents, most of them diplomatic papers.[75] At the very moment that Santo Domingo was gaining its independence, the French were conspiring to reestablish their dominion over the island; for this reason, they supported the Dominicans against Haiti. That the Dominicans sought this support, and that they later sought help or even a protectorate status or "annexation" to one of the great powers, proved irrefutably (to Price-Mars) that the majority of the Dominicans who "instigated" independence had as their goal "not so much the autonomy of the eastern region as the separation of said zone from the Republic of Haiti." Only a few—most notably Juan Pablo Duarte, "the expression of the purest ideology of Dominican nationalism"—opposed the pursuit of protectorate status or annexation.[76] But it was not the spirit of Duarte that prevailed in the Dominican government. Beginning in 1844, several attempts were made to attain protectorate status, the object being "not only to defend the Dominican community against any future Haitian domination but also to conclusively ensure white supremacy in the country and to prohibit for all time the supremacy of the black element."[77] According to the sources cited by Price-Mars, the geopolitical policy of the great powers—especially the United States—was to prevent "the establishment on the island of a pure-blooded people of the black race" that might then serve as a base for "a black empire" in the Caribbean; in this the powers were in agreement with the Dominican government.[78]

The "drama of the black man" in Hispaniola—to use the words of Price-Mars—was restricted by Dominican "Bovarism," which conspired with the white powers against Haiti and against what Haiti represented in the liberation process of Afro-Americans. "The Haitian-Dominican dispute took on a significance that went beyond the simple notion of a problem of the territorial indivisibility of the island of Haiti or of the right to national independence of the Dominican community; it broadened and deepened and took on the dramatic physiognomy of a racial antagonism. . . . It took on the stature of an ethical problem."[79] The dilemma was aggravated by a ring of slaveholding nations, from the southern U.S. states to Cuba and Puerto Rico, that seemed to be tightening around Haiti, the "international anomaly" because of its bastard origins. Haiti reflected, as in a fun house mirror, the nightmares of the powerful. Already besieged, the Haitians were alarmed by the annexationist tendencies that they were seeing in the principal political leaders of the Dominican Republic. Haiti stepped up its attempts to control eastern Hispaniola during the 1850s, but its defeat at the battle of Sabana Larga, in 1856, "put an end to the hopeless dream" of achieving "political union."[80] The Dominicans, however, did not give up their hopes of obtaining the protection of a foreign power. During the 1860s, the idea of a protectorate waned and that of "annexation" became more attractive.[81]

The first manifestation of this idea was the "annexation" of Santo Domingo to Spain, a measure arranged by Pedro Santana, a military caudillo who had played a crucial role in the separation from Haiti.[82] Santana negotiated the annexation to Spain on the grounds of the "Haitian threat," a stance that mitigated (in the eyes of an entire school of historiography) the surrender of national sovereignty.[83] The idea found expression later that same decade in the efforts—orchestrated this time by Buenaventura Báez—to be annexed to the United States.[84] In both cases, Price-Mars deplores the course of events. He characterizes the annexation to Spain in 1861 as a "crime" and a "catastrophe," because it allowed the in-stallation of an imperial power in the island; preventing such a thing had been a lodestar of Haitian policy since the coming of independence. Spanish control of Santo Domingo "presages the end of our freedom," declared Geffrard, who was president of Haiti at the time. His complaint had a double meaning: "freedom" de-fined as independence, the existence of the independent State of Haiti, and the "freedom" that had resulted from the abolition of slavery—freedom not granted to the "millions of our brothers and fellow citizens" enslaved in the Spanish colonies of Puerto Rico and Cuba. To crown Haiti's woes, the annexation had occurred just when Haitians were attempting to adapt "to the existence of a neighboring Dominican Republic that is free and independent."[85]

Interference from a European power in Hispaniola brought together roads that had previously forked apart. When an antiannexation movement arose in 1861 in the settlement of Moca, in the Cibao region of the Dominican Republic, Dominican rebels found a support base in Haiti against the Spanish forces. Groups of "Dominican patriots" would sally forth from Haiti, accompanied by Haitians, "who aided them in liberating the territory from foreign soldiers." In addition to regular soldiers, there were "volunteers" among the Haitians who fought alongside the Dominicans. Haitian solidarity with the Dominican cause brought on reprisals from the Spanish authorities, which obliged President Geffrard to assume "apparent neutrality." Secretly, however, he supplied the insurrectionists with provisions that, according to Price-Mars, helped extend the rebellion. Price-Mars also points out that Geffrard took a number of diplomatic actions designed to negotiate an armistice and the withdrawal of Spanish troops from Santo Domingo.[86]

In the view of Price-Mars, the War of Restoration (as the fight against annexation, 1863–65, is known) was a landmark event in the history of the two countries. In the first place, Dominicans and Haitians had come together, motivated by the fight against a common enemy. In the second place, the War of Restoration had initiated a new era in relations between the two countries at the level of State. Price-Mars writes that from the founding of the Republic of Haiti until the Geffrard administration, the prevailing doctrine had been that "indivisibility . . . was indispensable in order to defend the security of the government and of the people of the island," for which cause Haitian government leaders had been determined to gain control over the entire island territory.

> Until Geffrard the predominant feeling was . . . that said people and government were none other than those who, having risen from slavery, forged in the western part a fatherland for a sector of humanity [that is, the blacks] in whom the majority of men had not been willing to recognize any specifically human quality. . . .
> But [that feeling] was based on an illusion or an error, which

was to believe or suppose that in all the length of the territory, from Cabo Enga[ñ]o [in Santo Domingo] to Muelle Saint-Nicolas [in Haiti], there was a single group of humans, a single people, whose unanimous adherence to the ideal they pursued should become a reality in a single community.[87]

The differences between the two peoples had to do with the very geography of the island, according to Price-Mars, with valleys, rivers, and mountains that seemed to draw "a dividing line." But more than that, they had to do with two opposite and contradictory senses of identity. With a touch of bitterness, Price-Mars indicates that the inhabitants of the east invoke "a different human origin, . . . to which is ascribed the millennial iniquity that brought forth on the planet the enslavement of the black man by the white man." Acknowledging the differences that made "union" between the two societies impossible, Price-Mars insists that those who govern Haiti should do their part to help the Dominican Republic "live in independence and freedom," which would require as an indispensable condition that the country be freed from "every form of imperialism." That would have to be the "sacramental basis" for "reconciliation between the two peoples," a design frustrated by the political instability that reigned in Haiti, toppling Geffrard from power in 1867.[88] At the moment of possibility, when a definitive harmony might have embraced the two peoples, that reconciliation was frustrated by the ills weighing down the Haitian political system.

Once the Haitian government had abandoned the principle of the indivisibility of the island, a new conflict took its place in the 1870s: that which Price-Mars calls "the era of questions of limits," or border disputes. The flurry of diplomatic negotiations to define the boundaries of the two countries did little to diminish the mutual distrust between Dominicans and Haitians. In the Dominicans' view, Port-au-Prince's diplomatic strategy appeared to involve delaying any definitive solution of the "question of limits" in order to gain control over more territory along the border and claim it for Haiti.[89] Negotiations between the two governments, though often interrupted for years at a time, continued until 1935, when Presidents Rafael L. Trujillo and Sténio Vincent finally signed a treaty that it was hoped would resolve the border question. This treaty appeared to have brought to a close one of the most tortuous of the disputes that had clouded relations between the Dominican Republic and Haiti for several decades. "Unfortunately, it was not to be," writes Price-Mars, "and the hopes we had cherished in that regard were in vain."[90]

Prospects for the future were marred by the "rural exodus of Haitian proletarians toward Dominican territory"; this phrase, the title of the final chapter of Price-Mars's work, identifies the apple of discord between Haitians and Dominicans after the signing of the border treaty.[91] Demographic, economic, and social factors conspired against an end to Dominico-Haitian complaints. Demography and economy impelled poor Haitians across the border "in search of work." On Dominican soil, they lived "in a disguised form of bond service," in addition to what they suffered due to "racial prejudice." These two elements, one economic and the other "psychological," had been aggravated by the strained relations between the two countries "in these last twenty years"—that is, between 1935, when the border treaty was signed, and the mid-1950s, when Price-Mars published his work. In fact, it was barely two years after the signing, in 1937, when there was a massacre of Haitians on the Dominican side of the border territory, an event that Price-Mars describes as an "abominable drama," a "sinister episode," and a "terrible butchery."[92] The official Dominican version was that the "painful incidents" of 1937 took place "among Haitian marauders" who were looting and plundering Dominican settlers in the border region.[93] One of the most intriguing aspects of the entire matter was the relative ease with which the Haitian government agreed to a settlement with the Trujillo administration, a thorny issue about which Price-Mars suggests—citing a conversation he had with "a Dominican public figure" during his diplomatic service in Santo Domingo—that "eminent Haitians" had connived "in the perpetration of the drama."[94]

This was a moment when the destinies of the two countries appeared to fork apart for good. The massacre lived on in the Haitian popular imaginary as an utterly despicable act; for many Dominicans as well, it came to symbolize sheer barbarism.[95] Price-Mars saw the Massacre of 1937 as "a challenge, a provocation to war." Behind it was, precisely, that "emigration of the Haitian rural masses to the neighboring country." This would be, he said, "the exposed nerve" in all future relations between Haiti and the Dominican Republic. The Massacre of 1937 was a hallmark of the Trujillo policy regarding the Haitian population—a policy designed to prevent the contaminating effect of the emigrants.[96] "Agricultural colonies" were established along the border; one of their purposes was to "Dominicanize" the zone. While promoting agricultural development, Trujillo also intended to reinforce those institutions that could validate the Dominican government's claims for control over the borderlands.[97] There were several facets to the Dominicanization of the border: the human, the economic, and the political. From the perspective of Price-Mars, this policy was contradictory: Dominican migratory law permitted the use of Haitian labor in the sugar industry. Looking forward several decades to what is now an urgent dilemma, Price-Mars wondered what the nationality of children born to Haitian parents during their stay in the Dominican Republic would be.[98]

The real dilemma, however, lay not in treaties but in socioeconomic realities. Thus, to the migration made legitimate by the treaties signed by Haiti and the Dominican Republic, there was added, year after year, the "clandestine mass" that slipped across the border looking for work. And again in this drama we see the crisscrossing of demographic, ecological, and economic factors. In view of the magnitude of the problems, Price-Mars wonders, "Can any treaty in existence, no matter how well arranged it may be, presume to resolve them?" As a substratum to the drama of the Haitian migration to Dominican soil, there was also to be found that perennial "Dominican Bovarism": the incapacity to acknowledge that they were a people of black ancestry. This factor, according to Price-Mars, was an impediment to any solution of the grave dilemmas that the two collectivities had faced throughout their history. For this reason the "Haitian-Dominican federation" that might have been a solution for the problems he describes was a "utopia" (in the sense of an unattainable goal) from the perspective of either country. With his historical vision anchored in the centuries-old struggles of the Afro-Caribbean people, Price-Mars could not help but draw a parallel between his own times and the social situation of the old colony of Saint-Domingue. In the earlier period, the ethnosocial conflict led to a "unique solution": the destruction of one group (whites) by the other (blacks). In Price-Mars's times, the conflict between Haiti and the Dominican Republic also tended to be reduced to its "ethnic" dimensions. And the solution to the conflict was very similar to that of the old slave-holding colony. It is no wonder that Price-Mars concludes his work with a vision of "heavy storm clouds" on the horizon.[99] This vision, in apocalyptic tones, projects the future "on the basis of the model of the past, and the end as a reproduction of the origins."[100] Price-Mars's poetics of time, expressing at once the frustration of his utopia and his fears over future events, is a tangled labyrinth that ends up where it started.

A HISTORY (AND A FUTURE) OF SEVERAL PATHS

I leave to several futures (not to all) my garden of forking paths.
  Jorge Luis Borges

Virtually unknown in the Dominican Republic at the time of its publication in the 1950s, *La República de Haití y la República Dominicana* was contested by various intellectuals of the time, including Sócrates Nolasco, Emilio Rodríguez-Demorizi, and Ángel del Rosario-Pérez.[101] Save for a few minor discrepancies in emphasis, the positions assumed by these critics of Price-Mars differ little from the official history of the Trujillo dictatorship. In all three authors we find what Mateo has called the "great themes of the Trujillo ideology";[102] prominent among these themes are Hispanicism and anti-Haitianism. Price-Mars's work was judged in the light of these conceptions, which became virtual reasons of State during the Trujillo Era. That, far more than any deficiencies in his work, is why criticism from the Trujillo camp was bent on turning Price-Mars into "the enemy."[103] Jesús Zaglul writes of this process of making Haiti into "the enemy";[104] as a reflection of this demonizing, Price-Mars was vilified as the spokesman for the most bitter opposition to the Dominican Republic. Criticism covered the spectrum from his errors of scholarship regarding names, dates, and events to his interpretations, ideology, and methodology.

One of the main reasons for the Dominican critics' antagonism toward Price-Mars was the "negritude" at the center of his proposal regarding Haitian identity. Negritude emerged "initially" in the 1920s as (in the words of René Dépestre) "a form of revolt of the spirit against the historic vilification and denaturalization of a group of human beings, who, during the colonization process, were baptized generically and pejoratively as 'Negroes.' " Soon, however, negritude took on absolute dimensions, making cultural and social differences "evaporate into a somatic metaphysics."[105] Seen in this way, negritude was understood as a "totalizing" black identity, ennobling "black values" of African origin; it was an identity strategy that, like Trujillo's mythologized "Spanishness," crushed differences, concealed cracks, demolished diversity.[106]

But this trait was not exclusive to negritude. In the 1920s, the emblematic works on Latin American and Caribbean identity tended to be fundamentally exclusivist—or, at least, they strongly favored one ethnic or cultural tradition in particular. Dépestre reminds us that this trait was common to the identity proposal found in *So Spoke the Uncle* by Price-Mars, to the essay collection *Siete ensayos* by Mariátegui, and to the essay collection *Seis ensayos en busca de nuestra expresión* by Dominican author Pedro Henríquez-Ureña. "In none of the great books that we have just mentioned can we find the entirety of the sociohistoric roots of our Americanness. In them we find, planted in parallel rows, Mariátegui's 'Indian' trunk, the 'Black' trunk of Price-Mars, and the 'White Creole' trunk of Henríquez Ureña. In each one of the three studies the historically Creole unity of the American trunk of our common identity was absent. . . . None . . . has offered a definition of the self . . . useful *at once* to all the social types that have emerged from our common colonial tragedy."[107] Many were the routes leading to identity, but they tended to be narrow, not broad, and usually quite separate. Some, such as Hispanicism, were firmly anchored in ties to the European metropolis; identity proposals, in addition to their "racial" and cultural components, also had clearly classist origins. In Latin America and the Caribbean, this "cursed pair class/race" has been inseparable.[108] And both have been associated with colonialism. Determined upon a course of modernization for their respective societies, the Latin American and Caribbean elite felt that the future was impossible without their affiliations with Europe. Consequently, they stressed their differences from the "others," both within and without, who could push them toward the abyss with the slightest touch. Their construct of "differences" was an identity strategy. As Arcadio Díaz-Quiñones has said, "Differences illuminate, clarify; the 'others' are needed to buttress a respectable identity, which at the same time confesses to fear and revulsion."[109]

Fear and revulsion were also original components of those identities forged in subaltern sectors, such as indigenism and negritude, but in a very different manner: in negritude and indigenism, Dépestre's "cursed pair" was drastically different from that of Hispanicism. Above all, this revulsion was a reaction to discrimination based on skin color, to marginalization because of one's language or one's gods; this fear was of the return of the *gamonal* (cacique), the boss, the master. That is, negritude and indigenism both originated in response to the colonial power structures which, as Fanon has said, denied dark-skinned men and women their very humanity. The culture of these dark-skinned men and women was usually different from that of the dominant group, whether foreign or criollo;[110] as a result, in the majority of cases, their social substratum was substantially different from that of identity proposals based on Hispanicism. Of course, Hispanicism also flourished in the company of certain projects devoted to vindicating the "rural masses," projects articulated in identity proposals that used the pretext of the "white campesino" to exclude or marginalize from the national collective such sectors as did not fit the desired pattern. It should be sufficient to mention (as if any examples were needed) the defense of the *white* campesino propounded in Puerto Rico in the 1920s and 1930s by such authors as Antonio S. Pedreira and Tomás Blanco, or Ramiro Guerra's justification of the Cuban *guajiro*, who he claims was caught in the pincers of the foreign latifundio on one side and black migrant workers from Jamaica and Haiti on the other.[111] As a strategy designed to negate or minimize other identities, Hispanicism was, at first, a bastion of the elite. When it was articulated to include vindications of the masses, this was usually done from a fundamentally conservative (or even openly reactionary) perspective.

Despite their differences with Hispanicism—an identity proposal based on similarities with the former masters—indigenism and negritude have also been used for destructive purposes. Although their own social origins were frankly antiestablishment, Haitian government leaders developed a "new pathology of power," resulting in despotic structures turned against the very masses that had made possible their existence. In Duvalier and his supporters we see simply the culmination of that propensity to use discourse on negritude as a political strategy to seize power and then nail it down.[112] In Hurbon's words, "We see in Duvalier a consummation of the internalization of the European prejudice of racial superiority, while at the same time he proclaims himself the defender of the black race, as a leader sprung 'from the womb of the race,' and the new founder of 'civilization' in Haiti."[113] Ironies of history: the former disciple and collaborator of "the Uncle" became the new satrap of Haiti, reworking the doctrine of negritude—conceived by Price-Mars as the "tragedy of the black man"—but developing his own *noiriste* doctrine, designed according to factuality, rituals, and the simulacrum of power.[114] Following Marshall Berman, we may affirm that this intellectual and political adventure that was negritude, conceived as the heroic expression of modern struggles for human freedom, was transformed by the tyranny of the Duvalier regime into a deplorable emblem of the routine and the iconography of power.[115] In Haiti, in the twentieth century, the appeal to black identity occurred twice, as Marx would say: first as a tragedy, then as a farce.

In the Dominican Republic as well, government-sponsored identity played out as a farce. Based on the supposition that the island territory was divided between "two cultures/essences"— eternal enemies, never to be reconciled—the Dominican national identity was decreed to be "a prolongation . . . of the Spanish spirit." To this was added "a doctrine of retaliation" against Haiti.[116] This baroque ideological construct attributed all historical and cultural processes to the incompatibility of these two pure "essences." The Trujillo regime designed this identity construct most grandiloquently. Nor were its ornate contours forgotten with the end of the dictatorship: at that time new facets appeared, including the sham of a Haitian "bogeyman" to justify the need for a strong government. With his customary forcefulness, Mateo has defined that tactic as "fraudulent nationalism."[117]

Dominican Republic. Haiti. In both countries paeans have been sung to pure heritage, to the fatherland/landscape, to the nation as immutable essence. Enchanted by those melodies, power has been used, misused, and abused on both sides of the border, all in the name of "national identity." Both countries promote a "doctrine of retaliation." And so the never-ending conflict goes "riding into history"; it is a cause that has served its powerful champions well.

In the 1950s, Price-Mars foresaw a stormy future. His ominous prognosis has been at least partially, though not utterly, confirmed. In his labyrinth of time—which, like that of Borges, includes times gone by as well as those to come—the future appears to be rewriting the past. I am fond of Borges's image of history; he says, "Once in a while, the paths of that labyrinth converge; . . . in one of the possible pasts you are my enemy, in another my friend." And regarding the future: "Time forks, perpetually, into countless futures." And while it is true that in some of them "I am your enemy,"[118] in others there is still the possibility of hope, of utopia, of solidarity. For the Dominican Republic and Haiti, the routes they will take in the labyrinth of their stories will depend to a certain extent on roads already traveled; even more, though, it will depend on which paths, beginning in the present, they choose to explore. It may also require a change in the notions that the travelers have about themselves, and about those who may be traveling the same pathway (for, after all, on some of those paths there are companions). Depending upon the route chosen, a look over one's shoulder at the road behind may reveal tempests and the storm's ravages, or perhaps a less gloomy scene with much clearer skies. On a number of possible paths, the storm never strikes.

To Walter Cordero, for memories, "narrations," and friendship.

Storytelling the Nation

Memory, History, and Narration in Juan Bosch

MEMORY

Travel always changes some aspect of the life of the traveler.
  Juan Bosch, "Dos amigos"

*Childhood memories came to my mind, remnants of episodes
that I had believed forgotten.*
  Juan Bosch, "Rosa"

Memory becomes the vehicle for defining and fulfilling historical desire.
  David K. Herzberger, Narrating the Past *(Durham, 1995)*

A boy rides in his father's truck down the road that bisects the Dominican Republic from the Northwest Line to Santo Domingo. Along the route, the father acquires produce to sell in the city; once there, he loads the truck with merchandise to sell on the way back home. They stop at small country stores, where the campesinos come to choose a few basic necessities from sparsely stocked shelves, spending the meager proceeds from the sale of the fruits of their labor. The time is the 1920s. The Great Depression has not yet begun, but the price of agricultural products is already falling in parts of Latin America and the Caribbean. The crisis is particularly intense in the Cibao region from 1920 to 1922. The region is scourged by drought, making prices drop even more sharply; with good reason this time would be remembered, later in the decade, as "the instability of 1920."[1] The boy's father is one of thousands affected by the economic recession. Once a partner in a produce warehouse (later, in adulthood, his son would describe him in sociological terms as a "middle petit bourgeois"), he now owned a truck and served as a middleman.

Many years later—though not while facing a firing squad—Juan Bosch was to remember those long-ago days when he used to ride with his father to the capital. Unlike Colonel Aureliano Buendía, who recalled the first time he saw ice,[2] Bosch remembered selling hens, eggs, and other farm products. These trips are a central part of Bosch's childhood memories; he refers to them again and again when explaining the background for one of his stories. At the opening session (November 21, 1987) of the First National Colloquium on Literary Criticism, in speaking of the origin of "La mujer," he recalls, "From the time I was twelve until I was fourteen, I would go with my father on his trips to buy chickens, hens, and eggs in the Northwest Line and then sell them in the Capital." His "painful emotions" on observing "the destitution of those fields of the Northwest Line where I went with my father, and of the women— barefoot, ill-dressed, thin, gaunt," inspired the story, according to Bosch.[3] On other occasions he uses his memories of trips in his father's truck to illustrate some economic or social feature of the Dominican Republic in the early twentieth century. Thus, in 1959, he also calls to mind—this time for sociological rather than literary purposes—his trips with his father in the Ford pickup.[4] It is a recurring image. Is this mere chance, an inscrutable trick of the memory? Or do these recollections have a deeper significance, one that might allow us to understand the writings of Juan Bosch from a new perspective? What do these memories from his youth, practically from his childhood, evoke at different points in his long, complex, and prolific career? I do not expect to find in these memories an all-inclusive explanation. I do, however, believe that they are not unworthy of our attention as we examine the course of his evolution as a writer or try to see more clearly the paths that led him to his political and social ideology and to his historical narrative.

What relationship is there between Bosch's literary work, his social and political thought, and his historiographic work? The answer to this question may appear to be simple and obvious,[5] but it is actually difficult and complex. Let us remember that we are speaking of a body of work that began in the Dominican Republic with short stories set in the 1920s; that continued during a long and varied exile (1938–61) with both literature and essays, covering a broad range of subjects including biography, politics, culture, and travelogues; and that was resumed when he returned to his native land in 1961, primarily with works of a political nature. Once again in exile, during the late 1960s he wrote some of his most relevant political and historical texts, among them several that were particularly acclaimed in international circles.[6] When he returned to the Dominican Republic, this time for good, Bosch continued to write; in the 1970s and 1980s, his writings became decidedly political, although he never entirely abandoned literary, historical, and cultural topics.[7] In all, it is a massive oeuvre of extraordinary complexity, overwhelming in its sheer abundance and in its breadth, touching as it does on so many aspects of Dominican history and society in the most recent century of its existence.

How, then, are we to read the writings of Bosch and single out their defining features? Might it not make more sense to question whether his oeuvre can properly be viewed as monolithic—a seamless, homogeneous unit without contradictions or adulterations? If we reject that premise, then we must suggest criteria for outlining some of the contradictions, disparities, or changes that may be observed in his writing, beginning with its origins in La Vega in the late 1920s. Toward that end, I would like to suggest an interpretation of Bosch's work that, while postulating a break (or at least a shift), does, on the other hand, enable us to understand it as the evolution of a national modernizing project. This project consists of two great phases or stages, each marked by a particular type of writing or narration: The first stage, which begins in the Dominican Republic, is typified by his stories; the second stage begins in exile and continues into the 1960s with his return to his native land.

In the first phase, the modernizing project is incipient, expressed not as a fully articulated political proposal and economic and social design but in the tensions of encounters between modernity and Dominican premodernity.[8] The second stage is from the years when Bosch was in exile, beginning in 1938. At that time he turned toward the configuration of a political and social project of modernization. Two aspects of Bosch's experience in exile played decisive roles as he forged this project. The first was his encounter with the works of the Puerto Rican intellectual Eugenio María de Hostos, a figure of great importance in the history of the Dominican Republic.[9] Collaborating in Puerto Rico to publish the writings of Hostos, Bosch came in contact with what would become an intellectual and political paradigm. He was privy to Hostos's letters and his diary (what might be called his private texts) as well as his public writings; all of this gave Bosch a model of a committed intellectual, dedicated—body and soul—to a cause.[10]

The other experience crucial to the formation of his modernizing project was his lengthy sojourn in Cuba. While Bosch was still living in Puerto Rico, other exiles made contact with him; with them he founded the Dominican Revolutionary Party. From 1938 until the early 1950s, he resided in Cuba, where he began to be involved personally and directly in politics. In the 1940s and 1950s his modernizing project took shape, now channeled through a political program: first, because Bosch became an active participant in the movement against Rafael L. Trujillo's dictatorship in the Dominican Republic and, second, because his time in Cuba provided him with a model of society that would be fundamental in defining his aspirations for his native land. Of the countries of Latin America, in fact, two would become paradigms of Bosch's ambitions for his own country. One of these, obviously, was Cuba; the second was Costa Rica. In each case, a relatively small country with great economic potential won Bosch's admiration.[11] The outlines of the modernizing project he sought are to be found in his experiences in Cuba; his culture and his political practices were indelibly marked by what he learned in the "fascinating island." For its part, Costa Rica, though its impact was not as great as Cuba's, offered a model of an agrarian society with a respectable democratic tradition, which appealed directly to Bosch's yearnings for modernization in the early 1960s. The Dominican writer saw Cuba and Costa Rica as utopias of a sort, examples to be followed by the Dominican Republic.

The distinction between these two phases in the Bosch canon is not original with me; it may be considered a commonplace in analyses and commentaries on his written work. It is less common (perhaps even heretical) to maintain that Bosch's oeuvre, far from being understood in terms of a strict demarcation between his literary work—his fiction—and his political/historical works (which are grounded in reality and, in consequence, approach scientific discourse), should be understood on the basis of narrative expressions. That is, Bosch's political, historical, and sociological texts are also narrations. They are narrations in that they suggest or refer to an "imagined community," the utopian expression of the nation to which he aspires; they also contain, in counterpoint, images of the nation (or antination) that is to be replaced. After all, as Benedict Anderson has pointed out, the ideas of nation and nationalism "are cultural artifacts of a particular kind," one of whose constituent elements is the printed word.[12] Bosch's texts are also narratives in that, as Hayden White argues, the diverse expressions or "modes" of historiography "are in reality *formalizations* of poetic insights that analytically precede them and that sanction the particular theories used to give historical accounts the aspect of an 'explanation.' "[13] Thus we may say that the historical works of Juan Bosch, like any other text of this nature, are (as White would say) "literary artifacts" or "verbal fictions, the contents of which are as much *invented* as *found*."[14]

NARRATION

The nation is always conceived as a deep, horizontal comradeship.
    Benedict Anderson, Imagined Communities *(New York, 1996)*

It is a laborious madness and an impoverishing one, the madness of composing vast books—setting out in five hundred pages an idea that can be perfectly related orally in five minutes.
    Jorge Luis Borges, Collected Fictions *[1941] (New York, 1998)*[15]

His voice cast a spell, and one seemed to see the scenes.
    Juan Bosch, "El río y su enemigo"

Journeying through "the adventure of modernity," Marshall Berman takes us to many places far removed from the tropics, among them the gelid city of St. Petersburg during the nineteenth and early twentieth centuries. Berman turns his eyes toward St. Petersburg in his desire to approach the contradictions of "the modernism of underdevelopment"; above all, he wants us to see "the anguish of backwardness and underdevelopment" reflected in cultural expressions—particularly in Russian literature but also in social and political tensions. Berman's exercise is clearly comparative in nature: To him, czarist Russia—as an agrarian, feudal, authoritarian, premodern, patriarchal, archaic society—represents the "archetype of the emerging twentieth-century Third World."[16]

In its own way, the Dominican Republic of the early twentieth century also experienced "the anguish of backwardness and underdevelopment." The deep-seated angst of the clerisy stemmed from the "weight of infinite frustrations of the plans and projects for social regeneration, in their links to political power." One of the principal elements of that gloom was the failure to configure a stable, integrated nation according to the "paradigm of the bourgeois nation."[17] Unable to accomplish their dream of setting up a real-life "imagined community," the dominant and intellectual sectors in the Dominican Republic retreated behind the walls of a profound pessimism, seeking explanations for their failure in "race," biology, poor nutrition—that is, in anything that could be blamed on the "subaltern sectors" of the nation.[18] From that point of view, it was the campesinos—especially those who were black or mulatto—who bore the greatest responsibility for the Dominican Republic's backward state.

This "Dominican pessimism" was simply the expression of the ideas held by the lettered sectors about the rural masses. To the intelligentsia of the period, the economic, social, cultural, and religious practices of the campesinos were symptoms—visible and verifiable indicators—of a barbarism that their civilizing efforts could not eradicate. Even the "revolutions" that afflicted the country throughout the nineteenth century and into the twentieth—revolutions that contributed to the absence of a stable government able to guarantee the nation's sovereignty against foreigners, whether from Haiti, the United States, or Europe—were blamed on *conchoprimismo*, a derogatory term referring to the insurrectionary propensities of the rural sectors. The "imagined community" in the minds of the clerisy in the early twentieth century advocated, in contrast, the concept of a strong State that would be an administrator of people and spaces, a guarantor of national sovereignty, and, above all, a domesticator of the fickle campesino masses. To the intellectuals at the turn of the century, the peasantry was an internal "other," a "dangerous class" over which the State should immediately exercise its regenerating and civilizing will; the campesinos were that "fragment of the nation"—haphazard, unpredictable, unstable, and uncivilized, but necessary for their role in production—that would have to be subdued if the country aspired to play its part in the great symphony of civilized nations. Given those conditions, very few Dominican intellectuals could empathize with the campesino sectors; even fewer could grant them the capacity to articulate their own autonomous political or social projects, expressing their own aspirations, their culture, and their utopias.[19]

At the beginning of the twentieth century, the Dominican Republic found itself in a situation very similar to that of many post-independence Latin American countries: In the Dominican Republic, likewise, albeit for very different reasons, it appeared that "the chaos had only intensified." Here, too, writing "became a response to the necessity of overcoming . . . catastrophe"; it was a way to give shape to the dream of modernization, "*to civilize*, to order the randomness of . . . *barbarism*."[20] This was the intellectual climate in which Juan Bosch's thinking was developed. Scarred by the trauma of the U.S. occupation of 1916–24, the Dominican intelligentsia reacted against those factors that, in their view, weakened the nation.[21] Bosch and others who were to become leading actors in the Dominican cultural and political scene formed coteries and *peñas*, gathering for discussions that ranged freely from literature to politics.[22] Within these intellectual conclaves the country's social composition was no doubt spoken about as an impediment to the nation's progress. It was in these circles that the young Juan Bosch's social concerns were honed—concerns that, by his own testimony, he had begun to form in childhood and adolescence.

As Bosch himself has indicated, his social concerns were forged in the fires of his direct contact with the rural world of the Cibao, birthplace of the subject matter for his early stories. But what is the particular, specific link between Bosch's works and the Dominican countryside? I would like to emphasize certain links that, while they have been suggested in other studies, transcend (in my judgment) the relationships that have been established to date.[23] His stories with rural themes may be understood as a place where the intellectual—in search of a political project and marked by his generation's concerns for modernization—encounters a man critically identified with ("amazed and shadowed" by)[24] the campesino world that has, to a great extent, defined the experiences of his young life and that constantly haunts his memories. Fictional narrative becomes the medium for expressing the conflicts and tensions generated by his social concerns, marked by the encounters and divergences of modernity in the Dominican Republic.[25] In the political realm there is a tense encounter, charged with conflicts, between the premodernity of the rural *gavilla* (rebel band) and the "revolutions" of the caudillos, on the one hand, and modernity (represented by a State tending toward centralization, with a decided emphasis on the rationality of bourgeois order, emblematized in the law), on the other. There is also an encounter between the modern forms of capitalist exploitation of resources and labor—and of their derivatives in "backward" countries—and the traditional modalities of time, leisure, productive activity. There is, in sum, an encounter between an expanding modernity, surging with vigor, and the premodern (or, better, countermodern) forms in which human beings interrelate with each other and with the world about them.[26]

All of this represents some of the significance of Bosch's memories. But his memories are not his alone; they also contain the experiences, the beliefs, the fears, the narrations, and the stories—in short, the histories of the "others"—that were transmitted to him orally. In many of his stories there is "a voice that attempts to bring the event closer than his own memory, to make him speak the words of the others, [words] that in themselves have the value of an event."[27] In consequence, it is necessary to begin with orality and with the mediation between orality and the written word, representing modernity, in order to comprehend the configuration of Bosch's stories, in particular as a medium for the reconceptualization of their social content. Walter Ong, one of the pioneers in the study of the relationship between orality and literacy, has emphasized that orality presupposes a different "mentality" from that of cultures in which the written word prevails. Therefore, the transition from orality to literacy implies much more than permanently fixing sounds by means of writing; it involves, above all, seizing upon an episteme determined by a new technology—writing; in the process, the old oral episteme is transformed.[28] Such a transformation is not, however, a neutral act, the product of the mere application of a "new technology," more sophisticated and rational, that surpasses the knowledge that is founded in oral tradition. It is, on the contrary, a *political* process, since it implies a power relationship between groups who are able to wield the written word and those who are not or who are just being initiated into its mysteries. Orality is dominated by "lettered knowledge"; its concomitant is the "domestication of the savage mind."[29]

Patrick Hutton has indicated that to the same degree to which the replacement of orality by literacy implies changes in epistemes or paradigms, it also implies a transformation in the techniques of memory. According to Hutton, this transition contributed to the emergence of modern historiography, a written expression of the new forms of memory that accompany the advent of modernity—above all, the "memories of power" associated with the emerging forms of the State.[30] With the extension of literacy, the old collective memories—diverse, multiple, multifaceted—are subsumed, transformed, and subordinated, but they do not totally disappear. In fact, Hutton argues, in some works there occurs a "crossroads," an intersection of writing and orality. In such works tradition, "collective memory," and "oral literature" live on, sometimes concealed or disguised but recoverable in one way or another.[31] We must insist, however, that the incorporation of orality into letters is not done ingenuously, merely as a labor of transcribing the voice of the "other." It is, on the contrary, a complex process, usually linked to a civilizing project. Ángel Rama goes so far as to argue that "urban intellectuals" often look to the "rural cultures" that are "everywhere withering . . . under the extending influence of urban civilization" for the purpose of "hurr[ying] to collect endangered oral traditions." Because these traditions are on the road to extinction, Rama adds, "the books of letrados . . . entombed oral production, immobilizing and fixing [it] forever."[32]

All of this leads to a reading of the stories of Bosch—especially the earliest ones—as a crossroads at which a movement toward modernization encounters the rural society, dominated by orality, that is the object of his reflection and his literary praxis. A number of indications lead us to affirm that orality played a crucial role in the definition of Bosch's subject matter, his content, and perhaps even his narrative technique.[33] In the first place, we have his own testimony about his close contact, in childhood, with the campesinos. An unpretentious little store (*pulperiíta*), known as Villa Sinda, that Bosch's father opened somewhere in the Northwest Line was "a gathering place . . . [for] the campesinos from all over the zone." Wherever Bosch went, when he was "very small . . . , I heard the campesinos talking": "The campesinos would talk to me, would tell me things; they told me fabulous stories. . . . And then we went to live in Haiti. In Haiti Papá opened a store, and we had a man there at the store, a Dominican named Pablo Morillo, from here in Moca, who lived with us in the same house and worked as a clerk in the store, and every evening don Pablo would set me on his knee and tell me stories. They did the same thing back in Río Verde, poor Niño, . . . old Dumas and so many of those campesinos who would sit around telling stories, especially as night was falling."[34]

According to Rosario-Candelier, Bosch achieves "an objective narration" in his stories because the narrator is "almost always omniscient."[35] The voice that narrates, however, does not always adopt the same posture. Sometimes the narration appears to be almost a transcription of oral traditions, with the author as audience—as one who listens to a story being told, as opposed to one who testifies to what he has personally witnessed. This is especially true of those narrations referring to events of great portent, involving the supernatural world, that were part of the oral tradition in the early twentieth century or to characters, social customs, and situations typical of the rural world of that period.[36] In "La sangre," orality is the starting point of the narration: "Finally! Old Nelico was going to talk!" In others, it plays an important role in the tale. Thus, in "El abuelo," a semiautobiographical narrative, the grandfather of the title sets his grandson on his knee to tell him stories. In "La negación," an old campesino, who gives "the impression that he lived his life walking," would tell stories as he rolled tobacco leaves: "In my time there weren't any highways"—an evocation in which the highway, a symbol of modernity, becomes the line of demarcation between "back then" and "nowadays."[37] Other narrations interweave what is heard with what is witnessed or experienced; some suggest the author's presence on the scene, by means of the name of the main character.[38] The child who listens to the stories in "El abuelo" is named Juan, as is the young laborer in "Camino real," "Guaraguaos," and "Rosa." Bosch makes appearances, like the director's cameos in Hitchcock films, as a character in his stories. Sometimes he appears as a witness, taking a secondary role in the narration or moving through the scene without taking center stage in the plot ("El abuelo," "Guaraguaos"); in other stories "Juan" is the central character ("Camino real" and "Rosa"). There are even stories, such as "El río y su enemigo," in which the character of the narrator is an unspecified "Juan." Although this is a characteristic of Bosch's fictional narrative in many stories such as those mentioned above, stories in which the author's presence is emphasized by incorporating him as a character show a much more obvious intent to give a testimony, almost to write a chronicle.[39]

To point out the "testimonial" aspects of Bosch's narrative, or to affirm that in that narrative there is an intersection of campesino orality and writing, might appear to be a mere triviality. It is not so trivial a matter if we assume that this intersection is by no means a chance encounter, much less a careless one, but, on the contrary, a meeting of "possibilities in conflict," charged with tension and with ambivalent and even contradictory interpretations.[40] One might assert this reading for a number of reasons. Although Bosch certainly reveals in his stories his genuine admiration for some of the values held by the campesinos, he also takes critical stands against them. Various commentators have highlighted his stance in opposition to the "revolutions" of the early twentieth century, those bursts of rural violence that endangered the nation's political stability, upset the course of daily life, and threw into reverse the material progress so painfully achieved by the country. In fact, his first and best-known novel, *La mañosa*—based not only on the many stories about these events that he must have heard as a child but also on his personal experiences and recollections—is a sort of memoir or chronicle of the revolutions.[41]

But it is not—for no memoir ever is—a neutral memoir. The study of memory, as Hutton has indicated, leads us to the "politics of representation": "The images recollected are not evocations of a real past but only representations of it."[42] As David Herzberger writes, "Time is always corrosive, and memory can recoup never time itself but only the meaning of time for a remembering self."[43] Bosch's position relative to the "revolutions" and the ragtag *montonera* militias provides a fundamental key to understanding his modernizing and civilizing stance vis-à-vis the rural world of the early 1900s. In it we can clearly see how Bosch criticizes, how he distances himself from, barbarism—the "bloody specter of the revolution."[44] This stance denotes a move toward modernization, in keeping with the views of other Latin American and Dominican intellectuals, appalled by the "internal others," frequently "orientalized" (according to Said's conceptualization), due to their "Berber [that is, barbarian] spirit."[45] And while Bosch may have written that "the countryside was not to blame for being an arena for tragedies and a breeding ground for men unable to recognize themselves,"[46] still, the countryside bred uncommon and irrational forces, at least from the perspective of the modernizing intellectual. Bosch does not deny that "civilization is also pain,"[47] but at heart he believes that the civilizing element must prevail if happiness, stability, progress, triumph are to be won. In the story "Rosa," the main character (Juan, of course) renounces "bed, home, affection" and sets out "on the road" (symbolic of "the adventure of modernity," as Berman would say?) in spite of its "ruts" filled with "torrents of dirty water."[48] Might not these ruts, or the "unevenness" (*desniveles*) of the road, be a metaphor for the dangers and for the divergences of modernity of which Ramos writes? Would it be feasible to interpret the torrents of dirty water, which threaten to wipe out the very road and which endanger the life of the traveler, as a symbol of premodernity?

As a precondition to becoming a genuine source of human fulfillment, the countryside would have to be modernized. One had to "flee" from the "backcountry" (*monte*), for although it was "humid and cozy" there, these were "rude lands . . . , cruel like wicked men."[49] "Rude," uncouth, uncultivated land (*tierra inculta*): land in its natural state, land that has not been submitted to that pillar of civilization, systematic agriculture; land that has not yet been trampled by the permanent presence of humans; land that is untouched, primitive, barbaric, wild. Even when turned into farmland—cultivated land, land that has been subjected to the domesticating action of agriculture—the countryside was still a place where a certain mode of thought prevailed, a mode of thought that was not only different from modern thought but also, in many senses, opposed to it. The language was different, though that would eventually change with the adoption of "cultivated"—that is, modern—speech.[50] Human relationships and beliefs were permeated by premodernity, even in "the sugarmill, the pasture, and the ranch,"[51] agricultural lands that were subjected to economic exploitation—that is, to civilization.

But the civilizing process, far from eradicating barbarism, combined with premodernity to produce new forms of exploitation, subjugation, and despoliation. "El socio" (1940) exemplifies this "divergence" of modernity. The story tells of an affronted campesino's revenge against the local big shot, who had become "the owner of scads of land" through plunder and terrorist tactics.[52] In one scene of the story, Black Manzueta witnesses the arrival of the surveyors—heralds of modernity in the early 1900s, when premodern forms of landownership still prevailed in the Dominican Republic—and sees how some peons, at don Anselmo's orders, "brazenly threw up fences," stealing his land. In this act of despoliation, civilization and barbarism were combined: the surveyors' implements included some "colored sticks and a little gadget set up on three legs"; the peons carried sticks (*colines*), and their foreman had a revolver. Here was a modern technique of land measurement juxtaposed with the crudest symbols of violence; modernity allied to traditional expressions of terror as a means of carrying out injustice; modernity contributing to a new interpretation of the structures of power and exploitation. For such was don Anselmo: the landowner who—whether employing traditional, premodern forms or seizing upon the means provided by modernity—claimed the land occupied by the peasantry. In a play of contrasts, don Anselmo simultaneously represented the most oppressive facet of traditional society and the most destructive and unjust facet of the modernization of the countryside. On his lands, in contrast to the "rude" or "uncultivated" backcountry, "there were leagues of cattle pastures, plantain and cacao fields, enormous stretches of corn and pineapples." Thanks to the exploitation of the land, the new urban civilization—emblematized by the automobile, electric lights, the refrigerator, and the phonograph, all at don Anselmo's command—made its debut in the countryside.

To acquire his wealth and power, don Anselmo employed traditional resources, such as making a pact with the Devil, who became his "partner." Because of this pact, "everything worked out right" for don Anselmo: land, women, power—all things desirable—were his for the asking. Caught up in his newfound power, don Anselmo dared to repudiate the pact, claiming that money was his true partner. And that was when his misfortunes began. The Devil took his vengeance, making a new pact with old Adán Matías, who was incensed with the wealthy landowner for deceiving and seducing his adolescent granddaughter. Ironically, the traditional source of power—the Devil—turns out to be more democratic than money, for access to money was limited to certain groups within the society. The Devil, in contrast, requires only loyalty (which, of course, involves the loss of one's soul), a commonly accepted value among the campesinos. Don Anselmo had broken the alliance, clearing the way for Adán Matías to make his own pact with the Devil and consummate his revenge.[53]

The contradictory nature of modernization is clearly seen in the actions of the State (the agent of civilization par excellence), which usually have an adverse effect on the lives of the campesinos. "Forzados," one of the stories in *Camino real*, shows the moral outrage of the campesinos against the program of forced labor in public works that was established in the early decades of the twentieth century.[54] To recruit laborers, soldiers—some of whom looked and acted more like bandits—would sweep into a community and savagely beat the campesinos to intimidate them. The campesinos would then be taken, bound, to the work sites, where they would be forced to labor for four days building and repairing roads and highways. Due to this abuse, the end of the story (in which the main character returns to his *bohío* and unearths a revolver that he had hidden on his parcel of land [*conuco*]) seems to justify rural violence against the State and its representatives. This story emphasizes the oppressive face of the modernizing projects imposed by the power of the State. Since this power is of urban origin and its dominion over the countryside subverts and disrupts whatever redeeming value it might have, Bosch tends to condemn the extension of that power over the rural world, where the State is primarily a synonym for repression and persecution. In view of this State-sponsored oppression and violence—a manifestation of the city's exploitation of the countryside—Bosch adopts a less severe stance with respect to potential violence on the part of the rural masses.[55] A similar stance can be glimpsed in certain texts that make reference not to the power of the State but to local power structures, dominated by rural caciques. In "Lo mejor," two men who are determined to incite a rural uprising form a tacit agreement to assassinate the cacique of the region: "Ol' man Nano is in cahoots wit the gob'ment," a sympathizer explains to the conspirators. "Ya can't count on nobody long's he's around."[56] This story admits a reading in which the action of the rebels, reprehensible from an abstract moral perspective, is understandable in the light of political necessity. Although he stops short of openly justifying such acts, in "Lo mejor" and "Forzados" Bosch shows sympathy for what he would later come to label "revolutionary violence."

The presence of the power of the State brought about a growing confrontation with the forms and cultural expressions that had been, until then, predominant in the rural zone. We have already seen this in regard to the system of landownership, in "El socio"; in other texts, the confrontation occurs on the plane of beliefs, values, and the representation of reality and, consequently, the criteria for defining truth. The ironic title of "El muerto estaba vivo" (The Dead Man Was Alive, 1943) suggests a confrontation between two opposing notions of reality, two conflicting narrations. In the story Jesús Oquendo, a simple peon, adheres to his interpretation of a homicide even though his narration of the event contradicts the logic of the modern urban world, according to which the dead man cannot be alive. Modernization, emblematized in the story by the construction of a highway, was about to desecrate the grave of Pablo de la Mota. In defiance of the logic of progress, old Felicio, loyal to the dead man, opposes allowing the highway to disturb Pablo de la Mota's eternal rest, thus setting himself up as the champion of traditional rural beliefs and values. The confrontation culminates in the murder of Sergeant Felipe, who had instigated the construction of the highway through the cemetery because he stood to gain financially from it. In his explanation—his narration—of the events surrounding the murder of the sergeant, old Felicio, who has been accused of the crime, claims that "the dead man came to life," alleging that "nobody really dies long's there's somebody in the world that respects his memory."[57] Passed on orally, the memory of Pablo de la Mota is sufficient reason to justify his presence in the world of the living—that is, to explain events by a logic that does not coincide with that of modern knowledge, in which there are clearly defined boundaries between the worlds of the living and of the dead.

Bosch's fictional oeuvre may be seen as an attempt to codify the behaviors, beliefs, and social structures of the rural world; in that sense, it is similar to an ethnographic register.[58] Bosch's adoption of his anthropological view does not preclude him from taking a more critical, even ironic stance ("La nochebuena de Encarnación Mendoza" [1949], "El funeral" [1940], and "El río y su enemigo" [1940], in addition to "El muerto estaba vivo"). But it is in "Dos pesos de agua" (1937) that his ironizing of campesino culture and behaviors can best be seen.[59] In this narrative, a peasant woman prays to the "souls in purgatory" for help, promising to burn "two pesos' worth of candles" for them in exchange for an end to the drought that is devastating the region. The souls are initially deaf to her pleas, but they finally respond, unleashing torrential rains. The rains bring an end to the drought, but a mere "fifty centavos' worth" is enough to cause floods, and the overflowing rivers destroy the fields and sweep away bohíos, animals, and people, including old Remigia and her grandson. Adamant in their otherworldly reckoning, the "souls in purgatory" are unmoved by the floods, the suffering, and the devastation that they have caused, as they fervently cry, "More! More . . . ! It's two pesos, two pesos' worth of water!" In "Dos pesos de agua"—a tale that presents an aberrant logic, although we are never completely sure where the aberrance lies, in Remigia or in the souls—Bosch's irony is indicative of his move toward modernization.

But Bosch does not always take this stance in regard to campesino culture and society; in his catalog of behaviors he also vindicates certain aspects of rural life. In fact, there are moments when Bosch, in transcribing campesino orality, appropriates its possibilities for an antiestablishment polemic.[60] We have already seen this in "El socio," "El muerto estaba vivo," and "Lo mejor." In each of these stories there is a stance in opposition to the powers, whether traditional or modern, that undermine what is humane and admirable in campesino countermodernity. These stories offer an alternate reading to "official history"; "Forzados" is a good example. "La verdad" (1938), set in contrast to the "memory of power," is a more subversive appropriation of oral tradition.[61] The subject could not be more fitting: the death of the fugitive Enrique Blanco, a young soldier of campesino extraction, who hid out in the Cibao countryside after his desertion, receiving aid from the country people and becoming a symbol, in the 1930s, of resistance to Trujillo's forces of order. "La verdad" (The Truth) offers an alternative to the official explanation of Blanco's death, which claims that the fugitive was caught and killed by a campesino. Oral tradition (on which Bosch's story is based and which has been verified by recent research)[62] holds that Blanco committed suicide, possibly with the knowledge of the campesino who later claimed to have killed him. Needless to say, the Trujillo regime capitalized on Blanco's death for its propaganda value, ostentatiously exhibiting his body to illustrate the extent of the State's power over the Dominican population. In the Trujillo iconography, Blanco's corpse became an emblem of the irrefutable power of tyranny. As such, it carried a potent message "demonstrating" the advisability of submitting to the designs of those in power. Consequently, this Bosch story—fruit of the orality that had preserved and transmitted "the truth"—examines the management of facts in order to construct a "discourse of power."[63] In contrast to the official version found in the documents of the agencies of "law" and "order" and disseminated by the official-line press, Bosch's text is nourished by oral sources, which provide a different narration, a different truth. This is, in fact, a struggle over the representation of facts: a profoundly political conflict over the authority to represent what is real, not unrelated to Bosch's search for a civilizing model able to overcome a tyrant's falsification of reality.

An ironic stance, a "zeal for modernization" (with its consequent yearning for an order that would guarantee the existence of a prosperous, stable, integrated nation), a narrative that challenges accepted "truths," an ethnographic register, civilization and barbarism—all these are elements that come together in the tales of Juan Bosch. García-Cuevas has proposed the thought-provoking thesis that Bosch inherited and carried on the work of Pedro Francisco Bonó,[64] defender of the campesinos against the destructive wake of capitalist modernization as it stormed across the country in the late nineteenth century. As in Bosch, in Bonó can be found a "criticism of the ideology of progress"; his writings also include a "national/popular project" that was an attempt to legitimate the management of the country by its lettered sectors (transformed in this project into a political class) and that was destined to enable "bourgeois domination."[65] In each of these writers, "conceptions of nationality" (to follow Rama) were "enhanced by the humble oral productions of rural cultures."[66] The "appropriation" of "the knowledge of the other," as Julio Ramos has so accurately phrased it, enabled the intellectual who lacked any real, effectual power to be a mediator "between civilization and barbarism, modernity and tradition, writing and orality."[67] For this reason we find in Bosch a decided will to validate his voice, to define his position as a man of letters, to delimit his field of reflection and writing; literature becomes the hub of his (incipient) political *praxis*. Here Bosch finds—at a time when, thanks to the Trujillo dictatorship, the intelligentsia had few autonomous spaces—a loophole for action. If only in his narrations, Bosch is able to see himself as playing an important role in social and political vindications and, in consequence, in the restructuring of the nation.[68]

Few narrations express the tension between his "zeal for modernization," his posture in regard to power, and his political potential as an intellectual so well as "Camino real." Originally published in 1933 in the eponymous collection, it is unquestionably one of his most representative texts.[69] At the end of the tobacco harvest two men, Floro and—once again—Juan, meet and become acquainted on one of the many roads of the Cibao region. Both are looking for work, which they find at a foreigner's plantation. A strong bond of solidarity is quickly established between Juan and his companion, which is then extended to their fellow workers. In a long passage interrupting the train of the narration, the author harangues city dwellers—whom he calls "puny men" (*hombrecillos*) and "city sissies" (*mariquitas de ciudad*)—for looking down on the campesinos:

The lazy campesino? That campesino who pays all his taxes just the same as the rich man, but doesn't have a school or a theater or electricity? The campesino who they recruit and send off to the revolutions, to the slaughter! . . . The generous campesino, with his door open to any weary traveler, his table spread for anyone who's hungry, a hammock or a cot ready for anyone who's sleepy, his heart always willing to point the way to any wanderer lost in the hills or the meadows or the backcountry! The campesino who works from before sunup till after sundown, planting tobacco for the man in the city to smoke, planting cacao for candy and hot chocolate, planting coffee to feed the habit and for strength, planting beans and rice for food; who raises pigs and cows and chickens; who produces everything and sells it for a few measly centavos, so the rest can get rich, the others, the money changers who were driven out of the temple!

And still there are people who speak ill to me of the wretched man from the backcountry![70]

Bosch takes up a stance vindicating the "other"—the campesinos who constitute the nation's productive base. Shared sufferings and exploitation on the plantation establish a unifying link between the Juan of the story and the campesinos: "The burden of the entire country rests on *us*" (emphasis mine), Juan says to his fellow workers, bridging by means of that pronoun the gap that separates them. Juan himself recognizes that gap and continues to try to bridge it by disseminating the written word and by eradicating those beliefs that, according to him, help keep the country folk from recognizing their "right to rebel, to try for a better life." In this category he includes not only their belief "that all things come from a miraculous being" but also their inability to recognize that don Justo—the name that Bosch bestows, ironically, on the arbitrary and despotic plantation owner—is "a slave master." One night, after a heated discussion with his fellow workers, Juan has a dream. In it, he sees "thousands of little men weighed down by enormous burdens," and this fills him with a "violent desire . . . to run and help them." But finding himself "chained down, in the middle of the great plain that those little men were crossing," all he can do is scream at them, "You idiots! Throw off your burdens!" And the answer to this reproach, from "all those ravaged mouths," is "we're fine the way we are!"

The main character of this narration, whose mastery of "letters"—of the written word—differentiates him from the other workers, jockeys for position vis-à-vis both the campesino and the power elite; using his character as a mediator, Bosch as author sets his distance and demarcates his personal space. His self-portrayal as an agent of vindication confers ethical and political validity on his practice as a writer, as a man of letters;[71] thus he defines himself to those in power, and thus he authorizes himself to the (potential) objects of his political efforts and to the lettered sector, few of whom could see in campesino society any redeemable element whatsoever. Bosch, part of the "new generation of intellectuals" in Latin America, "set about using [his] political influence to orient the rest of society,"[72] those sectors that had not yet (according to those same intellectuals, it should be noted) "come to full self-awareness."[73] To accomplish that purpose, he takes on the role of advocate for the masses—acting, of course, on the premise that the masses need an advocate since, in their circumstances, they are unable to create their own agendas and utopias.[74] It falls to the man of letters to develop or complete the consciousness of the masses—a consciousness that is shadowed, fragmented, incomplete, inapposite, or altogether lacking. In a typical enlightened gesture, in "Camino real" Juan sets himself the task of teaching "letters" to the plantation workers; these lessons, along with the harangues on social justice that frequently accompany them, explain (according to don Justo) "why people aren't happy working here any more." Juan, the character, breaks the rules, becoming an agent of liberation through his efforts as a teacher—a prototype of the intellectual imparting knowledge, "enlightenment," "consciousness." The conflict between Juan and don Justo—landowner, but also "owner" of lettered culture—revolves, above all, around the use of the written word. Don Justo defends "letters" as a privilege and, in consequence, a "mechanism of control and social subordination"; Juan transgresses on this privilege, which is an element of the power that "decided the distance—and the struggle—between the ruling classes and the campesinos, between those who could and could not write" (or read).[75] In his enlightened version of the ancient myth of Prometheus stealing fire from the gods, Bosch takes up a stance on the side of the campesinos and rural laborers, in a vindicating posture typical of the modernizing radical intellectual. In the enlightened myth, the written word is an agent of civilization, a symbol of the new modern order, and consequently an indispensable element of progress and liberation.

But in the Dominican Republic the 1930s was not an opportune time for staging great social projects in defense of the campesinos. Bosch chose a different path from that of other intellectuals of his generation who also yearned for changes in the social structure: while they, in the end, became integrated into the power schemes of the Trujillo dictatorship, Bosch went into exile.[76] In his narratives of the 1930s, journeys are a recurring theme: here we have another venerable mythical theme, in which the hero must go through many trials and vicissitudes along his way. In modern literature, Ramos writes, "the voyage is a *prospective* exercise, a displacement to the future that propels the subject beyond the insufficiencies of the present."[77] In the stories written before the exile, Bosch's travelers—including his fictional "Juan"—traversed the Cibao, "so rich and so large" and crisscrossed by so many roads, as he wrote in "Camino real." Beginning in 1938, it would be Bosch himself who would journey down many roads, this time the roads of exile. Along the way, his incipient project of modernization would become (re)defined, acquiring new elements. Little by little, the themes of rural life and campesinos were left behind; progressively, Bosch changed his narrative: the fictional story was replaced by the political/historical essay. In the end, it seems that, truly, "travel always changes some aspect of the life of the traveler."

HISTORY

History has become the unavoidable element in our thought.
    Michel Foucault, The Order of Things *(New York, 1994)*

To historize any structure, to write its history, is to mythologize it: either in order to effect its transformation by showing how "unnatural" it is . . . , or in order to reinforce its authority by showing how consonant it is with its context, how adequately it conforms to the "order of things."
    Hayden White, Tropics of Discourse *(Baltimore, 1986)*

I had learned something that made me different from them.

  Juan Bosch, "Rosa"

Writing speaks of the past only in order to inter it. Writing is a tomb in the double sense of the word in that, in the very same text, it both honors and eliminates.

  Michel de Certeau, The Writing of History *(New York, 1988)*

Following Italo Calvino, Carlos Fuentes asserts that "literature is necessary to politics when it gives a voice to something that has no voice, or gives a name to something that is as yet anonymous."[78] Lacking a voice of their own (or at least, so reputed among the lettered and the powerful), the campesinos are represented with complexity, contradictorily, problematically—disturbingly, in many ways—in Bosch's stories. In exile, Bosch continued to give a name to the plight of the campesinos; at that time he also began to do so openly in political essays. Only two years after leaving the Dominican Republic, Juan Bosch wrote a short essay that is one of his least known but perhaps most telling texts, revealing much about his political ideology during that period. This very brief text—almost a story, if you will—is a prologue to one of the first works to attempt an interpretation of Dominican history: Juan Isidro Jimenes-Grullón's *La República Dominicana: Análisis de su pasado y su presente.* As Roberto Cassá has indicated, in this prologue Bosch presents a "populist *campesinismo*" and advocates leading the campesino masses toward the annihilation of "the *pueblitas* as a ruling class."[79]

In these assertions we can see a reflection of several of the principles observed in Bosch's rural stories. First of all, there is the social struggle between the campesinos and the pueblitas. In an explanatory note to the second edition of Jimenes-Grullón's work, Bosch identifies the pueblitas as those who, in the "rustic consciousness," occupy "a despicable moral position: that of exploiter or aspiring exploiter," usually of urban origin or affiliation. Following Jimenes-Grullón, Bosch recommends organizing "the natural enemies of 'los pueblitas,' . . . the great campesino mass," a task to be carried out by a "Partido Revolucionario" (Revolutionary Party) that would "influence the masses" in order to "bring about the aspirations of the people from a position of Power."

A second "reflection" seen in this prologue is the vindicatory stance that Bosch takes, as he had previously done in "Camino real." The task of influencing the masses of campesinos and laborers to accomplish their own regeneration would be assigned to a dedicated and "limited number of pure-hearted men of conscience" who loved their fatherland as a noble "duty." Unlike those whose love of country was solely for personal economic gain (that is, the ones whom it was necessary to oppose), these devoted men desired that the Dominican Republic become "that which its founders intended for it to be: a prosperous, cultivated, and happy fatherland."[80] The venerable Jacobin ideal of leading the masses, "the people," toward their own liberation is firmly established in his allusion to the "founding fathers," an evocation with strong mythic connotations, thus legitimizing and granting authority to his political position along genealogical lines.[81]

Agrarian populism, patriotism, nationalism, and social vindication thus come together in Bosch's proposal. Within this apparent congruence, so much in keeping with that of other political programs in Latin America and the Caribbean during those years,[82] elements begin to creep in that belong to a discourse different from that which is present in his stories. The social proposal in the above-mentioned essay, "Un pueblo en un libro," is directly linked to a political project of opposition to the Trujillo regime—a possibility that was, of course, unthinkable within the country at the time. One begins to catch a glimpse—at a distance and still overshadowed by the strong appeal to agrarianist populism—of the new agents who will soon take center stage in his narrative. This is, in fact, a transitional text, in which we can see Bosch's narration edging toward other historical agents, other social forces—other stories.[83] One of these new historical forces is the party, modifying agent par excellence of Latin American politics in the early twentieth century, in particular the polyclassist parties headed by modernization-minded men of letters, who hoped to democratize public debate, as well as the avenues of access to and the ways of exercising power. Expressed in these parties (discursively, at least, since party structures retained much of the traditional social hierarchies) was a new solidarity: that of the *correligionario*—the fellow party member, the comrade, the true believer.[84] To the solidarity that we saw in the stories, based on the world of labor and on shared life experiences and narrations, is now added (although evidently in the process of eventual substitution) a solidarity based on common cause and common political militancy.

A crucial element in this new and novel alliance between the masses and the radical men of letters (an alliance that, in the case of the Dominican Republic, is strictly confined to the plane of discourse, due to the impossibility of carrying it out in practice) is its stance vis-à-vis power. In Bosch's essay, the existing power structure is stigmatized for its inability to bring the "conquests of civilization" to the campesino masses and to urban laborers. The power to which Bosch aspires, on the one hand, would make of them "complete men," enabling them to take part in "the enjoyment of civilization."[85] The illegitimacy of power originates in its defense of an exclusivist order in which civilization is taken over and enjoyed by only the limited numbers of the pueblitas. In contrast, the political legitimacy and ethical authority of the new power stem from its willingness to extend and democratize the benefits of civilization. One of the consequences of this agenda of regeneration of the masses (and therefore of the nation) was to make the State the linchpin of Boschian discourse. Although still a many-headed, many-faced monster, the Leviathan of this essay is not, exclusively, the demonized figure of the stories, in which the State signifies repression, extortion, exploitation: to a great extent, it signifies opposition to civilization—or, at least, its distortion and dilution. But extending to the masses the "conquests of civilization" (which would be accomplished by those in power) would mean returning to them "the rights that had been confiscated for four centuries."[86] In this prologue Bosch sees in the State a potential civilizing agent and thus an agent for the reconstruction of the nation.

Equally revealing are some of the concrete proposals that Bosch, following Jimenes-Grullón, advances as part of his modernizing project. In a passage in the story "Camino real" Bosch had written (referring to the railroads of the Cibao), "I have seen . . . the remains of a powerful English engine smothered by grass and weeds, taken over by the wilderness. The backcountry of the Cibao has become master over civilization. Nothing that does not come from this land's very heart can ever hold sway over it."[87] Later, however, in his 1940 essay, industrialization (which brought the railroad to the Cibao) appears as one of the potential agents of the country's regeneration. It should be stressed that, according to Bosch, the economic transformation that he proposes could not be accomplished by the pueblitas: "A century of failure disqualifies them for any such weighty task." It was the new generations of "pure-hearted men of conscience" who, from a position of power and with the support of the masses, would be fit to carry out the protean task of achieving such an economic mutation; their disinterested political will would enable them to overcome the "failure of the people organized into a State," a consequence of the hegemony of the pueblitas.[88] Together with proposals for democratization, these economic changes would make it possible to extend the benefits of civilization to all and to reinforce national solidarity, a solidarity founded not on that "gaze upon the earth" of which Silvia Álvarez-Curbelo speaks, but rather on a broadening of "the city," on the transformation of "rustics" into "citizens."

Although Bosch stops far short of assuming that the nation is solely or even primarily the State, still the State becomes, beginning with this brief essay, an ever more prominent force in his political/social interpretations and, in consequence, in his historical narrative.[89] Also stepping into more visible roles are social classes or groups other than the peasantry. In fact, in Bosch's post-1940 texts, campesinos play an ever-diminishing role; in the 1940s the displacement of social actors becomes patent, not only in his stories but also in his other works. The political possibilities (and impossibilities as well) imposed by his exile provide a partial explanation of this displacement; their concomitant was the reconfiguration of his modernization project. In that same 1940 essay that I have been discussing, the pueblitas (although defined somewhat eclectically) are a sort of counterfigure to the campesino in Bosch's interpretation of social conflicts in the Dominican Republic. In later works, however, the term disappears from his historical/social interpretations; along with "pueblitas," and as a dialectical counterpart to their evanescence as an analytic category, the peasantry disappears as a social player. During the 1960s and 1970s, the place of the campesino in Bosch's historical narratives becomes less and less significant. At the same time that his political project is undergoing modernization, a shift is occurring in regard to historical actors, fields of social action, and the configuration of politics. Modern classes replace premodern ones in his narrative.

This shift is visible in his *Trujillo, causas de una tiranía sin ejemplo*, a text from the late 1950s. Weak from the historiographic standpoint and in regard to the mastery of sociological theories, this work is nonetheless interesting, first, for its political content and, second, because it constitutes Bosch's first attempt at presenting an integrated interpretation of Dominican history.[90] For that reason this text is crucial in examining the evolution of his thought and his narrative expressions; in it are reflected the principal transformations undergone in the development of Bosch's modernizing project, on both the political and the discursive planes (that is, the construction of his narrations). He sets out to explicate the tyrannical Trujillo regime, which in his view is unparalleled in the Americas, as not "a political tyranny" but rather a "ruthless capitalist enterprise" spanning the entire Dominican population and territory. Therefore, "in good sociological technique, Trujillo's Santo Domingo does not qualify as a nation; its inhabitants are not a people; the power to which they are subjected cannot be called a government."[91]

Bosch turns to history to explain the origins of the Trujillo dictatorship; it is "Santo Domingo's historical backwardness, determined by causes foreign to the will of the people," that has resulted in such a regime. He places particular emphasis on the consequences for Dominican society of "foreign military interventions," beginning with the colonization by Spain. Following a strong intellectual tradition in the Caribbean, Bosch views Dominican history as resulting from the impact of external forces on the country (and on the region in general). Internal historical processes then appear as reflections, mere echoes of those forces.[92] Although the two texts were written two decades apart, in *Trujillo* we find that Bosch's vision of the Caribbean as an "imperial frontier" (the central thesis of his history of the region) is still inchoate. This thesis—venerable in the Dominican Republic, wielded by some of the most representative political figures and intellectuals of the twentieth century—emphasizes the adverse effects of invasions on the country. Bosch argues that each of the invasions inflicted on Santo Domingo left its particular sediment—political, social, cultural, even biological— that had a negative impact on the country's destiny and, in the long run, led to the Trujillo dictatorship, the "political regime . . . [that is] the fruit of the national tree."[93] Like other authors of his generation, such as Joaquín Balaguer and Manuel A. Peña-Batlle, Bosch constructs Dominican history on the foundation of an "origin myth" in which a "golden age" turns into "decadence." Narrated as a tragedy, Dominican history is seen as a series of failures brought on by the invasions.[94]

It is these invasions that are responsible for the "deformation" of Dominican society. The Spanish Conquest brought about "the birth of a society deviated from its natural order" (although this "natural order" is not clearly defined), resulting in a caste system in which "second-class people" would be forever frustrated in their ambition to become "first-class people." That frustration, a permanent feature of Dominican society, distorted the country's history, its social hierarchy, and the mentality of its inhabitants, including the psychology of Trujillo himself: a "sick" psyche, Trujillo's, that led him in "his avid desire to set himself above all Dominicans" to initiate a reign of terror that would bring him both wealth and revenge on "the social medium that had humiliated him."[95] Politically and socially, the dictator was "the personification of the country," but he was its personification in other senses as well, in that he expressed (and exploited for his personal benefit) "the psychological dissatisfaction of the Dominicans," based on the same causes that had produced the deformation of Trujillo. The lack of any "national vocation," an unhealthy "oversensitivity," and envy were, according to Bosch, some of the fundamental features of the Dominican personality.[96] Reducing Dominican history and the national collective to their essence, Bosch offers a teleological view of their evolution; he traces the particular, specific processes that the country has endured from their origins in the Spanish Conquest of the sixteenth century, and represents those processes as instances of a unique, predetermined, and immanent movement toward the inevitable result of a brutal totalitarian order. Although the point of departure in Bosch's analysis is the formation of a social hierarchy, with particular attention to the theory of castes, in this book he diverges toward an emphatically psychologistic interpretation that, in the end, permeates and even to a great extent determines his historical narrative.[97] And his psychological explanations are not limited to Trujillo. Bosch interprets *caudillismo* in general in the light of the "feminine response" of the masses toward the caudillos. Unable to consummate sexually their "attraction to the caudillo," the masses, like "infatuated females," sublimated their relationship to him, transforming it in "idolatry."[98]

Paradoxically, this psychologism, in conjunction with his teleological view of Dominican history, leads Bosch to assume positions that, on the one hand, represent a sort of inversion of the messianism embraced by the exegetes of the Trujillo doctrine and, on the other, border on the anti-Haitianism that was State policy under the dictatorship. As we know, the epigoni of the Trujillo era—including figures of the intellectual sophistication of Peña-Batlle—presented the tyrant as one sent by Providence to rescue the Dominican Republic from its history of failure. According to this logic, Trujillo's iron hand was necessary in order to establish a genuine national State with the strength to safeguard Dominican territory and sovereignty (especially against Haiti), guarantee economic prosperity and political stability, and even preserve the country's ethnocultural configuration with its purported Spanish roots.[99] In his demonization of Trujillo, Bosch sees the tyrant as the ineluctable product of the Dominican past. Thus, Trujillo's social resentment against the "first-class people" is already contained in the social structure of the colony; his "maternal seed . . . arrived with the Haitian occupation of 1822," and his paternal seed with the Spanish occupation of 1861. "Two foreign occupations," Bosch argues, "were to produce biologically the future Dominican dictator."[100] A third foreign occupation, by the United States in 1916–24, would give Trujillo the opportunity to begin his climb through the ranks of the military; this completes the cycle of interventions of which Trujillo is merely the "fruit." Bosch concludes, therefore, that "Trujillo was the net result of Dominican history itself."[101] Of course, unlike the ideologues of the regime, who present Trujillo as a savior, Bosch sees him as a tragic figure. Yet Bosch, like them, presents a Trujillo who is immanent in the nation's destiny, already contained in the fundamental events of its past. In this "inverted

messianism," Trujillo does not fail to take on superhuman proportions, resulting in a type of Hegelian historical "cunning of reason"
in which what is real is rational simply because it exists; therefore,
it is also necessary.

Another relevant element in this work is Bosch's position on
Haiti, expressed obliquely in his references to the legacy of the occupation of 1822–44: the "seed" in Trujillo's lineage that came to
Santo Domingo in the person of his great-grandmother, Diyetta
Chevalier. Besides the fact that this interpretation is biologistic in
nature (which is usually associated with conservative and racist
ideologies), it actually approaches the reactionary nationalism of
the Trujillo dictatorship, noted for its characterization of Haiti as
"the enemy" and for maintaining that the emergence of Haiti in
colonial times has continuously been central to Santo Domingo's
woes.[102] An overview of some of the principal historical narratives
produced by the traditional intelligentsia and hegemonized by the
dictatorship shows significant points of contact with Bosch's perspective. Without claiming that this list is exhaustive, we may note
their respective views on: the existence, during the colonial period,
of an endless conflict between Spanish Santo Domingo and French
Saint-Domingue; the negative effects of the Haitian Revolution on
the Spanish part of the island, including "the exodus of the wealthy,
cultured families"—a point favored (and perhaps exaggerated and
mythicized) by traditional historiography; the terror among the
Dominican population caused by Haitian incursions; and the thesis
of Spain's neglect of its colony during the seventeenth and eighteenth centuries, which is a notion that forms the cornerstone of
tragic interpretations of the country's history, according to the prevailing historiography of the period.[103]

But to my mind, the most interesting argument in *Trujillo* is the
concept that Bosch calls "the Dominican historical arrhythmia."
This concept is intriguing not so much for its originality as for the
fact that despite being reconstructed and resemanticized later in
the light of different historical/social theories and conceptions and
in other political and cultural circumstances, it would become a
constant of Bosch's interpretations of Dominican history. In this
conception, during the colonial period Santo Domingo lost "the
rhythm of history," falling behind the other countries of the Ameri-

cas in the diverse orders of collective life.[104] And what is this arrhythmia, produced by Santo Domingo's backwardness? To use
Bosch's own words, it consists of "not having entered into the great
current of capitalist development"; just at the right moment, that
possibility was blocked, and the country was left "out of that current that engulfs and, in its historical sense, renews."[105] Santo
Domingo, he argues, had a chance to "synchronize its history to the
rhythm of the Americas" during the period of the Bourbon reforms, "an opportunity that came to nothing due to the interference
of outside forces . . . loosed in Haiti by the French Revolution." In
the late nineteenth century there was another opportunity, when
several factors, such as the expansion of the exportation economy,
the liberal policies of the Blue Party, and the educational reforms of
de Hostos came together to foment a degree of advancement. But
this second opportunity also miscarried due to the power hunger
of Ulises Heureaux (popularly known as Lilís), who diverted "the
progressivist current" of that moment, although Bosch makes it
clear that had there been "a healthier and more normal development," it would not have been within the dictator's power to squan-
der that opportunity to correct the "historical arrhythmia."[106]

"A healthier and more normal development": Bosch means this
in the capitalist sense of development, the insufficiency of which, in
his opinion, distinguishes Santo Domingo from the other countries
of the Americas. In this context it would be useful to highlight some
of Bosch's thoughts on those two Latin American countries that he
considered (as I pointed out at the beginning of this essay) models
or paradigms for Santo Domingo to imitate: Cuba and Costa Rica.
Bosch says that Cuba did not suffer the same deformations as Santo
Domingo because Cuba "succeeded in taming its own past despite . . . [the] corrupt colonial regime that gave it birth."[107] In the
colonial period, Cuba attained a notable degree of development of
its resources, which made it the focus of the most powerful "creative
forces that propelled the rise of capitalism in the Western world."[108]
Based on tobacco and sugar, Cuba's wealth formed the basis for the
emergence of a criollo social sector, strongly nationalistic and legit-
imately proud of its fatherland, that played leading roles in the
national struggles of the nineteenth century and in the fight against
semicolonial subordination in the twentieth. In the 1950s, when

Bosch was writing this book, those "criollo capitalists" were retaking control of the sugar industry, which they had lost to U.S. investors at the turn of the century. Both Bosch and the "criollo capitalists" viewed the future optimistically; Cuban control over sugar would enable the launching of other industries and provide job security and "a decent salary" for the workers. In sum, the criollo bourgeoisie could see "more clearly that the good of all rests on the security of the great masses." Bosch concludes his tour of the "fascinating island" with a lyrical and bucolic paean to the Cuban bourgeoisie, whom he deemed capable of forging a future in which laborers would be able to show their children, with confidence and hope, "the land illuminated by the stars."[109]

In the case of Costa Rica, Bosch highlights this society's ability to find positive solutions to its internal conflicts, without going through the shocks, the intolerable violence, or the excessive oppression that the majority of Latin American countries have suffered. Costa Rica's economic evolution is an example of a singular harmony, once again in the light of the experiences of the other countries of the region. With what Bosch calls "astoundingly natural ease," Costa Rican society went through a series of economic phases from the "stage of the small farm owner" to that of the "capital financier," with the "criollo capital financier" allied, as a "junior partner," to the foreign investor. During this latter phase, and with the help of foreign investment, the "proletarian class, properly speaking," emerged; the Costa Rican proletariat, however, continued "behaving like a small business owner" who (as Bosch had said earlier) was known for a "strong feeling and tradition of equality." From the political point of view, the most important consequence of this evolution was that despite the social conflicts that arose throughout its history, in Costa Rica the "national character," tempered in the crucible of the small campesino property, "obstructed the formation of a tyranny of class," that is, of an oligarchic structure such as that which developed in Venezuela, a country that Bosch contrasts with Costa Rica. He concludes, therefore, that in comparison "with that of other American countries whose chain of events resembles a rough, untamed terrain, the history of Costa Rica appears to us as a welcoming landscape, with shady forests and refreshing streams."[110]

"Land illuminated by the stars"—Cuba; welcoming shady for-est—Costa Rica: these are earth metaphors expressing Bosch's ad-miration for these two countries and embracing his vision of their respective histories, in contrast with that of the Dominican Re-public, which is clearly included among those countries whose histories are a rough, untamed terrain. Unlike Bosch's tragic re-construction of the history of the Dominican Republic, his books about Cuba and Costa Rica (published in 1955 and 1963, respec-tively) give an optimistic view of those countries' historical pro-cesses. Narrated as a tragedy, Dominican history is a sequence of failures to form a ruling class who would, as in Cuba and Costa Rica, organize society along bourgeois principles. We might say that there is in Bosch a nostalgia for a bourgeoisie, a class that he believes could bring about the modernization of the society and of the State.[111] The absence of that class is the result of the various economic failures that the country had endured throughout its history. Thus, in the sixteenth century, the failure of the sugarcane industry was accompanied by the "*death* of that nucleus of a sugar oligarchy that was beginning to take shape in our island, and that death, in turn, was to have *fatal* consequences in all of our history." One of these disastrous consequences was the emergence of a *hatero* (herding, livestock-raising) society, in which "social author-ity" fell to the owners of the *hatos*; this was another "tragedy" because of the "descent" that it implied in the "social function of the men who had acquired in the [sugar] mills skills and work habits corresponding to the highest level of the time." With this transition, Santo Domingo took "a twisted, obscure footpath, that of the precapitalist slaveholding oligarchy," a "descent" toward a more primitive form of social organization that, according to Bosch, obstructed the "road of capitalist development" and was to determine "all of our history."[112]

For the following two centuries, continues Bosch in his narra-tive, the hateros held their position as the centers of "social author-ity"; the colony's other economic activities were not conducive to the formation of social sectors or institutions able to counteract that power. From the *estancias* or small farms, he writes, "no social sector arose during the seventeenth and eighteenth centuries"—a surprising statement, since it was those very estancias that witnessed the birth of the Dominican campesino, the lead actor in Bosch's early narratives.[113] Although bogged down by the economic inertia of Spain (itself held back by its feudal structures), reduced in territory by the establishment of the French colony on the western part of the island, and harassed by Spain's enemies, Santo Domingo enjoyed a brief interlude of progress around the middle of the eighteenth century due to small booms in the trade economy, especially in the production of sugar. It was a wasted opportunity to find the "road that had been lost"—that is, the road to a capitalist development similar to that seen in other Caribbean colonies, including Haiti. These other colonies had fit into the network of the infant world economy by means of the exportation of sugar and, of course, by the establishment of slaveholding societies.[114] It is interesting to note that while Bosch, in the case of Costa Rica and from a historical/social point of view, considers the failure of the slaveholding latifundio economy to be a positive element—"I would propose erecting a monument in gratitude to the failure of the cacao planters of Matina," he exclaims with enthusiasm[115]—in Santo Domingo he views it as a factor contributing to the country's backward state. The failure of their Dominican counterparts was, according to Bosch, what made the country different from Cuba, Venezuela, and Haiti, countries with powerful slaveholding latifundio sectors for which wealth consisted of producing rather than possessing and which were, in addition, a source of authority that was substantially different from that of the hateros.

Imbued with a productivist discourse of a clearly enlightened stamp, according to which production for the market is synonymous with progress, modernity, and civilization, Bosch anathematizes anything that impeded, obstructed, or frustrated the insertion of Santo Domingo into the formative currents of the capitalist economy. For this reason he emphasizes the destructive effects of the Haitian Revolution, whose "events . . . disrupted all of Dominican life," reinforcing "social organization based on the hatero."[116] Only the launching of the tobacco economy in the Cibao region in the early nineteenth century, which gave rise to a society of harvesters and merchants, partially counteracted the effects of the revolution and of the Haitian Domination (1822–44). But not even the emergence of a "petite bourgeoisie"—a term that Bosch uses very broadly to define different types of social sectors—following that economic activity was sufficient to produce a "class with defined ideas and purposes" to take the country's reins at the moment of independence in 1844; therein lay the "intrinsic weakness of the Republic."[117] During the decades that followed, political conflicts would reflect the struggles between the petite bourgeoisie and the hateros and, later, between the various "layers" of the petite bourgeoisie, none of whom aspired to leading the country but rather to climbing socially and economically; the Republic was not, in fact, a bourgeois regime. It was not until the 1870s and 1880s, with a new impetus in the sugar industry and with the government under the administration of Ulises Heureaux (1882–99), that the bases were established for the emergence of an order of that sort. Once again the road twisted and the process of forming a bourgeoisie was aborted; when no bourgeois society emerged, modernization was aborted as well. "At the beginning of the twentieth century, in the country there was no . . . Dominican industrial bourgeoisie, and there was no financial bourgeoisie, whether foreign or criollo."[118]

It is that absence of a bourgeoisie that, in the end, explains for Bosch the weakness of the institutions of State. Following the death of Heureaux, who by means of his dictatorship had succeeded in creating "centers of social authority," the country sank back into the chaos of "revolutions" and "montoneras." Lacking a ruling class at a national level on both the political and the economic plane, the country was easy prey for U.S. imperialism: this is the origin of the occupation of 1916–24. Although the occupiers had an impact on the economic base of the Dominican Republic, they had no significant effect on its social structure, which continued in its lack of a proper bourgeoisie and, in consequence, of a class capable of taking on a leadership role in society. One accomplishment of the occupation, however, was the reestablishment of "the centers of social authority, lost practically since the death of Lilís [Heureaux]."[119] Because of the changes to the State wrought by the U.S. occupation, this ostensible move toward bourgeois order facilitated the ascension of Rafael L. Trujillo, who "was the first Dominican to come to power prepared to use that power to become an authentic bourgeois"; his was a bourgeois regime "in its crudest form."[120] Bosch concludes that it is the "Dominican historical arrhythmia" that explains the "late appearance of an industrial bourgeoisie" in the country and the fact that, well into the twentieth century, Trujillo used the "brutal methods" of domination that the European bourgeoisie had employed in the eighteenth and nineteenth centuries. And that arrhythmia continued, even after Trujillo's death, to generate contradictions that are unique in the Latin American context.[121]

Death, fatalism: these themes, typical of the tragedy, appear repeatedly in Bosch's historical essays. With the language in *Composición social* resemanticized in light of theories of "modes of production" and "social formations," Bosch's "story" of Dominican history retains some of the themes and explanations that were already present in his previous historical works.[122] In this work we find interpretations that approach his notion of the "petrification" of the social structure in the colonial period, a fundamental argument in his *Trujillo*; likewise, he reverts to his thesis of a "historical arrhythmia." In his historical works, his stories take on the trappings of science, the archetypal knowledge of the modern tradition,[123] distinct from the other types of knowledge that permeate his rural narratives. But above all, there is a palpable shift in his narrative toward those historical actors who represent the urban setting and the possibility of industrialization and of a democratic/bourgeois political order—in fact, everything that to Bosch emblematizes modernity.[124] Narrated early in the century as a "horizontal community" together with the campesino masses—a community founded on the solidarity of labor and of shared memories and stories—still Bosch's national utopia always contained an element of hierarchy, originating in a nation that is *imagined* as a bourgeois society. And in his vision, the bourgeoisie, which does not exist (giving more than a touch of irony to his interpretation), is the *camino real*—the high, or royal, road—to civilization and modernity. There is a Dominican proverb that says, *Camino real no se abandona por vereda* (You don't leave the *camino real* and take a footpath). For that reason, then, like a "twisted, obscure footpath," left behind as mere memories, ever less relevant to his modernizing project, were the rural world and the campesinos that had been, when he began to write, the favorite setting and the principal actors in Juan Bosch's stories.

NOTES

Introduction: A Kind of Sacred Writing

1. Silvia Álvarez-Curbelo, "Terrores de fin de siglo," in Silvia Álvarez-Curbelo and Antonio Gaztambide-Géigel (eds.), *Historias vivas: Historiografía puertorriqueña contemporánea* (San Juan, P.R., 1996), 207–10.

2. Raúl Dorra, *Profeta sin honra: Memoria y olvido en las narraciones evangélicas* (Mexico City, 1994), 242.

3. Michel de Certeau, *The Writing of History*, trans. Tom Conley (New York, 1988), esp. 147–68; Joyce Appleby, Lynn Hunt, and Margaret Jacob, *Telling the Truth about History* (New York, 1994), esp. 15–43; Michel Foucault, *Discipline and Punish: The Birth of the Prison*, trans. Alan Sheridan (New York, 1979).

4. Thomas S. Kuhn, *The Structure of Scientific Revolutions* (2nd ed.; Chicago, 1994).

5. Appleby, Hunt, and Jacob, *Telling the Truth*, 52–90; Hayden White, *Metahistory: The Historical Imagination in Nineteenth-Century Europe* (Baltimore, 1973).

6. Edward Hallett Carr, *What Is History?* (New York, 1961), 5; Sir George Clark, *The Listener*, June 19, 1952, p. 992, quoted in ibid., 7.

7. De Certeau, *Writing of History*; Appleby, Hunt, and Jacob, *Telling the Truth*, esp. 91–125; Benedict Anderson, *Imagined Communities: Reflections on the Origin and Spread of Nationalism* (rev. ed.; New York, 1996); Partha Chatterjee, *The Nation and Its Fragments: Colonial and Postcolonial Histories* (Princeton, 1993).

8. Andrés L. Mateo, *Al filo de la dominicanidad* (Santo Domingo, 1996), 43, and *Mito y cultura en la Era de Trujillo* (Santo Domingo, 1993).

9. David K. Herzberger, *Narrating the Past: Fiction and Historiography in Postwar Spain* (Durham, N.C., 1995), 17.

10. Carr, *What Is History?*, esp. 3–35; White, *Metahistory*, xii. [The title of this section, "The Poetics of History," is from White, *Metahistory*, 1. Trans.]

11. Hayden White, *Tropics of Discourse: Essays in Cultural Criticism* (2nd printing; Baltimore, 1986), 105, quoted in George E. Marcus and Dick Cushman, "Ethnographies as Texts," *Annual Review of Anthropology* 11 (1982): 56.

12. Dorra, *Profeta sin honra*, 234.

13. Ibid., 11–14; Mateo, *Mito y cultura*.

14. White, *Tropics of Discourse*; Hayden White, *The Content of the Form: Narrative Discourse and Historical Representation* (2nd printing; Baltimore, 1992).

15. These terms are taken, respectively, from the essay by Marilyn Strathern, "Out of Context: The Persuasive Fictions of Anthropology," *Current Anthropology* 28, no. 3 (1987): 251–81, and from a fictional work by Ana Lydia Vega, *Falsas crónicas del sur* (Río Piedras, P.R., 1991).

16. Herzberger, *Narrating the Past*, 84.

17. Dorra, *Profeta sin honra*, 14.

18. Marcus and Cushman, "Ethnographies as Texts," 54, 56.

19. Patrick H. Hutton, *History as an Art of Memory* (Hanover, N.H., 1993); Roger Chartier, *The World as Representation*, published as *El mundo como representación: Estudios sobre historia cultural* (2nd ed.; Barcelona, 1995).

20. Dorra, *Profeta sin honra*, 156–57.

21. Chartier, *El mundo como representación*, esp. 107–62.

22. Hutton, *History as an Art of Memory*, xxi.

23. Clifford Geertz, *Local Knowledge: Further Essays in Interpretive Anthropology* (New York, 1983), 36–54. [The quotation is from the title of Geertz, *Local Knowledge*, chap. 2, p. 36. Trans.]

24. Herbert Marcuse, *Eros and Civilization: A Philosophical Inquiry into Freud* (Boston, 1955).

25. Michael Agar, *Speaking of Ethnography* (Beverly Hills, Calif., 1986), 19.

The Imagined Colony: Historical Visions of Colonial Santo Domingo
This essay is an expanded version of a paper presented before the Seventh Dominican History Congress, National Museum of History and Geography, Santo Domingo, October 16–19, 1995.

1. Hayden White, *Metahistory: The Historical Imagination in Nineteenth-Century Europe* (Baltimore, 1973), x, 7. See also *Tropics of Discourse: Essays in Cultural Criticism* (2nd printing; Baltimore, 1986), and *The Content of the Form: Narrative Discourse and Historical Representation* (2nd printing; Baltimore, 1992). In addition to White's works, the following are also relevant: Ana Lydia Vega et al., *Historia y literatura* (San Juan, P.R., 1995), and David K. Herzberger, *Narrating the Past: Fiction and Historiography in Postwar Spain* (Durham, N.C., 1995).

2. Antonio Sánchez-Valverde, *Idea del valor de la isla Española*, annotated and ed. by Emilio Rodríguez-Demorizi and Fray Cipriano de Utrera (Santo Domingo, 1971) (cited hereinafter as *Idea*, followed by the corresponding page number[s]).

3. Ibid., 158.

4. Ibid., 169, 174–75.

5. The historical sections of *Idea* are found primarily in chaps. 11–15, apparently a summary of more extensive research conducted by Sánchez-Valverde, since he states at the beginning of his work, "I have produced a compleat History of the Island" (ibid., 5; in Emilio Rodríguez-Demorizi's note 3, this work is said to be lost). For evaluations of Sánchez-Valverde's work, see Roberto Cassá, "Historiografía de la República Dominicana," *Ecos: Órgano del Instituto de Historia de la Universidad Autónoma de Santo Domingo* 1, no. 1 (1993): 10–12, and Máximo Rossi Jr., *Praxis, historia y filosofía en el siglo XVIII: Textos de Antonio Sánchez Valverde (1729–90)* (Santo Domingo, 1994).

6. This type of discursive strategy was common in the colonial period. See the shrewd analysis by Severo Martínez-Peláez, *La patria del criollo: Ensayo de interpretación de la realidad colonial guatemalteca* (3rd ed.; San José, Guat., 1975).

7. *Idea*, 98.

8. In his annotations to *Idea*, Rodríguez-Demorizi, who can hardly be suspected of trying to diminish the grandeur of Santo Domingo in colonial days, alludes to these exaggerations. See, for example, nn. 116 and 118.

9. See Roberto Cassá and Genaro Rodríguez, "Algunos procesos formativos de la identidad nacional dominicana," *Estudios Sociales* 25, no. 88 (1992): 67–98.

10. Jacques Le Goff, *El orden de la memoria: El tiempo como imaginario* (Barcelona, 1991), 11.

11. [That is, the apportionment of native laborers among the Spanish colonizers. Trans.]

12. *Idea*, 107.

13. The term is borrowed from Samuel Stone, *La dinastía de los conquistadores: La crisis del poder en la Costa Rica contemporánea* (3rd ed.; San José, C.R., 1982).

14. See San Miguel, "Racial Discourse and National Identity: Haiti in the Dominican Imaginary," in this volume.

15. Ibid. I take the term "criollo homeland" from Martínez-Peláez, *La patria del criollo*.

16. Rossi, *Praxis, historia y filosofía*. On the configuration of "criollo patriotism," see Martínez-Peláez, *La patria del criollo*; Jacques Lafaye, *Quetzalcóatl and Guadalupe: The Formation of Mexican National Consciousness, 1531–1813*, trans. Benjamin Keen (Chicago, 1976); David A. Brading, *Los orígenes del nacionalismo mexicano*, trans. Soledad Loaeza-Grave (2nd ed.; Mexico City,

1991); and Enrique Florescano, *Memoria mexicana* (2nd ed.; Mexico City, 1994).

17. For general context, see Eric Williams, *From Columbus to Castro: The History of the Caribbean, 1492–1969* (2nd printing; New York, 1973), esp. 255–79, and Gordon K. Lewis, *Main Currents in Caribbean Thought: The Historical Evolution of Caribbean Society in Its Ideological Aspects, 1492–1900* (Baltimore, 1987), 94–170. For studies of the islands mentioned, see Manuel Moreno-Fraginals, *The Sugarmill: The Socioeconomic Complex of Sugar in Cuba, 1760–1860*, trans. Cedric Belfrage (New York, 1976), and Francisco A. Scarano, *Sugar and Slavery in Puerto Rico: The Plantation Economy of Ponce, 1800–1850* (Madison, 1984).

18. This argument is based on Raymundo González, *Bonó, un intelectual de los pobres* (Santo Domingo, 1994), esp. 39–83.

19. I am indebted to Silvia Álvarez-Curbelo for suggesting this parallelism. On Michelet, see White, *Metahistory*, 135–62; Georges Lefebvre, *El nacimiento de la historiografía moderna*, trans. Alberto Méndez (Barcelona, 1974), 195–213; Josefina Vázquez–de Knauth, *Historia de la historiografía* (2nd ed.; Mexico City, 1973), 108–9; Josep Fontana, *Historia: Análisis del pasado y proyecto social* (Barcelona, 1982), 121–22; and Patrick H. Hutton, *History as an Art of Memory* (Hanover, N.H., 1993), 131–33.

20. Fontana, *Historia*, 121.

21. Hutton, *History as an Art of Memory*, 132.

22. See Cassá, "Historiografía," 18–19.

23. See Pedro Francisco Bonó, "Apuntes sobre las clases trabajadoras dominicanas" (1881), in Emilio Rodríguez-Demorizi (ed.), *Papeles de Pedro F. Bonó: Para la historia de las ideas políticas en Santo Domingo* (Santo Domingo, 1964), 190–245 (cited hereinafter as *Papeles*, followed by the corresponding page number[s]).

24. Ibid., 217–18.

25. Ibid., 217.

26. Ibid., 219.

27. See Frank Tannenbaum, *Slave and Citizen: The Negro in the Americas* (New York, 1946), and Laura Foner and Eugene D. Genovese (eds.), *Slavery in the New World: A Reader in Comparative History* (Englewood Cliffs, N.J., 1969).

28. *Papeles*, 219.

29. Ibid., 199.

30. On the Braudelian concept of "historical times," see Fernand Braudel,

On *History*, trans. Sarah Matthews (Chicago, 1980), esp. 25–54 and 64–82, and Bernard Lepetit et al., *Segundas jornadas braudelianas: Historia y ciencias sociales* (Mexico City, 1995).

31. *Papeles*, 179, quoted in González, *Bonó*, 107–8.

32. *Papeles*, 179.

33. González finds in his search for progress *with* justice one of the fundamental differences between Bonó and the rest of the Dominican liberals of his time, and one of the keys to his thinking.

34. Cassá, "Historiografía," 14–15. On Ranke, see White, *Metahistory*, 163–90; Lefebvre, *El nacimiento*, 275–78; Vázquez-de Knauth, *Historia*, 131–34; and Fontana, *Historia*, 127–31.

35. White, *Metahistory*, 172.

36. On nineteenth-century liberalism, see Fernando Pérez-Memén, *El pensamiento dominicano en la Primera República (1844–1861)* (2nd ed.; Santo Domingo, 1995).

37. Cassá, "Historiografía," 14.

38. José Gabriel García, *Compendio de la historia de Santo Domingo* (4 vols., 5th ed.; Santo Domingo, 1982), 1:24 (cited hereinafter as *Compendio*, followed by the corresponding volume and page number[s]).

39. Ibid., 1:32.

40. Ibid., 1:33.

41. Ibid., 1:109.

42. On these notions in Western thought, see Edward W. Said, *Orientalism* (New York, 1979); Tzvetan Todorov, *On Human Diversity: Nationalism, Racism, and Exoticism in French Thought*, trans. Catherine Porter (Cambridge, Mass., 1993); David Spurr, *The Rhetoric of Empire: Colonial Discourse in Journalism, Travel Writing, and Imperial Administration* (Durham, N.C., 1993); and Eduardo Subirats, *El continente vacío: La conquista del Nuevo Mundo y la conciencia moderna* (Mexico City, 1994).

43. *Compendio*, 1:45.

44. Ibid., 1:55.

45. Ibid., 1:62.

46. Cassá refers to García's "assimilation of history into politics" ("Historiografía," 14).

47. *Compendio*, 1:63–64.

48. Ibid., 1:68.

49. On "indigenism" in nineteenth-century Dominican literature, see Bruno Rosario-Candelier, *Tendencias de la novela dominicana* (Santiago, D.R.,

1988); and Concha Meléndez, "El *Enriquillo* de Manuel de Jesús Galván," in Manuel de Jesús-Galván, *Enriquillo: Leyenda histórica dominicana (1503–1533)* (Mexico City, 1976), vii–xxv.

50. *Compendio*, 1:73.

51. Ibid., 1:103–4.

52. Ibid., 1:114.

53. Ibid., 1:141–42.

54. Ibid., 1:142, 145, 147–49.

55. Ibid., 1:148–49.

56. Ibid., 1:151.

57. Ibid., 1:176–80.

58. Ibid., 1:188.

59. Ibid., 1:193–223; the quotation is from p. 216.

60. Ibid., 1:222.

61. Ibid., 1:229–30.

62. Among others, Cordero-Michel cites the nineteenth-century historian Antonio del Monte y Tejada, who rates Toussaint's regime very favorably, in contrast to García's evaluation. See *La Revolución Haitiana y Santo Domingo* (2nd ed.; Santo Domingo, 1974). See also Franklin J. Franco, *Los negros, los mulatos y la nación dominicana* (5th ed.; Santo Domingo, 1977). It should be mentioned that García's interpretations have greatly influenced a number of historians. For example, Roberto Cassá holds that slaves accustomed to the patriarchal slavery of the Spanish showed little enthusiasm for the abolition decreed by Toussaint (*Historia social y económica de la República Dominicana* [2 vols.; Santo Domingo, 1982], 1:156). However, he does not consider the possibility that this putative lack of enthusiasm—an argument that, in itself, requires more scrutiny—might be due to the *libertos'* ["freedmen," freed slaves] having a different agenda from that of the revolutionary leader, including a goal of becoming independent campesinos rather than plantation laborers, as envisioned by Toussaint.

63. *Compendio*, 1:264ff.

64. Ibid., 1:332.

65. Although the term is imprecise, I choose to speak of the "dominant sectors"; I am attempting to suggest that the criteria for identity were not homogeneous among the Dominicans, as certain authors aver, assuming that identity was based on exclusive criteria, especially "Spanishness," in which case racial conflicts would have been virtually nonexistent. Such a vision presupposes a broad-based ethnic, racial, and cultural consensus among the inhabitants of colonial Santo Domingo, a notion that is completely inconsis-

tent with the latest research on colonial societies in Latin America and the Caribbean. These investigations tend, on the contrary, to reveal diversity in the criteria for identity among the inhabitants of these countries. On this point, consult the classic work by Magnus Mörner, *Race Mixture in the History of Latin America* (Boston, 1967), and Harry Hoetink, *Santo Domingo y el Caribe* (Santo Domingo, 1994), esp. 131–201. In the Dominican context, the following essays are also useful: Cassá and Rodríguez, "Algunos procesos formativos"; Roberto Cassá et al., *Actualidad y perspectivas de la cuestión nacional en la República Dominicana* (Santo Domingo, 1986); and Roberto Cassá and Otto Fernández, "Cultura y política en República Dominicana: La formación de la identidad histórica," in Hugo Zemelman (coord.), *Cultura y política en América Latina* (Mexico City, 1990), 228–55.

66. I take this idea from Christopher Hill's classic study *The World Turned Upside Down: Radical Ideas during the English Revolution* (New York, 1972). The study by C. L. R. James, *The Black Jacobins: Toussaint L'Ouverture and the San Domingo Revolution* (2nd ed.; New York, 1963), continues to be the best work for transmitting the sensation of the disrupted world produced by the revolution. For comparisons with other social movements that produced a similar commotion among the dominant groups of Latin America, in this case in relation to indigenous revolts and rebellions, see Nelson Reed, *The Caste War of Yucatan* (Stanford, 1964); Antonio García-de León, *Resistencia y utopía* (2 vols.; Mexico City, 1989); Steve J. Stern, *Peru's Indian Peoples and the Challenge of Spanish Conquest: Huamanga to 1640* (2nd ed., Madison, Wis., 1993); and Alberto Flores-Galindo, *Buscando un inca: Identidad y utopía en los Andes* (Mexico City, 1993).

67. Laënnec Hurbon, *El bárbaro imaginario*, trans. Jorge Padín-Videla (Mexico City, 1993), 12, 29–35, 53–55; the quotations are from pp. 12 and 53.

68. Ibid., 188.

69. Andrés L. Mateo, *Mito y cultura en la Era de Trujillo* (Santo Domingo, 1993), 52.

70. See Raymundo González, "Ideología del progreso y campesinado en el siglo XIX," *Ecos: Órgano del Instituto de Historia de la Universidad Autónoma de Santo Domingo* 1, no. 2 (1993): 25–43; Pedro L. San Miguel, "Storytelling the Nation," in this volume, and "Una perspectiva histórico-social sobre las relaciones entre el Estado y el campesinado en la República Dominicana," in *Secuencia: Revista de Historia y Ciencias Sociales* (Instituto Mora, Mexico City), Nueva época, 40 (1998): 43–67.

71. Mörner, *Race Mixture*; Nicolás Sánchez-Albornoz, *The Population of Latin America: A History*, trans. W. A. R. Richardson (Berkeley, 1974), 146–81;

and Richard Graham (ed.), *The Idea of Race in Latin America, 1870–1940* (Austin, 1990).

72. Jesús M. Zaglul, "Una identificación nacional *defensiva*: El antihaitianismo nacionalista de Joaquín Balaguer. Una lectura de *La isla al revés*," *Estudios Sociales* 25, no. 87 (1992): 29–65. See also San Miguel, "Racial Discourse," in this volume, and Hoetink, *Santo Domingo y el Caribe*, 113–29, 159–201.

73. The phrase is from the title of one of the best-known works dealing with the kind of argument discussed in this section. See Joaquín Balaguer, *La isla al revés: Haití y el destino dominicano* (5th ed.; Santo Domingo, 1989). [This title has been variously translated as "The Island in Reverse," "The Island Inside Out," the "Upside-Down Island," and "The Backward Island." A clue to Balaguer's intended meaning might be that the book was published with a reversed or mirror image of Hispaniola on the cover. I thank Dr. Máximo Rossi for pointing this out, although I should mention that he prefers "The Island Inside Out." Trans.]

74. On Peña-Batlle's thought, see Mateo, *Mito y cultura*; Raymundo González, "Peña Batlle y su concepto histórico de la nación dominicana," *Ecos: Órgano del Instituto de Historia de la Universidad Autónoma de Santo Domingo* 2, no. 3 (1994): 11–52; and Juan Daniel Balcácer et al., *El pensamiento de Manuel Arturo Peña Batlle* (Santo Domingo, 1988).

75. Manuel A. Peña-Batlle, *Ensayos históricos* (Santo Domingo, 1989), 60–61 (cited hereinafter as *Ensayos*, followed by the corresponding page number[s]).

76. Ibid., 61–62.

77. Ibid., 157–59.

78. See San Miguel, "Racial Discourse," in this volume.

79. The idea of a "postapocalyptic paradise," applied to the Franco regime in Spain, derives from Herzberger, *Narrating the Past*, 35–37. Reading this work evokes clear similarities between the historiography of Franco's and Trujillo's partisans.

80. See San Miguel, "Racial Discourse," in this volume.

81. Meindert Fennema and Troetje Loewenthal, *La construcción de raza y nación en la República Dominicana* (Santo Domingo, 1987).

82. See San Miguel, "Racial Discourse," in this volume.

83. Balaguer, *La isla al revés*, 103–4 (cited hereinafter as *Isla*, followed by the corresponding page number[s]).

84. See San Miguel, "Racial Discourse," in this volume.

85. *Isla*, 59–61.

86. Ibid., 59–62 and photographs between 192 and 193.

87. Roberto Cassá, *Capitalismo y dictadura* (Santo Domingo, 1982), 765.

88. See Mateo, *Mito y cultura*, and Diógenes Céspedes, "El efecto Rodó. Nacionalismo idealista vs. nacionalismo práctico: Los intelectuales antes de y bajo Trujillo," *Cuadernos de Poética* 6, no. 17 (1989): 7–56. Two extremely valuable resources on the general Latin American sphere are Ángel Rama, *The Lettered City*, ed. and trans. John Charles Chasteen (Durham, N.C., 1996), and Julio Ramos, *Divergent Modernities: Culture and Politics in Nineteenth-Century Latin America*, trans. John D. Blanco (Durham, N.C., 2000).

89. Among the noteworthy historical works of Jimenes-Grullón are *La República Dominicana: Análisis de su pasado y su presente* [1940] (3rd ed.; Santo Domingo, 1974); *La República Dominicana: Una ficción* (Merida, Venezuela, 1965); and *Sociología política dominicana: 1844–1966* [1976], vol. 1 (4th ed.; Santo Domingo, 1982), and vol. 2 (3rd ed.; Santo Domingo, 1981). Although the terms are imprecise, I refer to "democratic authors" or to "authors (or intellectuals) of the democratic persuasion (or tradition)" to distinguish them from those intellectuals who were associated with the Trujillo model and/or ideologically similar intellectual and political traditions. To a great extent, this democratic tradition flowered in exile; for some sense of its complex (and contradictory) history, see Franklin J. Franco, *Historia de las ideas políticas en la República Dominicana* (Santo Domingo, n.d.), and Roberto Cassá, *Movimiento obrero y lucha socialista en la República Dominicana (Desde los orígenes hasta 1960)* (Santo Domingo, 1990).

90. See Bruno Rosario-Candelier, *La narrativa de Juan Bosch* (Santo Domingo, 1989), and Eugenio de J. García-Cuevas, *Juan Bosch: Novela, historia y sociedad* (San Juan, P.R., and La Vega, D.R., 1995).

91. Juan Bosch, "Un pueblo en un libro," in Jimenes-Grullón, *La República Dominicana: Análisis*, 7–15.

92. Juan Bosch, *Trujillo, causas de una tiranía sin ejemplo* (5th ed.; Santo Domingo, 1991) (cited hereinafter as *Trujillo*, followed by the corresponding page number[s]).

93. For further comments on the historiography of Bosch, see Cassá, "Historiografía," 35–36; Franco, *Historia de las ideas políticas*, 261–66; San Miguel, "Storytelling the Nation," in this volume; and A. H. Alcántara-E. and I. R. Lawrence-Mazara, "La interpretación materialista de la historia y la sociedad dominicana en Juan Bosch" (thesis, Universidad Católica Madre y Maestra, 1984).

94. *Trujillo*, 37.

95. Ibid., 38–39.

96. Ibid., 40.

97. Ibid., 40, 41.

98. Ibid., 42.

99. Ibid., 70.

100. See Manuel A. Peña-Batlle, *La Isla de la Tortuga: Plaza de armas, refugio y seminario de los enemigos de España en Indias* [1951] (3rd ed.; Santo Domingo, 1988).

101. *Trujillo*, 72 (emphasis mine). Bosch's vision here has clear parallels to Peña-Batlle's, even to the periods into which he divides Dominican history.

102. Ibid., 80.

103. Works giving evidence of intra-Caribbean trade include Cornelio C. Goslinga, *Los holandeses en el Caribe* (Havana, 1983); Héctor R. Feliciano-Ramos, *El contrabando inglés en el Caribe y el Golfo de México (1748–1778)* (Seville, 1990); and Arturo Morales-Carrión, *Puerto Rico y la lucha por la hegemonía en el Caribe: Colonialismo y contrabando, Siglos XVI–XVIII* (San Juan, P.R., 1995). For Santo Domingo in particular, the following are useful: Frank Peña-Pérez, *Antonio Osorio: Monopolio, contrabando y despoblación* (Santiago, D.R., 1980) and *Cien años de miseria en Santo Domingo, 1600–1700* (Santo Domingo, [1985]); and Antonio Gutiérrez-Escudero, *Población y economía en Santo Domingo (1700–1746)* (Seville, 1985).

104. *Trujillo*, 86–87.

105. Ibid., 92.

106. For an overview of Bosch's writings, I recommend Guillermo Piña-Contreras, *Juan Bosch: Bibliografía (Precedida de una cronología)* (Santo Domingo, 1990).

107. Juan Bosch, *Pentagonism, a Substitute for Imperialism*, trans. Helen R. Lane (New York, 1968), and *De Cristóbal Colón a Fidel Castro: El Caribe, frontera imperial* [1971] (5th ed.; Santo Domingo, 1986).

108. Juan Bosch, *Composición social dominicana: Historia e interpretación* [1970] (30th ed.; Santo Domingo, 1983).

109. See San Miguel, "Storytelling the Nation," in this volume.

110. Michel de Certeau, *The Writing of History*, trans. Tom Conley (New York, 1988), xxvii (emphasis in the original).

111. See Partha Chatterjee, *The Nation and Its Fragments: Colonial and Postcolonial Histories* (Princeton, 1993); Benedict Anderson, *Imagined Communities: Reflections on the Origin and Spread of Nationalism* (rev. ed.; New York, 1996); and Eric Hobsbawm and Terence Ranger (eds.), *The Invention of Tradition* (Cambridge, Eng., 1988).

112. Juan Gelpí, *Literatura y paternalismo en Puerto Rico* (Río Piedras, P.R., 1993), 1–16; the quotation is from p. 5.

113. Ibid., 136.

114. For examples, see John Womack Jr., *Zapata and the Mexican Revolution* (New York, 1968); Marcello Carmagnani, *El regreso de los dioses: El proceso de reconstitución de la identidad étnica en Oaxaca. Siglos XVII y XVIII* (Mexico City, 1988); and Alain Breton and Jacques Artaud (coords.), *Los mayas: La pasión por los antepasados, el deseo de perdurar* (Mexico City, 1994).

Racial Discourse and National Identity: Haiti in the Dominican Imaginary
Originally published in *Op Cit.: Boletín del Centro de Investigaciones Históricas* 7 (1992–93). Permission of the editors to reprint the essay in this book is gratefully acknowledged.

1. See Gordon K. Lewis, *Main Currents in Caribbean Thought: The Historical Evolution of Caribbean Society in Its Ideological Aspects, 1492–1900* (Baltimore, 1987). For accounts of the region's history that highlight the influence of slavery, see Eric Williams, *From Columbus to Castro: The History of the Caribbean, 1492–1969* (2nd printing; New York, 1973), and Franklin W. Knight, *The Caribbean: The Genesis of a Fragmented Nationalism* (2nd ed.; New York, 1990).

2. On mestizaje, see Magnus Mörner, *Race Mixture in the History of Latin America* (Boston, 1967), and Nicolás Sánchez-Albornoz, *The Population of Latin America: A History*, trans. W. A. R. Richardson (Berkeley, 1974), esp. 86–145. For the Caribbean in particular, see H. Hoetink, *Caribbean Race Relations: A Study of Two Variants*, trans. Eva M. Hooykaas (Oxford, 1971), and his restatement of the theme in "*Race* and Color in the Caribbean," in Sidney W. Mintz and Sally Price (eds.), *Caribbean Contours* (Baltimore, 1985), 55–84.

3. Roger Bastide, *African Civilisations in the New World*, trans. Peter Green (New York, 1971); Manuel Moreno-Fraginals (ed.), *Africa in Latin America: Essays on History, Culture, and Socialization*, trans. Leonor Blum (New York, 1984); Jean Casimir, *La cultura oprimida* (Mexico City, 1981); and Herbert S. Klein, *African Slavery in Latin America and the Caribbean* (New York, 1986), 163–241. For Santo Domingo in particular, see the thought-provoking essay by Roberto Cassá and Genaro Rodríguez, "Algunos procesos formativos de la identidad nacional dominicana," *Estudios Sociales* 25, no. 88 (1992): 67–98.

4. Among the few available studies about free blacks and mulattoes, see David W. Cohen and Jack P. Greene (eds.), *Neither Slave nor Free: The Freedmen of African Descent in the Slave Societies of the New World* (Baltimore, 1972);

Jerome Handler, *The Unappropriated People: Freedmen in the Slave Society of Barbados* (Baltimore, 1974); and Edward L. Cox, *Free Coloreds in the Slave Societies of St. Kitts and Grenada, 1763–1833* (Knoxville, 1984). According to Barbara Bush, as the Afro-Caribbeans became more criollo, their notions about freedom changed accordingly. See *Slave Women in Caribbean Society, 1650–1838* (Kingston, 1990), 79.

5. Klein, *African Slavery*, 163–87; Hilary McD. Beckles, "Slaves and the Internal Market Economy of Barbados: A Perspective on Non-violent Resistance," *Historia y Sociedad* 2 (1989): 9–30, and *Natural Rebels: A Social History of Enslaved Black Women in Barbados* (New Brunswick, N.J., 1989). For a broader discussion of the mechanisms and implications of the ways in which slaves adapted, see Eugene D. Genovese, *Roll, Jordan, Roll: The World the Slaves Made* (New York, 1976); John W. Blassingame, *The Slave Community: Plantation Life in the Antebellum South* (rev. ed.; New York, 1979); and Charles Joyner, *Down by the Riverside: A South Carolina Slave Community* (Urbana, 1984).

6. Klein, *African Slavery*, 189–215; Richard Price (ed.), *Maroon Societies: Rebel Slave Communities in the Americas* (Garden City, N.Y., 1973); Eugene D. Genovese, *From Rebellion to Revolution: Afro-American Slave Revolts in the Making of the Modern World* (New York, 1981); Carlos Esteban Deive, *Los guerrilleros negros: Esclavos fugitivos y cimarrones en Santo Domingo* (Santo Domingo, 1989); and Richard Hart, *Slaves Who Abolished Slavery* (Kingston, 1980).

7. C. L. R. James, *The Black Jacobins: Toussaint L'Ouverture and the San Domingo Revolution* (2nd ed.; New York, 1963); Robert Conrad, *The Destruction of Brazilian Slavery, 1850–1888* (Berkeley, 1972); and Rebecca J. Scott, *Slave Emancipation in Cuba: The Transition to Free Labor, 1860–1899* (Princeton, 1985).

8. The term "natal alienation" is used by Orlando Patterson in *Slavery and Social Death: A Comparative Study* (Cambridge, Mass., 1982), 5–10.

9. Lewis, *Main Currents*, 149–54; José A. Saco, *Historia de la esclavitud* (condensed ed.; Buenos Aires, 1965); Mildred de la Torre, "Las ideas sobre la esclavitud (1790–1878)," in Instituto de Ciencias Históricas, *La esclavitud en Cuba* (Havana, 1986), 42–58, and "Posiciones y actitudes en torno a la esclavitud en Cuba, 1790–1830," in *Temas acerca de la esclavitud* (Havana, 1988), 71–95. See also the influential work by Raúl Cepero-Bonilla, *Azúcar y abolición* (Barcelona, 1976).

10. Pedro Irizarri, "Informe de Don Pedro Irizarri, Alcalde ordinario de San Juan, sobre las instrucciones que debían darse a Don Ramón Power,

Diputado por Puerto Rico ante las Cortes españolas . . . , 1809," in Eugenio Fernández-Méndez (ed.), *Crónicas de Puerto Rico: Desde la Conquista hasta nuestros días (1493–1955)* (2nd ed.; Río Piedras, P.R., 1969), 352–56. For a perceptive analysis of the circumstances behind this report and the view of the labor problem taken by diverse sectors of the colonial elite, see Arturo Morales-Carrión, "La Revolución Haitiana y el movimiento antiesclavista en Puerto Rico," in Blanca G. Silvestrini (ed.), *Politics, Society and Culture in the Caribbean* (San Juan, P.R., 1983), 203–20.

11. See Alberto Cibes-Viadé, *El Gobernador Pezuela y el abolicionismo puertorriqueño (1848–1873)* (Río Piedras, P.R., n.d.), and Arturo Morales-Carrión, *Auge y decadencia de la trata negrera en Puerto Rico (1820–1960)* (San Juan, P.R., 1978).

12. Lewis, *Main Currents*, esp. 171–320.

13. On the historical context of the Devastations, see Roberto Cassá, *Historia social y económica de la República Dominicana* (2 vols.; Santo Domingo, 1983), 1:93–112; Frank Moya-Pons, *Historia colonial de Santo Domingo* (Santiago, D.R., 1974), 109–226; Juan Bosch, *Composición social dominicana: Historia e interpretación* (30th ed.; Santo Domingo, 1983), 43–62, and *De Cristóbal Colón a Fidel Castro: El Caribe, frontera imperial* (5th ed.; Santo Domingo, 1986), 183–237; and Frank Peña-Pérez, *Antonio Osorio: Monopolio, contrabando y despoblación* (Santiago, D.R., 1980), and *Cien años de miseria en Santo Domingo, 1600–1700* (Santo Domingo, [1985]).

14. James, *Black Jacobins*, and Casimir, *La cultura oprimida*.

15. Cassá, *Historia social y económica*, 1:113–37; Moya-Pons, *Historia colonial*, 229–310; Antonio Gutiérrez-Escudero, *Población y economía en Santo Domingo (1700–1746)* (Seville, 1985); and Carlos Esteban Deive, *La esclavitud del negro en Santo Domingo (1492–1844)* (2 vols.; Santo Domingo, 1980).

16. Sidney W. Mintz, *Caribbean Transformations* (Chicago, 1974), 131–56; Pedro L. San Miguel, "The Making of a Peasantry: Dominican Agrarian History from the Sixteenth to the Twentieth Century," *Punto y Coma: Revista Interdisciplinaria de la Universidad del Sagrado Corazón* 2, nos. 1–2 (1990): 143–62; and Rubén Silié, *Economía, esclavitud y población* (Santo Domingo, 1976).

17. Hugo Tolentino, *Raza e historia en Santo Domingo: Los orígenes del prejuicio racial en América* (2nd ed.; Santo Domingo, 1992); Franklin J. Franco, *Los negros, los mulatos y la nación dominicana* (5th ed.; Santo Domingo, 1977).

18. On the concept of the "other," see Tzvetan Todorov, *The Conquest of America: The Question of the Other*, trans. Richard Howard (New York, 1984), and *On Human Diversity: Nationalism, Racism, and Exoticism in French*

Thought, trans. Catherine Porter (Cambridge, Mass., 1993); Edward W. Said, *Orientalism* (New York, 1979); and Peter Hulme, *Colonial Encounters: Europe and the Native Caribbean, 1492–1797* (New York, 1986).

19. For more-detailed analyses, see Franklin J. Franco, "Antihaitianismo e ideología del Trujillato," and Hugo Tolentino, "El fenómeno racial en Haití y en la República Dominicana," both in Gérard Pierre-Charles et al., *Problemas domínico-haitianos y del Caribe* (Mexico City, 1973), 83–109 and 111–44, respectively; Lil Despradel, "Las etapas del antihaitianismo en la República Dominicana: El papel de los historiadores," in Gérard Pierre-Charles (ed.), *Política y sociología en Haiti y la República Dominicana* (Mexico City, 1974), 83–108; Pablo A. Maríñez, *Relaciones domínico-haitianas y raíces histórico culturales africanas en la República Dominicana: Bibliografía básica* (Santo Domingo, 1986); and Agapito Bautista Betances, "El racismo integrante del antihaitianismo dominicano," *Estudios Sociales* 18, no. 59 (1985): 61–76. Also relevant are Wilfredo Lozano (ed.), *La cuestión haitiana en Santo Domingo: Migración internacional, desarrollo y relaciones inter-estatales entre Haití y República Dominicana* (Santo Domingo, 1992), and Orlando Inoa, *Bibliografía haitiana en la República Dominicana* (Río Piedras, P.R., 1994).

20. Manuel Arturo Peña-Batlle, *Ensayos históricos* (Santo Domingo, 1989); Joaquín Balaguer, *La isla al revés: Haití y el destino dominicano* (5th ed.; Santo Domingo, 1989). For evaluations of these authors in the context of Trujillo's regime and ideology, see José Alcántara-Almánzar, *Los escritores dominicanos y la cultura* (Santo Domingo, 1990), 183–97; Diógenes Céspedes, "El efecto Rodó. Nacionalismo idealista vs. nacionalismo práctico: Los intelectuales antes de y bajo Trujillo," *Cuadernos de Poética* 6, no. 17 (1989): 7–56; Andrés L. Mateo, *Mito y cultura en la Era de Trujillo* (Santo Domingo, 1993); and Raymundo González, "Peña Batlle y su concepto histórico de la nación dominicana," *Ecos: Órgano del Instituto de Historia de la Universidad Autónoma de Santo Domingo* 1, no. 1 (1993): 9–39.

21. The works cited in notes 17 and 19 are useful in the elucidation of this issue. In addition, works that aid in restating the theme of the black presence in colonial times include Deive, *Esclavitud del negro*; Silié, *Economía, esclavitud y población*; and Carlos Larrazábal-Blanco, *Los negros y la esclavitud en Santo Domingo* (Santo Domingo, 1975). Other works attempt to evaluate the Afro-Dominican presence in more-recent times; these include Carlos Esteban Deive, "La herencia africana en la cultura dominicana actual," in Bernardo Vega et al., *Ensayos sobre cultura dominicana* (2nd ed.; Santo Domingo, 1988), 105–41, and *Vodú y magia en Santo Domingo* (2nd ed.; Santo

Domingo, 1988); and Fradique Lizardo, *Cultura africana en Santo Domingo* (Santo Domingo, 1979).

22. Antonio Sánchez-Valverde, *Idea del valor de la Isla Española*, annotated and ed. by Emilio Rodríguez-Demorizi and Fray Cipriano de Utrera (Santo Domingo, 1971) (cited hereinafter as *Idea*, followed by the corresponding page number[s]). For a fuller study on Sánchez-Valverde, see Máximo Rossi Jr., *Praxis, historia y filosofía en el siglo XVIII: Textos de Antonio Sánchez Valverde (1729–90)* (Santo Domingo, 1994). Sánchez-Valverde's work is akin to other colonial texts. For example, see Fray Agustín Íñigo Abbad–y Lasierra, *Historia geográfica, civil y natural de la isla de San Juan Bautista de Puerto Rico,* preliminary study by Isabel Gutiérrez del Arroyo (3rd ed.; Río Piedras, P.R., 1970).

23. *Idea*, 158 (emphasis in the original).

24. Ibid., 160 (emphasis in the original). For a modern perception that coincides with Sánchez-Valverde's indications of the economic importance of Haiti vis-à-vis the Spanish colonies, see David A. Brading, "Bourbon Spain and Its American Empire," in Leslie Bethell (ed.), *Colonial Spanish America* (Cambridge, Eng., 1987), 140–41, 149.

25. *Idea*, 168 (emphasis in the original).

26. Ibid., 169 (emphasis in the original).

27. Ibid., 174–75 (emphasis in the original).

28. Ibid., 164–65.

29. Fray Cipriano de Utrera, "Antonio Sánchez Valverde," in *Idea*, 7*–39* [*sic*]. The allusion to Sánchez-Valverde's skin color is from a document cited by Utrera on p. 26*; Sánchez-Valverde himself mentions his "Hacienda de Villegas" (p. 43).

30. *Idea*, 170–71.

31. Blaming slave women for relations with their owners was a common stratagem in the eighteenth-century Caribbean. See Bush, *Slave Women*, 18.

32. *Idea*, 171–72.

33. Ibid., 172–73.

34. Ibid., 166 (emphasis in the original).

35. Ibid., 167.

36. Arguments of this type were common among colonial writers, although differences with the "mother country" were also pointed out. See Severo Martínez-Peláez, *La patria del criollo: Ensayo de interpretación de la realidad colonial guatemalteca* (3rd ed.; San José, Guat., 1975); David A. Brading, *Los orígenes del nacionalismo mexicano*, trans. Soledad Loaeza-Grave (2nd

ed.; Mexico City, 1991); Jacques Lafaye, *Quetzalcóatl and Guadalupe: The Formation of Mexican National Consciousness, 1531–1813*, trans. Benjamin Keen (Chicago, 1976); and Enrique Florescano, *Memoria mexicana* (2nd ed.; Mexico City, 1994). For discussion of the ethnic composition of colonial Santo Domingo, with a criticism of the traditional view of the subject, see Cassá and Rodríguez, "Algunos procesos formativos."

37. *Idea*, 7 (emphasis in the original).

38. Ibid., 111.

39. On the Haitian Revolution, see James, *Black Jacobins*; José L. Franco, *Historia de la revolución de Haití* (2nd ed.; Santo Domingo, 1971); Emilio Cordero-Michel, *La Revolución Haitiana y Santo Domingo* (2nd ed.; Santo Domingo, 1974); and David Geggus, *Slavery, War, and Revolution: The British Occupation of Saint Domingue, 1793–1798* (Oxford, 1982).

40. Despradel, "Las etapas del antihaitianismo."

41. Frank Moya-Pons, *La Dominación Haitiana, 1822–1844* (3rd ed.; Santiago, D.R., 1978); Bosch, *Composición social*, 143–61; and Cassá, *Historia social y económica*, 1:173–89.

42. Literature on these events is plentiful. For a synthesis, see Cassá, *Historia social y económica*, 2:39–120.

43. For a chronology and a biography of Bonó, see Emilio Rodríguez-Demorizi (ed.), *Papeles de Pedro F. Bonó: Para la historia de las ideas políticas en Santo Domingo* (Santo Domingo, 1964), 5–15 and 17–58, respectively (cited hereinafter as *Papeles*, followed by the corresponding page number[s]).

44. Ibid., 5–58; Raymundo González, *Bonó, un intelectual de los pobres* (Santo Domingo, 1994); Wilfredo Lozano, in collaboration with Ivette Sabbagh, "La sociología dominicana: Una evaluación," in *Ciencias Sociales en la República Dominicana. Sociología, demografía, economía: Evolución y bibliografía* (Santo Domingo, 1989), 19–21; Juan I. Guerra, "Concepción antropológica-fisiológica en el pensamiento de Pedro Francisco Bonó," *Eme-Eme* 11, no. 64 (1983): 33–76; and Roberto Cassá, "Historiografía de la República Dominicana," *Ecos: Órgano del Instituto de Historia de la Universidad Autónoma de Santo Domingo* 1, no. 1 (1993): 18–19.

45. González, *Bonó*, esp. 15–38, 85–103, and Freddy Peralta, "La sociedad dominicana vista por Pedro Francisco Bonó," *Eme-Eme* 5, no. 29 (1977): 13–54.

46. *Papeles*, 84.

47. Ibid., 82–83.

48. Ibid., 89–90.

49. Ibid., 610.

50. Ibid., 343–44.

51. Ibid., 91.

52. Ibid., 394.

53. Ibid., 219.

54. Frank Moya-Pons, *La Española en el siglo XVI, 1493–1520* (Santiago, D.R., 1971), 70–71, and *Historia colonial*, 71–89; Cassá, *Historia social y económica*, 1:65–70; Deive, *Esclavitud del negro*, 1:51–102; and José Chez-Checo and Rafael Peralta-Brito, *Azúcar, encomiendas y otros ensayos históricos* (Santo Domingo, 1979), 13–54. See also Carlos Esteban Deive, *La Española y la esclavitud del indio* (Santo Domingo, 1995).

55. On the economic and social peculiarities of plantation systems, see Klein, *African Slavery*, 21–137; Sidney W. Mintz, "Slavery and Emergent Capitalisms" and "Labor and Sugar in Puerto Rico and Jamaica, 1800–1850," in Laura Foner and Eugene D. Genovese (eds.), *Slavery in the New World: A Reader in Comparative History* (Englewood Cliffs, N.J., 1969), 27–37 and 170–77, respectively; Jean Benoist, "La organización social de las Antillas," in Manuel Moreno-Fraginals (ed.), *África en América Latina* (Mexico City, 1977), 77–102; Ciro F. Santana-Cardoso, "El modo de producción esclavista colonial en América," in Carlos Sempat-Assadourian et al., *Modos de producción en América Latina* (3rd ed.; Buenos Aires, 1975), 193–242; Eric R. Wolf and Sidney W. Mintz, "Haciendas y plantaciones en Mesoamérica y las Antillas," in Enrique Florescano (coord.), *Haciendas, latifundios y plantaciones en América Latina* (Mexico City, 1975), 493–531; Ciro F. S. Cardoso and Héctor Pérez-Brignoli, *Historia económica de América Latina* (2 vols.; Barcelona, 1979), 1:185–208; Robert W. Fogel, *Without Consent or Contract: The Rise and Fall of American Slavery* (New York, 1989), 17–80; and Philip Curtin, *The Rise and Fall of the Plantation Complex* (Cambridge, Eng., 1990).

56. Hoetink, "*Race* and Color in the Caribbean," 55–68; Deive, *La esclavitud del negro*, 1:51–154, and *Los guerrilleros negros*, 135; and Franc Báez-Evertsz, *La formación del sistema agroexportador en el Caribe: República Dominicana y Cuba, 1515–1898* (Santo Domingo, 1986), 43–80.

57. Deive, *Los guerrilleros negros*.

58. *Papeles*, 610.

59. González, *Bonó*, and Peralta, "La sociedad dominicana."

60. *Papeles*, 92.

61. The idea of regenerating Latin American countries by means of immigration and contact with European civilization became a common theme among the intelligentsia of the region. For a discussion of racial ideas in Latin America and, in particular, of the relation between those ideas and national

development and regeneration projects, see Richard Graham (ed.), *The Idea of Race in Latin America, 1870–1940* (Austin, 1990).

62. *Papeles*, 394.

63. Relatively few works deal systematically with the history of ideas in the Dominican Republic during the nineteenth century. Important elements may be found in Franklin J. Franco, *Historia de las ideas políticas en la República Dominicana* (Santo Domingo, n.d.); Juan I. Jimenes-Grullón, *Sociología política dominicana, 1844–1966* (4th ed.; Santo Domingo, 1982), vol. 1; and Fernando Pérez-Memén, *El pensamiento dominicano en la Primera República (1844–1861)* (2nd ed.; Santo Domingo, 1995).

64. Jimenes-Grullón, *Sociología política*, 1:49–112; Jaime de Jesús Domínguez, *La anexión de la República Dominicana a España* (Santo Domingo, 1979); and Mu-Kien A. Sang, *Buenaventura Báez: El caudillo del Sur (1844–1878)* (Santo Domingo, 1991), 39–56.

65. Franklin Franco, *Los negros, los mulatos y la nación dominicana*, 115–62, and "La sociedad dominicana de los tiempos de la independencia," in F. Franco et al., *Duarte y la independencia nacional* (Santo Domingo, 1976), 10–36.

66. *Papeles*, 199 (emphasis in the original).

67. On Bonó's attachment to the popular sectors of Dominican society, see González, *Bonó*.

68. H. Hoetink, *El pueblo dominicano (1850–1900): Apuntes para su sociologia histórica* (3rd ed.; Santiago, D.R., 1985), 50–56; the essays by José del Castillo and Patrick E. Bryan in Manuel Moreno-Fraginals, Frank Moya-Pons, and Stanley L. Engerman (eds.), *Between Slavery and Free Labor: The Spanish-Speaking Caribbean in the Nineteenth Century* (Baltimore, 1985), 215–34 and 235–51, respectively.

69. José del Castillo, "La inmigración de braceros a la industria azucarera, 1900–1930," *Cuadernos del CENDIA* (1978), and Bruce J. Calder, *The Impact of Intervention: The Dominican Republic during the U.S. Occupation of 1916–1924* (Austin, 1984), 91–99.

70. On this "mask" metaphor, see Rosalba Campra, *América Latina: La identidad y la máscara* (Mexico City, 1987).

71. This is evidenced in two novels: Jacques Roumain, *Masters of the Dew*, trans. Langston Hughes and Mercer Cook (Oxford, 1978), and Anthony Lespès, *Las semillas de la ira*, trans. Diógenes Céspedes (Santo Domingo, 1990) [original French title: *Les semences de la colère*].

72. An enormous amount has been written on the Trujillo regime. For examples, see Jesús de Galíndez, *The Era of Trujillo, Dominican Dictator* (Tuc-

son, 1973); José R. Cordero-Michel, *Análisis de la Era de Trujillo (Informe sobre la República Dominicana, 1959)* (5th ed.; Santo Domingo, 1987); Robert D. Crassweller, *Trujillo: The Life and Times of a Caribbean Dictator* (New York, 1966); and Roberto Cassá, *Capitalismo y dictadura* (Santo Domingo, 1982).

73. Peña-Batlle, *Ensayos históricos*, 60–61 (cited hereinafter as *Ensayos*, followed by the corresponding page number[s]).

74. Ibid., 61–62.

75. Ibid., 155.

76. Ibid., 157–59.

77. Ibid., 160.

78. Ibid., 164.

79. Ibid., 179–81.

80. Ibid., 56.

81. Ibid., 67.

82. Ibid., 191.

83. This phrase, which summarizes the Hispanophile spirit represented by Peña-Batlle and other writers, is picked up in Ramón Marrero-Aristy's *La República Dominicana: Origen y destino del pueblo cristiano más antiguo de América* (2 vols.; Ciudad Trujillo, D.R., 1957). For a critical view of this interpretation, see Cassá and Rodríguez, "Algunos procesos formativos."

84. *Ensayos*, 229.

85. Ibid., 69.

86. Ibid., 190.

87. Ibid., 191.

88. Ibid., 230.

89. Ibid., 192, 194.

90. Ibid., 335–48, and Peña-Batlle, *La frontera de la República Dominicana con Haití* (Ciudad Trujillo, D.R., 1946); Bernardo Vega, *Trujillo y Haití: 1930–1937* (Santo Domingo, 1988); and José Israel Cuello (comp.), *Documentos del conflicto domínico-haitiano de 1937* (Santo Domingo, 1985).

91. *Ensayos*, 369–70.

92. Cassá, *Capitalismo y dictadura*, 765.

93. Cuello, *Documentos*, 499–503. On the massacre, see Vega, *Trujillo y Haití*, 271–412, and the testimonial novels of Lespès, *Las semillas de la ira*, and Freddy Prestol-Castillo, *El Masacre se pasa a pie* (5th ed.; Santo Domingo, 1982).

94. On this point, see Bernardo Vega, *Nazismo, fascismo y falangismo en la República Dominicana* (Santo Domingo, 1985).

95. This work was originally published in 1947 under the title of *La*

realidad dominicana. On this point, see Roberto Cassá et al., *Actualidad y perspectivas de la cuestión nacional en la República Dominicana* (Santo Domingo, 1986), 108 n. 70, and Roberto Cassá, *Los doce años: Contrarrevolución y desarrollismo* (Santo Domingo, 1986), 394–416. I owe much to several recent studies on *La isla al revés*, including Carlos Dore-Cabral, "La inmigración haitiana y el componente racista de la cultura dominicana: Apuntes para una crítica de *La isla al revés*," *Ciencia y Sociedad* 10, no. 1 (1985): 61–70; Meindert Fennema and Troetje Loewenthal, *La construcción de raza y nación en la República Dominicana* (Santo Domingo, 1987); and Jesús M. Zaglul, "Una identificación nacional *defensiva*: El antihaitianismo nacionalista de Joaquín Balaguer. Una lectura de *La isla al revés*," *Estudios Sociales* 25, no. 87 (1992): 29–65. Balaguer's book cited hereinafter as *Isla*, followed by the corresponding page number(s). [Balaguer's title has been variously translated as "The Island in Reverse," "The Island Inside Out," the "Upside-Down Island," and "The Backward Island." A clue to Balaguer's intended meaning might be found in the fact that the book was published with a reversed or mirror image of Hispaniola on the cover. I thank Dr. Máximo Rossi for pointing this out, although I should mention that he prefers "The Island Inside Out." Trans.]

96. Fennema and Loewenthal, *Construcción de raza y nación*.

97. *Isla*, 206–12. The exaltation of Spanish elements in Dominican culture has been a dominant theme in the works of other writers. For example, see Carlos Dobal, "Herencia española en la cultura dominicana de hoy," in Vega et al., *Ensayos sobre cultura dominicana*, 61–104. One of the facets of Dominican racial discourse is the use of the term *indio*, or "Indian," to refer to mulattoes—a practice that is in evidence in the work of Sánchez-Valverde. On this point, a scholar of the indigenous past has said, "The greatest and most frequent presence of the *indio* in our contemporary culture is where he does not exist. Our curious system of cultural values has obliged us to create . . . a mirage, to use a sophism, in order to try to conceal our national prejudice. A large proportion of our population demands to be typified as *indios* or *indias*, instead of mulattoes or mulattas, when they have no *indio* genes at all." Bernardo Vega, "La herencia indígena en la cultura dominicana de hoy," in Vega et al., *Ensayos sobre cultura dominicana*, 52–53. See also Cassá and Rodríguez, "Algunos procesos formativos," 67–88.

98. *Isla*, 96 (emphasis mine).

99. Ibid., 31–33.

100. Ibid., 35–36; Fennema and Loewenthal, *Construcción de raza y nación*, 39–41; and Zaglul, "Identificación nacional," 38–48. A good number of

works examine various aspects of the Haitian migrations to the Dominican Republic, including Maríñez, *Relaciones domínico-haitianas*; del Castillo, "La inmigración de braceros"; Lozano, *La cuestión haitiana*; Inoa, *Bibliografía haitiana*; André Corten et al., *Azúcar y política en la República Dominicana* (3rd ed.; Santo Domingo, 1981); Maurice Lemoine, *Bitter Sugar: Slaves Today in the Caribbean*, trans. Andrea Johnston (Chicago, 1985); Suzy Castor, *Migración y relaciones internacionales (El caso haitiano-dominicano)* (Santo Domingo, 1987); José Manuel Madruga, *Azúcar y haitianos en la República Dominicana* (Santo Domingo, 1986); Franc Báez-Evertsz, *Braceros haitianos en la República Dominicana* (2nd ed.; Santo Domingo, 1986); Frank Moya-Pons et al., *El batey: Estudio socioeconómico de los bateyes del Consejo Estatal del Azúcar* (Santo Domingo, 1986); Rafael E. Yunén, *La isla como es: Hipótesis para su comprobación* (Santiago, 1985); Wilfredo Lozano and Franc Báez-Evertsz, *Migración internacional y economía cafetalera: Estudio sobre la migración estacional de trabajadores haitianos a la cosecha cafetalera en la República Dominicana* (Santo Domingo, 1985); and André Corten and Isis Duarte, "Quinientos mil haitianos en República Dominicana," *Estudios Sociales* 27, no. 98 (1994): 7–36.

101. *Isla*, 41.

102. Ibid., 45, 48–53.

103. On this point, see Dore-Cabral, "La inmigración haitiana," and Fennema and Loewenthal, *Construcción de raza y nación*.

104. Arcadio Díaz-Quiñones, "Tomás Blanco: Racismo, historia, esclavitud," preliminary study in Tomás Blanco, *El prejuicio racial en Puerto Rico* (3rd ed.; Río Piedras, P.R., 1985), 38–39.

105. *Isla*, 36.

106. Ibid., 40.

107. Dore-Cabral, "La inmigración haitiana"; Zaglul, "Identificación nacional"; and Fennema and Loewenthal, *Construcción de raza y nación*.

108. *Isla*, 103–4. The demographic history of the Dominican Republic has not yet been written. Nevertheless, one of the favorite arguments of traditional Dominican historiography is that the Haitian Revolution supposedly caused a demographic crisis, due to emigration as well as to slaughters. Without denying that both occurred, we must be careful with such assessments. For example, a more recent study calls into question whether there really were as many emigrations to Cuba as previously believed. See Carlos Esteban Deive, *Las emigraciones dominicanas a Cuba (1795–1808)* (Santo Domingo, 1989). Two of the few available studies on demographic history are Frank Moya-Pons, "Nuevas consideraciones sobre la historia de la población

dominicana: Curvas, tasas y problemas," *Eme-Eme* 3, no. 15 (1974): 3–28, and Roberto Marte, *Cuba y la República Dominicana: Transición económica en el Caribe del siglo XIX* (Santo Domingo, [1998]), 51–144.

109. *Isla*, 104.

110. Marte, *Cuba y la República Dominicana*, 57. There are clear indicators showing that the relative stability of the period of 1822–44 served as a stimulating factor to the Dominican population and economy, particularly among the campesinos. See San Miguel, "The Making of a Peasantry," and Roberto Marte, *Estadísticas y documentos históricos sobre Santo Domingo (1805–1890)* (Santo Domingo, 1984), 1–50.

111. *Isla*, 59–61, 130 (emphasis mine).

112. Díaz-Quiñones, "Tomás Blanco"; Antonio S. Pedreira, "La actualidad del jíbaro" [1935], in Enrique A. Laguerre and Esther M. Melón (eds.), *El jíbaro de Puerto Rico: Símbolo y figura* (Sharon, Conn., 1968), 7–24; and José Luis González, "Literatura e identidad nacional en Puerto Rico," in Ángel G. Quintero-Rivera et al., *Puerto Rico: Identidad nacional y clases sociales (Coloquio de Princeton)* (Río Piedras, P.R., 1979), 67–73. ["La actualidad del jíbaro," by Antonio S. Pedreira, has also been published separately (Río Piedras, P.R., 1935). Trans.]

113. *Isla*, 188. Included in this work is a series of photographs of campesino families, supposedly white, from the Cibao region. No information is given anywhere indicating to what degree these families or the communities to which they belonged were representative of the general population.

114. Ibid., 59–62.

115. Ibid., 55.

116. Ibid., 96 n. 40.

117. For a fuller discussion of Balaguer's views on mestizaje, see Zaglul, "Identificación nacional," 46–48.

118. Dore-Cabral, "La inmigración haitiana," and Zaglul, "Identificación nacional."

119. At the end of his work, Balaguer proposes the creation of a "confederation between the two countries." This proposal, however, must be examined in the light of the role he played in Dominican public life following the fall of Trujillo's dictatorship (Cassá, *Los doce años*). In other passages of *Isla*, Balaguer's suggestions revolve around containing the Haitians within their borders and strengthening the Dominican Republic, economically and demographically.

120. Fennema and Loewenthal, *Construcción de raza y nación*, 47–50, and Zaglul, "Identificación nacional."

121. *Isla*, 98–99, and Zaglul, "Identificación nacional," 52–54.

122. See Cassá et al., *Actualidad y perspectivas*, 7–20; Cassá and Rodríguez, "Algunos procesos formativos"; and Pierre Vilar, *Iniciación al vocabulario del análisis histórico* (Barcelona, 1980), 161–200. The debate over "the national problem" and nationalism has currently been reopened. For examples, see Todorov, *On Human Diversity*, esp. 171–263; Benedict Anderson, *Imagined Communities: Reflections on the Origin and Spread of Nationalism* (rev. ed.; New York, 1996); Homi K. Bhabha (ed.), *Nation and Narration* (London, 1993); Partha Chatterjee, *The Nation and Its Fragments: Colonial and Postcolonial Histories* (Princeton, 1993); and Ernest Gellner, *Culture, Identity, and Politics* (Cambridge, Eng., 1987).

123. Vilar, *Iniciación al vocabulario*, 161–65.

124. Anderson, *Imagined Communities*.

125. These questions are treated more thoroughly in Heraclio Bonilla, "The Indian Peasantry and 'Peru' during the War with Chile," in Steve J. Stern (ed.), *Resistance, Rebellion, and Consciousness in the Andean Peasant World: Eighteenth to Twentieth Centuries* (Madison, 1987), 219–31; Florencia E. Mallon, "Nationalist and Antistate Coalitions in the War of the Pacific: Junín and Cajamarca, 1878–1902," in Stern, *Resistance, Rebellion*, 232–79, and *Peasant and Nation: The Making of Postcolonial Mexico and Peru* (Berkeley, 1995); and José Luis Rénique, *Los sueños de la sierra: Cusco en el siglo XX* (Lima, 1991).

126. Todorov, *Conquest of America*, 3.

127. Martin Lienhard, *La voz y su huella: Escritura y conflicto étnico-social en América Latina (1492–1988)* (Havana, 1990).

128. Zaglul, "Identificación nacional," 35–39.

129. Hugues Portelli, *Gramsci y el bloque histórico* (Buenos Aires, 1973).

130. See Walter Cordero, "El tema negro y la discriminación racial en la República Dominicana," *Ciencia* 2, no. 2 (1975): 151–62; Carlos Esteban Deive, "El prejuicio racial en el folklore dominicano," *Boletín del Museo del Hombre Dominicano* 8 (1977): 75–96; Lauren Derby, "Haitians, Magic, and Money: *Raza* and Society in the Haitian-Dominican Borderlands, 1900 to 1937," *Comparative Studies in Society and History* 36, no. 3 (1994): 488–526; and Equipo Onè Respe, *El otro del nosotros* (Santiago, D.R., 1995).

131. Todorov, *Conquest of America*, 3.

The Island of Forking Paths: Jean Price-Mars and the History of Hispaniola

1. Jorge Luis Borges, "The Garden of Forking Paths," in *Collected Fictions: Jorge Luis Borges*, trans. Andrew Hurley (New York, 1998), 126–27.

2. Jacques Le Goff, *El orden de la memoria: El tiempo como imaginario*

(Barcelona, 1991), 11. See also Paul Ricoeur, *Time and Narrative*, trans. Kathleen McLaughlin and David Pellauer (3 vols.; Chicago, 1994–98).

3. Jean Price-Mars, *La República de Haití y la República Dominicana: Diversos aspectos de un problema histórico, geográfico y etnológico* [1953], trans. Martín Aldao and José Luis Muñoz-Azpiri (1st Spanish ed.; Santo Domingo, 1995) (cited hereinafter as *República*, followed by the corresponding page number[s]).

4. Juan Daniel Balcácer, "Hacia una historia comparativa de Santo Domingo y Haití: La contribución de Price-Mars," in *República*, xii–xiii. See also Fernando Ortiz, *Ensayos etnográficos*, selected by Miguel Barnet and Ángel L. Fernández (Havana, 1984); Jorge Ibarra, "La herencia científica de Fernando Ortiz," *Revista Iberoamericana* 152–53 (1990): 1339–51; Diana Iznaga, *Transculturación en Fernando Ortiz* (Havana, 1989); Gilberto Freyre, *The Masters and the Slaves*, trans. Samuel Putnam (2nd English ed.; Berkeley, 1986); and José Carlos Mariátegui, *Siete ensayos de interpretación de la realidad peruana* (26th ed.; Lima, 1973). For Price-Mars's place in the context of Haitian historiography, see Patrick Bellegarde-Smith, "Eddies in the Stream: Issues for Haitian History and Historiography," *Historia y Sociedad* (Department of History, University of Puerto Rico, Río Piedras) 8 (1995–96): 31–49.

5. Jean Price-Mars, *So Spoke the Uncle*, trans. and introduction by Magdaline W. Shannon (Washington, 1983) (cited hereinafter as *Uncle*; references to the Spanish translation, *Así habló el Tío*, trans. Virgilio Piñera, prólogo by René Dépestre [Havana, 1968], will be cited as *Tío*, followed by the corresponding page number[s]).

6. *Tío*, 37–39.

7. René Dépestre, prólogo to *Tío*, ix–x, and "Hello and Goodbye to Negritude," in Manuel Moreno-Fraginals (ed.), *Africa in Latin America: Essays on History, Culture, and Socialization*, trans. Leonor Blum (New York, 1984), 251–72.

8. Richard Graham (ed.), *The Idea of Race in Latin America, 1870–1940* (Austin, 1990). For Haiti specifically, see J. Michael Dash, *Literature and Ideology in Haiti, 1915–1961* (Totowa, N.J., 1981), 43–128.

9. Suzy Castor, *La ocupación norteamericana de Haití y sus consecuencias (1915–1934)* (Mexico City, 1971); David Nicholls, *From Dessalines to Duvalier: Race, Colour and National Independence in Haiti* (Cambridge, Eng., 1979), 142–52.

10. Jean Price-Mars, *La vocation de l'elite* (Port-au-Prince, 1919), 55–90 (cited hereinafter as *Vocation*, followed by the corresponding page number[s]).

11. Jacques Carmeleau Antoine, *Jean Price-Mars and Haiti* (Washington,

D.C., 1981), 101–2, 171–72. It is of interest to examine the similarities between these premises of Price-Mars and those developed by Juan Bosch in his historical works concerning the absence of an authentic ruling class in the Dominican Republic. See "Storytelling the Nation," in this volume.

12. Nicholls, *From Dessalines to Duvalier*, 156.

13. Patrick Bellegarde-Smith, "Dantès Bellegarde o la fe en occidente," in Dantès Bellegarde, *La nación haitiana* (Santo Domingo, 1984), 7–13, and Bellegarde-Smith, *In the Shadow of Powers: Dantès Bellegarde in Haitian Social Thought* (Atlantic Highlands, N.J., 1985).

14. Ángel Rama, *The Lettered City*, ed. and trans. John Charles Chasteen (Durham, N.C., 1996), 60–68; the quotation is from p. 65.

15. José Luis Rénique, *Los sueños de la sierra: Cusco en el siglo XX* (Lima, 1991).

16. Francisco A. Scarano, "The *Jíbaro* Masquerade and the Subaltern Politics of Creole Identity Formation in Puerto Rico, 1745–1823," *American Historical Review* 101, no. 5 (1996): 1398–431.

17. *Vocation*, 41–42. On the coffee economy and mechanisms for the exploitation of campesinos, see Christian A. Girault, *El comercio del café en Haití*, trans. Ana Maritza de la Mota (Santo Domingo, 1985), and Mats Lundahl, *Peasants and Poverty: A Study of Haiti* (London, 1979), and *Politics or Markets?: Essays on Haitian Underdevelopment* (London, 1992), 110–39, 200–254. Lundahl employs the apt term "predator State" in describing the exploitation of the campesinos.

18. *Vocation*, 163–209.

19. Ibid., 1–24, 131–61, 211–69.

20. *República*, 11.

21. Ibid., 12–13.

22. Ibid., 15.

23. Erich Kahler, *The Meaning of History* (New York, 1964), 18.

24. See the pamphlet by Jean Price-Mars, *La contribution haïtienne à la lutte des Amériques por les libertés humaines* (Port-au-Prince, 1942), and Benedetto Croce, *History as the Story of Liberty*, trans. Sylvia Sprigge (Indianapolis, 2000). [Croce's book, *La storia come pensiero e come azione*, in the original Italian, is known as *La historia como hazaña de la libertad* in its Spanish incarnation. Trans.]

25. [That is, the flight of slaves from their masters. Escaped slaves became known as *cimarrones*, or Maroons, and frequently banded together to form fugitive communities. *Cimarronaje* is occasionally called *marronage* in English-language texts. Trans.]

26. *República*, 19. Few studies have been made of cimarronaje and other forms of resistance to slavery in Haiti. Sources that may be consulted include Gabriel Debien, "Marronage in the French Caribbean," in Richard Price (ed.), *Maroon Societies: Rebel Slave Communities in the Americas* (Garden City, N.Y., 1973), 107–34; C. L. R. James, *The Black Jacobins: Toussaint L'Ouverture and the San Domingo Revolution* (2nd ed.; New York, 1963), 6–26; and Jean Casimir, *La cultura oprimida* (Mexico City, 1981), 51–57. Other, more general interpretations may be found in Eugene D. Genovese, *From Rebellion to Revolution: Afro-American Slave Revolts in the Making of the Modern World* (New York, 1981), esp. 82–125, and Herbert S. Klein, *African Slavery in Latin America and the Caribbean* (New York, 1986), 189–215. For additional bibliographic references, see Horácio Gutiérrez and John M. Monteiro (comp.), *A escravidão na América Latina e no Caribe: Bibliografia básica* (São Paulo, 1990), esp. 53–54.

27. *República*, 25.

28. Manuel A. Peña-Batlle, "Orígenes del Estado haitiano," in *Ensayos históricos*, comp. and introduction by Juan Daniel Balcácer (Santo Domingo, 1989), 160. Peña-Batlle's opinion was very similar to that of Máximo Coiscou-Henríquez, who referred to Haitian colonial society as an "unorganized assemblage" (cited in Balcácer, "Hacia una historia comparativa," in *República*, xvi n. 9). On Peña-Batlle's debates with Price-Mars, especially in regard to *So Spoke the Uncle*, see Andrés L. Mateo, *Mito y cultura en la Era de Trujillo* (Santo Domingo, 1993), 175–78.

29. I am using the concepts of "imagined community" or "imaginary community" and "invention of tradition" in application to resistance efforts by subaltern sectors. For more on these concepts, see, respectively, Benedict Anderson, *Imagined Communities: Reflections on the Origin and Spread of Nationalism* (rev. ed.; New York, 1996), and Eric Hobsbawm and Terence Ranger (eds.), *The Invention of Tradition* (New York, 1988).

30. Diógenes Céspedes has emphasized the importance of "oral culture" in the formation of an independent Haitian State (*Lenguaje y poesía en Santo Domingo en el siglo XX* [Santo Domingo, 1985], 349, cited in Mateo, *Mito y cultura*, 177 n. 37).

31. Price-Mars, *La contribution haïtienne*, 25–26, and *República*, 23–24.

32. Peña-Batlle, "Orígenes," 160.

33. Ibid., 160–81.

34. *República*, 27–28.

35. Ibid., 25, 47.

36. As an example of the fear of "contagion" in Puerto Rico and of the measures taken by the island's colonial authorities, see Carlos D. Altagracia-

Espada, "La utopía del territorio perfectamente gobernado: Miedo y poder en la época de Miguel de la Torre" (master's thesis, Department of History, University of Puerto Rico, Río Piedras, 1997).

37. [The phrase is from the title of an English-language version of *Les damnés de la terre*: Frantz Fanon, *The Wretched of the Earth*, trans. Constance Farrington (New York, 1963). The phrase used by San Miguel, "condenados de la tierra," reflects the title of the same book in Spanish: Fanon, *Los condenados de la tierra*, trans. Julieta Campos (Mexico City, 1963). Trans.]

38. *República*, 46–47.

39. Barrington Moore Jr., *Social Origins of Dictatorship and Democracy: Lord and Peasant in the Making of the Modern World* (Boston, 1967).

40. See Emilio Rodríguez-Demorizi (ed.), *Cesión de Santo Domingo a Francia* (Ciudad Trujillo, D.R., 1958).

41. José Gabriel García, *Compendio de la historia de Santo Domingo* (4 vols., 5th ed.; Santo Domingo, 1982), 1:222, 229–30.

42. For a variety of opinions on his work, consult Balcácer, "Hacia una historia comparativa"; Dépestre, prólogo to *Tío*; Antoine, *Price-Mars and Haiti*; Magdaline W. Shannon, introduction to *Uncle*, ix–xxviii; and Manuel Núñez, *El ocaso de la nación dominicana* (Santo Domingo, 1990), 63–132.

43. *República*, 59–61.

44. On the subject of the border, see Orlando Inoa, *Bibliografía haitiana en la República Dominicana* (Río Piedras, P.R., 1994), esp. 120–40; Frank Moya-Pons, "Las tres fronteras: Introducción a la frontera dominico-haitiana," and "Contribución a la bibliografía de la frontera dominico-haitiana, la presencia haitiana en Santo Domingo y las relaciones dominico-haitianas," in Wilfredo Lozano (ed.), *La cuestión haitiana en Santo Domingo: Migración internacional, desarrollo y relaciones inter-estatales entre Haití y República Dominicana* (Santo Domingo, 1992), 17–32 and 33–68, respectively; and Carlos Altagracia-Espada, "La nación desde los bordes: Imaginación geográfica y paisaje fronterizo en la República Dominicana durante la Era de Trujillo" (doctoral thesis, Department of History, University of Puerto Rico, Río Piedras, 2001).

45. *República*, 67–78.

46. Ibid., 78–79.

47. Ibid., 79–80.

48. Ibid., 81–86.

49. [J. R. Beard, *Toussaint L'Ouverture: A Biography and Autobiography* (Boston, 1863), 233, in *Documenting the American South*, University of North Carolina at Chapel Hill, 2001, <http://docsouth.unc.edu neh/beard63/beard63.html>. "© This work is the property of the University of North

Carolina at Chapel Hill. It may be used freely by individuals for research, teaching and personal use as long as this statement of availability is included in the text." Trans.]

50. *República*, 30–36.

51. Ibid., 50, 97–99.

52. Ibid., 57, 97–100. See also Emilio Cordero-Michel, *La Revolución Haitiana y Santo Domingo* (2nd ed.; Santo Domingo, 1974), 81–106.

53. Price-Mars's assessments of the "Domination," which he calls the period of "National Unity," are found primarily in *República*, 187-328. The quotations are from pp. 245, 258, and 291, respectively. For more on this historical period, see García, *Compendio*, 2:89–223; Frank Moya-Pons, *La Dominación Haitiana, 1822–1844* (3rd ed.; Santiago, D.R., 1978); Juan Bosch, *Composición social dominicana: Historia e interpretación* (30th ed.; Santo Domingo, 1983), 143–61; and Roberto Marte, *Estadísticas y documentos históricos sobre Santo Domingo (1805–1960)* (Santo Domingo, 1984). This last work includes a variety of statistical information on the period of the Haitian occupation, useful in considering some of its effects on the Dominican economy. The first chapter of my book *Los campesinos del Cibao: Economía de mercado y transformación agraria en la República Dominicana, 1880–1960* (San Juan, P.R., 1997) includes some of my own assessments of its economic and social consequences.

54. Emilio Rodríguez-Demorizi (ed.), *Papeles de Pedro F. Bonó: Para la historia de las ideas políticas en Santo Domingo* (Santo Domingo, 1964), 89–90, 610. See also my essay "Racial Discourse and National Identity: Haiti in the Dominican Imaginary," in this volume. In his weighty study *El pensamiento dominicano en la Primera República (1844–1861)* (2nd ed.; Santo Domingo, 1995), Fernando Pérez-Memén makes little reference to race, a crucial aspect of Latin American and Caribbean thought in the nineteenth century. One of the few allusions Pérez-Memén does make is in reference to the ideas of Juan Pablo Duarte on the "equality of the races." In light of the attention given to racial questions during that period, fuller comprehension might have resulted from presenting conceptions regarding "racial inequalities."

55. *República*, 299–300.

56. On the notion of "decline" or "decay," see Le Goff, *El orden de la memoria*, 87–127. The quotation is from p. 126 (emphasis in the original).

57. For a discussion of racial relations in the Caribbean, with emphasis on Santo Domingo, see Harry Hoetink, "*Race* and Color in the Caribbean," in Sidney W. Mintz and Sally Price (eds.), *Caribbean Contours* (Baltimore, 1985), 55–84.

58. Charles Hale, "Political and Social Ideas," in Leslie Bethell (ed.), *Latin America: Economy and Society, 1870–1930* (Cambridge, Eng., 1989), 254–67, and Thomas Skidmore, "Racial Ideas and Policy in Brazil, 1870–1940," in Graham, *The Idea of Race*, 7–36. Other relevant works include Tzvetan Todorov, *On Human Diversity: Nationalism, Racism, and Exoticism in French Thought*, trans. Catherine Porter (Cambridge, Mass., 1993), esp. 90–170, and Hannah Arendt, *The Origins of Totalitarianism* (2nd ed.; Cleveland, 1958), 158–221.

59. One of many possible examples is Ángel S. del Rosario-Pérez, *La exterminación añorada* (Ciudad Trujillo, D.R., 1957).

60. Hayden White, *Tropics of Discourse: Essays in Cultural Criticism* (2nd printing; Baltimore, 1986), 152.

61. Laënnec Hurbon, *El bárbaro imaginario*, trans. Jorge Padín-Videla (Mexico City, 1993), 13.

62. García, *Compendio*, 2:90.

63. Magnus Mörner, *Race Mixture in the History of Latin America* (Boston, 1967), 75–90. For more on the subject of the "revolts of the nonwhites," see Genovese, *From Rebellion to Revolution*, and Steve J. Stern (ed.), *Resistance, Rebellion, and Consciousness in the Andean Peasant World: Eighteenth to Twentieth Centuries* (Madison, 1987). On conflicts between "castes" (that is, races) in the independence period, John Lynch, *The Spanish American Revolutions, 1808–1826* (New York, 1973), is still a useful work.

64. Alberto Flores-Galindo, *Buscando un inca: Identidad y utopía en los Andes* (Mexico City, 1993); José L. Franco, *Historia de la Revolución de Haití* (2nd ed.; Santo Domingo, 1971), 168–72; David Geggus, "Slave Resistance Studies and the Saint Domingue Slave Revolt: Some Preliminary Considerations" (Occasional Papers Series no. 4, Latin American and Caribbean Center, Florida International University, 1983); Gabriel Debien, "Assemblées nocturnes d'esclaves a Saint-Domingue (La Marmelade, 1786)," offprint from *Annales Historiques de la Révolution* (1972): 273–84; and Dantès Bellegarde, *La nación haitiana*, 85–87. Information on the "Comegente" is from personal communication with Raymundo González. Regarding the sense of persecution due to the actions of fugitive slaves and cimarrones, the thought-provoking book by Carlos Esteban Deive, *Los guerrilleros negros: Esclavos fugitivos y cimarrones en Santo Domingo* (Santo Domingo, 1989), may be helpful.

65. Luis Martínez-Fernández, *Torn between Empires: Economy, Society, and Patterns of Political Thought in the Hispanic Caribbean, 1840–1878* (Athens, Ga., 1994), esp. 114–49, 187–226; the quotation is from p. 141. See also Eric Williams, *From Columbus to Castro: The History of the Caribbean, 1492–1969*

(2nd printing; New York, 1973), esp. 237–346, 392–407; Franklin W. Knight, *The Caribbean: The Genesis of a Fragmented Nationalism* (2nd ed.; New York, 1990), 159–274; and Gordon K. Lewis, *Main Currents in Caribbean Thought: The Historical Evolution of Caribbean Society in Its Ideological Aspects, 1492–1900* (Baltimore, 1987), 239–320.

66. I employ the term "protonational" to refer to debates about the *possibilities* of the creation of the nations of the Caribbean, which (according to the models in vogue in the nineteenth century) should be as culturally, ethnically, and "racially" homogeneous as possible. On elements contributing to the emergence of nations and nationalities, see Anderson, *Imagined Communities.*

67. Julio Ramos, *Divergent Modernities: Culture and Politics in Nineteenth-Century Latin America,* trans. John D. Blanco (Durham, N.C., 2000), 255–59 (emphasis added). [The quotation is from p. 259. Trans.] This work is fundamental for understanding debates on the construction of the nations of the New World.

68. Ibid., 259.

69. Raymundo González, *Bonó, un intelectual de los pobres* (Santo Domingo, 1994). Regarding the debates and political discussions in nineteenth-century Santo Domingo, see Pérez-Memén, *El pensamiento dominicano.*

70. *República,* 326–28.

71. Ibid., 379.

72. Ibid., 381–83.

73. Fernando Picó, "La constitución del narrador en los textos historiográficos puertorriqueños: Algunos ejemplos," in Ana Lydia Vega et al., *Historia y literatura* (San Juan, P.R., 1995), 80.

74. Hayden White, *The Content of the Form: Narrative Discourse and Historical Representation* (2nd printing; Baltimore, 1992), esp. 58–82. This discursive strategy is typical of the documentalist tradition that is so deeply rooted in the Dominican Republic, as can be seen in the dozens of volumes edited by Emilio Rodríguez-Demorizi. Apart from their undeniable historiographic value, such works attempt to convey a sense of objectivity based on the "truth" that springs inevitably from the documents presented. Forgotten is the suggestion of Edward H. Carr, that documents "speak" only in response to the questions asked of them (*What Is History?* [New York, 1961]).

75. The bulk of these documents is reproduced in *República,* 387–541.

76. Ibid., 518, 520.

77. Ibid., 583.

78. The quotations are from William R. Manning, *Diplomatic Correspon-*

dence of the United States: Inter-American Affairs, 1851–1860 (Washington, D.C., 1935), 46, cited in ibid., 585.

79. *República*, 586.

80. Ibid., 622–23.

81. Pérez-Memén, *El pensamiento dominicano*, 397–444. For an overview of Dominican annexationism, see Martínez-Fernández, *Torn between Empires*, 120–21, 141–44. See also Mu-Kien A. Sang, *Buenaventura Báez: El caudillo del Sur (1844–1878)* (Santo Domingo, 1991), esp. 39–56, 113–46, for an interpretation of annexationism from the standpoint of this important political leader.

82. On Santana, see Pérez-Memén, *El pensamiento dominicano*; Frank Moya-Pons, *Manual de historia dominicana* (4th ed.; Santiago, D.R., 1978), 297–320; and Emilio Rodríguez-Demorizi (ed.), *Papeles del General Santana* (Rome, 1955). On the historical context of the annexation to Spain, see Emilio Rodríguez-Demorizi (ed.), *Antecedentes de la Anexión a España* (Ciudad Trujillo, D.R., 1955); Roberto Cassá, *Historia social y económica de la República Dominicana* (2 vols., 3rd ed.; Santo Domingo, 1982), 2:39–96; Jaime de Jesús Domínguez, *Economía y política en la República Dominicana, 1844–1861* (Santo Domingo, 1977); *La anexión de la República Dominicana a España* (Santo Domingo, 1979); and Juan I. Jimenes-Grullón, *Sociología política dominicana, 1844–1966*, vol. 1 (4th ed.; Santo Domingo, 1982), 19–142. [Also available from Frank Moya-Pons in English is *The Dominican Republic: A National History* (New Rochelle, N.Y., 1995). The author states, "This volume is based on my *Manual de historia dominicana*. . . . Yet, this is an entirely new book with a different structure. It is the only complete Dominican history available in English" (10–11). Corresponding to the section of the *Manual* cited above would be pp. 165–83 of the English-language work. Trans.]

83. For views critical of this interpretation, see Domínguez, *Anexión*, 81–84, and Jimenes-Grullón, *Sociología política*, 1:100–105.

84. See Sang, *Buenaventura Báez*, 113–46; Jimenes-Grullón, *Sociología política*, 1:165–99; and Emilio Rodríguez-Demorizi (ed.), *Informe de la Comisión de Investigación de los E.U.A. en Santo Domingo en 1871* (Ciudad Trujillo, D.R., 1960).

85. *República*, 634 and 629, respectively. The first two quotations are words of Geffrard reproduced by Price-Mars.

86. Ibid., 650–61. On annexation and the fight against it, see Domínguez, *Anexión*; Pedro M. Archambault, *Historia de la Restauración* (4th ed.; Santo Domingo, 1981); Juan Bosch, *La Guerra de la Restauración* (3rd ed.; Santo Domingo, 1984); Luis Álvarez, *Dominación colonial y guerra popular, 1861–*

1865 (Santo Domingo, 1986); and Hugo Tolentino-Dipp, *Gregorio Luperón: Biografía política* (Havana, 1979), 26–85.

87. *República*, 659–60.

88. Ibid., 659–61. On this phase of Haitian history, see Nicholls, *From Dessalines to Duvalier*, 108ff., and Dantès Bellegarde, *La nación haitiana*, 143–61. Also useful is the view of Haitian politics presented in James G. Leyburn, *The Haitian People* (New Haven, 1941), 211–49.

89. Among the many Dominican works on the subject, see Manuel A. Peña-Batlle, *Historia de la cuestión fronteriza domínico-haitiana* (Ciudad Trujillo, D.R., 1946).

90. Price-Mars's presentation on the border question is found in *República*, 742–75. The quotation is from p. 775.

91. On the migration of Haitians to the Dominican Republic, see José del Castillo, "La inmigración de braceros a la industria azucarera, 1900–1930," *Cuadernos del CENDIA* (1978); Suzy Castor, *Migración y relaciones internacionales (El caso haitiano-dominicano)* (Santo Domingo, 1987); Lozano, *La cuestión haitiana*; and Frank Moya-Pons et al., *El batey: Estudio socioeconómico de los bateyes del Consejo Estatal del Azúcar* (Santo Domingo, 1986).

92. *República*, 776–79. The Massacre of 1937 has been the subject of several studies in recent years. Noteworthy among these are José Israel Cuello (comp.), *Documentos del conflicto domínico-haitiano de 1937* (Santo Domingo, 1985); Robin L. Derby and Richard Turits, "Historias de terror y los terrores de la historia: La masacre haitiana de 1937 en la República Dominicana," *Estudios Sociales* 27, no. 92 (1993): 65–76; and Bernardo Vega, *Trujillo y Haití* (2 vols.; Santo Domingo, 1988 and 1995). In the second volume of Vega's work, he evaluates the different death counts that have been put forth for the Massacre of 1937, concluding that the correct figure must be between five and six thousand.

93. Del Rosario-Pérez, *La exterminación*, 353–60.

94. *República*, 778–79.

95. These two attitudes are revealed in two novels: the first by a Haitian author, the second by a Dominican. See Anthony Lespès, *Las semillas de la ira*, trans. Diógenes Céspedes (Santo Domingo, 1990) [original French title: *Les semences de la colère*], and Freddy Prestol-Castillo, *El Masacre se pasa a pie* (5th ed.; Santo Domingo, 1982).

96. *República*, 781–86, 799. See also C. Harvey Gardiner, *La política de inmigración del dictador Trujillo* (Santo Domingo, 1979).

97. Christian Girault, "Las relaciones entre la República de Haití y la

República Dominicana: Un enfoque geográfico," in Lozano, *La cuestión haitiana*, 69–77; Orlando Inoa, *Estado y campesinos al inicio de la Era de Trujillo* (Santo Domingo, 1994), 157–80; and Lauren Derby, "Haitians, Magic, and Money: *Raza* and Society in the Haitian-Dominican Borderlands, 1900 to 1937," *Comparative Studies in Society and History* 36, no. 3 (1994): 488–526.

98. *República*, 800. For a contemporary perspective, see Carmen Cedeño, "La nacionalidad de los descendientes de haitianos nacidos en la República Dominicana," in Lozano, *La cuestión haitiana*, 137–43.

99. *República*, 792–813.

100. Le Goff, *El orden de la memoria*, 84.

101. See Emilio Rodríguez-Demorizi, "Al margen de la obra del Dr. Price Mars," and Sócrates Nolasco, "Comentarios a la historia de Jean Price Mars," in *República*, 815–38 and 839–66, respectively; and del Rosario-Pérez, *La exterminación*, a hefty volume dedicated exclusively to refuting the Haitian scholar. As Balcácer has pointed out ("Hacia una historia comparativa," xxv), a good many of Rodríguez-Demorizi's works published during the 1950s can be seen as replies to Price-Mars. The following volumes, in order of publication, are among those edited by Rodríguez-Demorizi during those years: *Invasiones haitianas de 1801, 1805 y 1822* (Ciudad Trujillo, D.R., 1955); *La Era de Francia en Santo Domingo* (Ciudad Trujillo, D.R., 1955); *Relaciones dominicoespañolas (1844–1859)* (Ciudad Trujillo, D.R., 1955); *Antecedentes de la Anexión* (1955); *Guerra dominico-haitiana* (Ciudad Trujillo, D.R., 1957); and *Cesión de Santo Domingo* (1958). The common theme of all of these is the "misfortune" that the existence of Saint-Domingue / Haiti has represented for Santo Domingo.

102. Mateo, *Mito y cultura*, esp. 127–60.

103. Balcácer, "Hacia una historia comparativa," xxiii–xxix.

104. Jesús M. Zaglul, "Una identificación nacional *defensiva*: El antihaitianismo nacionalista de Joaquín Balaguer. Una lectura de *La isla al revés*," *Estudios Sociales* 25, no. 87 (1992): 29–65. [Zaglul's felicitous term, "enemización," cannot readily be rendered in English. Trans.]

105. Dépestre, "Hello and Goodbye," 251.

106. These criticisms of "negritude" have already been presented in texts by Frantz Fanon—for example, in *Wretched*, esp. 211–17, as Edward Said points out in *Culture and Imperialism* (New York, 1994), 267–81.

107. Dépestre, "Hello and Goodbye," 263 (emphasis in the original). For light on the historical context in which the indigenist thought of Mariátegui was developed, see Flores-Galindo, *Buscando un inca*, 293–346, and Rénique,

Los sueños de la sierra, esp. 99–135. Regarding Henríquez-Ureña, see Arcadio Díaz-Quiñones, "Pedro Henríquez Ureña: Modernidad, diáspora y construcción de identidades," in Gilberto Giménez and Ricardo Pozas (eds.), *Modernización e identidades sociales* (Mexico City, 1994), 59–117.

108. Dépestre, "Hello and Goodbye," 272.

109. Arcadio Díaz-Quiñones, *La memoria rota* (Río Piedras, P.R., 1993), 79–80.

110. Fanon, *Wretched*, and G. R. Coulthard, "Parallelisms and Divergences between *Negritude* and *Indigenism*," *Caribbean Studies* 8, no. 1 (1968): 31–55.

111. Arcadio Díaz-Quiñones, "El enemigo íntimo: Cultura nacional y autoridad en Ramiro Guerra y Sánchez y Antonio S. Pedreira," *Op. Cit.: Boletín del Centro de Investigaciones Históricas* 7 (1992): 9–65, and "Tomás Blanco: Racismo, historia, esclavitud," in Tomás Blanco, *El prejuicio racial en Puerto Rico* (3rd ed.; Río Piedras, P.R., 1985), 13–91.

112. Lundahl, *Politics or Markets?*, 255–309; Casimir, *La cultura oprimida*; Nicholls, *From Dessalines to Duvalier*; and Said, *Culture and Imperialism*, 264–65.

113. Hurbon, *El bárbaro imaginario*, 55.

114. Nicholls, *From Dessalines to Duvalier*, 212–38; Dash, *Literature and Ideology*, 98–128; Laënnec Hurbon, *Culture et dictature en Haïti: L'imaginaire sous contrôle* (Paris, 1979); G. R. Coulthard, "Negritude: Reality and Mystification," *Caribbean Studies* 10, no. 1 (1970): 12–51; Franklin J. Franco, *Haití: De Dessalines a nuestros días* (Santo Domingo, 1988), 91–110; Michael Dash, "Blazing Mirrors: The Crisis of the Haitian Intellectual," in Alistair Hennessy (ed.), *Intellectuals in the Twentieth-Century Caribbean* (2 vols.; London, 1992), 2:175–85. The book by Antoine, reputed to be the most complete biography of Price-Mars, scarcely mentions his relationship with Duvalier (*Price-Mars and Haiti*, 171–74, 185–87, 190). It was only at the close of his life, in the late 1960s, when the Uncle distanced himself from Duvalier's regime, which had honored him in various ways. To Dépestre, Price-Mars's withdrawal from Duvalier and his doctrines was a rehabilitation of sorts after a "long guilty silence" ("Prólogo," in *Tío*, xxiii–xxxi).

115. Marshall Berman, *All That Is Solid Melts into Air: The Experience of Modernity* (New York, 1988).

116. Andrés L. Mateo, *Al filo de la dominicanidad* (Santo Domingo, 1996), 47–49.

117. Ibid., 77–88.

118. Borges, "Garden of Forking Paths," 125, 127.

Storytelling the Nation: Memory, History, and Narration in Juan Bosch

This essay is an expanded version of a paper presented at the 28th Conference of the Association of Caribbean Historians, Bridgetown, Barbados, April 14–19, 1996.

1. Santiago Chamber of Commerce, letter from various Santiago property owners to the Secretary of State of Internal Revenue and Trade, November 24, 1927.

2. [The reference is to the novel by Gabriel García-Márquez, *One Hundred Years of Solitude*, trans. Gregory Rabassa (New York, 1970). Trans.]

3. Juan Bosch, "La literatura y la crítica literaria," in Bruno Rosario-Candelier, *La narrativa de Juan Bosch* (Santo Domingo, 1989), 259. Bosch recalls those trips on various occasions. See, for example, "Entrevista con Juan Bosch," an interview reproduced in *La narrativa*, esp. pp. 226, 228.

4. Juan Bosch, *Trujillo, causas de una tiranía sin ejemplo* [1959] (5th ed.; Santo Domingo, 1991), 201–2.

5. Rosario-Candelier analyzes Bosch's works as a seamless unit based on the "human and social background" that this critic detects in Bosch's texts (*La narrativa*, 267). He states, "There is no rupture between Bosch the creator of fictional texts and Bosch the creator of nonfictional texts" (80).

6. I refer to *El pentagonismo, sustituto del imperialismo* (Mexico City, 1968); *Composición social dominicana: Historia e interpretación* [1970] (30th ed.; Santo Domingo, 1983); and *De Cristóbal Colón a Fidel Castro: El Caribe, frontera imperial* [1971] (5th ed.; Santo Domingo, 1986). [At least the first of these has been translated into English: *Pentagonism, a Substitute for Imperialism*, trans. Helen R. Lane (New York, 1968). Trans.]

7. In tracing Bosch's trajectory I have used Rosario-Candelier, *La narrativa*; Franklin J. Franco, *Historia de las ideas políticas en la República Dominicana* (Santo Domingo, [1981–]), 254–87; Mildred Guzmán-Madera, *Introducción al pensamiento político de Juan Bosch* (Santo Domingo, 1992), 5–16; Eugenio de J. García-Cuevas, *Juan Bosch: Novela, historia y sociedad* (San Juan, P.R., and La Vega, D.R., 1995); and the very helpful work of Guillermo Piña-Contreras, *Juan Bosch: Bibliografía (Precedida de una cronología)* (Santo Domingo, 1990).

8. On his role in the modernization of Dominican narrative, see Rosario-Candelier, *La narrativa*, 27–36. Of course, the two phases or stages to which I refer do not signify an absolute break; for that reason I have included several of his stories written in exile in the section with my analysis of Bosch's view of rurality and peasantry. For a more precise analysis of the stages of his intel-

lectual and political career, see García-Cuevas, *Juan Bosch*, 57–77. García-Cuevas alludes to Bosch's modernizing views, which he identifies with a political project with "liberal revolutionary" or "liberal nationalist revolutionary" roots.

9. Emilio Rodríguez-Demorizi (ed.), *Hostos en Santo Domingo* (Ciudad Trujillo, D.R., 1939); José Alcántara-Almánzar, *Los escritores dominicanos y la cultura* (Santo Domingo, 1990), 103–15; and Andrés L. Mateo, *Mito y cultura en la Era de Trujillo* (Santo Domingo, 1993), 51–63. Compare García-Cuevas, *Juan Bosch*, 67–69.

10. Juan Bosch, *Hostos, el sembrador* [1939] (Río Piedras, P.R., 1976), 7–8. Earlier studies have emphasized the influence of Hostos over Bosch; his own testimony may be seen in the prologue to the new edition of this work. Bosch's knowledge of Hostos's private life is reflected in *Mujeres en la vida de Hostos* (Women in the Life of Hostos) (San Juan, P.R., 1938), originally given as a speech. I am grateful to Christie Capetta of the Instituto de Estudios Hostosianos of the University of Puerto Rico for providing me with a copy of this work.

11. Bosch wrote about each of these countries: *Cuba, la isla fascinante* [1955] (2nd ed.; Santo Domingo, 1988), and *Una interpretación de la historia costarricense* [1963] (Santo Domingo, 1984).

12. Benedict Anderson, *Imagined Communities: Reflections on the Origin and Spread of Nationalism* (rev. ed.; New York, 1996), 4, 37–46; the quotation is from p. 4.

13. Hayden White, *Metahistory: The Historical Imagination in Nineteenth-Century Europe* (Baltimore, 1973), xii (emphasis in the original). White's theories spring from his study of the modes of historical representation, a theme that he also develops in *The Content of the Form: Narrative Discourse and Historical Representation* (2nd printing; Baltimore, 1992).

14. Hayden White, *Tropics of Discourse: Essays in Cultural Criticism* (2nd printing; Baltimore, 1986), 81–82 (emphasis in the original).

15. [English translation by Andrew Hurley: Jorge Luis Borges, foreword to *Fictions*, in *Collected Fictions: Jorge Luis Borges*, trans. Andrew Hurley (New York, 1998), 67. Trans.]

16. Marshall Berman, *All That Is Solid Melts into Air: The Experience of Modernity* (New York, 1988), 173–286. The quotations are from the section title and p. 175. It is worth mentioning, if only in passing, that Bosch read Russian authors in his youth (Rosario-Candelier, *La narrativa*, 165).

17. Mateo, *Mito y cultura*, 52, 69.

18. See my essay "Racial Discourse and National Identity," in this volume,

and José Ramón López, "La alimentación y las razas," in *Ensayos y artículos* (Santo Domingo, 1991), 9–61. On the concept of "subaltern sectors," see Ranajit Guha and Gayatri Chakravorty Spivak (eds.), *Selected Subaltern Studies* (New York, 1988), esp. 3–44.

19. This paragraph summarizes some of the arguments that I put forth in "Un libro para romper el silencio: Estado y campesinos al inicio de la Era de Trujillo, de Orlando Inoa," *Estudios Sociales* 27, no. 98 (1994): 83–92. See also Mateo, *Mito y cultura*, 49–89; García-Cuevas, *Juan Bosch*, esp. 19–34; and Diógenes Céspedes, "El efecto Rodó. Nacionalismo idealista vs. nacionalismo práctico: Los intelectuales antes de y bajo Trujillo," *Cuadernos de Poética* 6, no. 17 (1989): 7–56. On the concept of the "other," see Edward W. Said, *Orientalism* (New York, 1979), and Tzvetan Todorov, *The Conquest of America: The Question of the Other*, trans. Richard Howard (New York, 1984), and *On Human Diversity: Nationalism, Racism, and Exoticism in French Thought*, trans. Catherine Porter (Cambridge, Mass., 1993). The term "fragment of the nation" is from Partha Chatterjee, *The Nation and Its Fragments: Colonial and Postcolonial Histories* (Princeton, 1993), esp. 158–72. The existence of internal "others" has been a phenomenon occurring in every country of Latin America and the Caribbean, from the Conquest to the present. On this subject, see Martin Lienhard, *La voz y su huella: Escritura y conflicto étnico-social en América Latina (1492–1988)* (Havana, 1990). [A recent book by the author discusses in greater detail the implications of rural rebellions. See Pedro L. San Miguel, *La guerra silenciosa: Las luchas sociales en la ruralía dominicana* (Mexico City, 2004). Trans.]

20. Julio Ramos, *Divergent Modernities: Culture and Politics in Nineteenth-Century Latin America*, trans. John D. Blanco (Durham, N.C., 2000), 4 (emphasis in the original).

21. For enlightenment on the relationships between politics and the intellectual climate of the period, see Céspedes, "El efecto Rodó"; Mateo, *Mito y cultura*; Franco, *Historia de las ideas políticas*, 79–112; García-Cuevas, *Juan Bosch*; Juan I. Jimenes-Grullón, *Sociología política dominicana, 1844–1966*, vol. 2 (3rd ed.; Santo Domingo, 1981); Francisco Antonio Avelino, "Elogio y crítica del pensamiento de Américo Lugo," *Ecos: Órgano del Instituto de Historia de la Universidad Autónoma de Santo Domingo* 1, no. 2 (1993): 101–27; Raymundo González, "Peña Batlle y su concepto histórico de la nación dominicana," *Ecos: Órgano del Instituto de Historia de la Universidad Autónoma de Santo Domingo* 2, no. 3 (1994): 11–52; and Arcadio Díaz-Quiñones, "Pedro Henríquez Ureña: Modernidad, diáspora y construcción de identidades," in Gilberto Giménez and Ricardo Pozas (eds.), *Modernización e identidades so-*

ciales (Mexico City, 1994), 59–117. A useful essay in the field of historiography proper is by Roberto Cassá, "Historiografía de la República Dominicana," *Ecos: Órgano del Instituto de Historia de la Universidad Autónoma de Santo Domingo* 1, no. 1 (1993): 9–39.

22. Rosario-Candelier, *La narrativa*, 29–31, and García-Cuevas, *Juan Bosch*, 41. The poet Héctor Incháustegui-Cabral describes the atmosphere of "La Cueva" (The Cave), a *peña* in which Bosch participated in the 1930s, in his autobiographical work *El pozo muerto* (Santiago, D.R., 1980), although he mentions Bosch only obliquely.

23. For example, Rosario-Candelier, *La narrativa*, esp. 27–46, 83–92, and García-Cuevas, *Juan Bosch*, 62–67.

24. It is Bosch himself who uses the term *asombrado* to describe his reaction to the early-twentieth-century campesino: see "Entrevista," 226. [The word "asombrado," chosen by Bosch, has a number of meanings, and San Miguel stresses that more than one apply here. It can mean "darkened," "shadowed," "overshadowed"; "astounded" or "astonished"; "amazed," "lost in admiration"; even "frightened" or "in dread." Trans.]

25. Ramos, *Divergent Modernities*, and Ángel Rama, *The Lettered City*, ed. and trans. John Charles Chasteen (Durham, N.C., 1996), esp. 50–126.

26. On the tensions generated between State and society due to such "encounters," see Ramonina Brea, *Ensayo sobre la formación del Estado capitalista en la República Dominicana y Haití* (Santo Domingo, 1983). Following Néstor García-Canclini, we can define modernization projects succinctly: (1) They include an "emancipating project" based on "the rationalization of social life and increasing individualism"; (2) in an "expansive project" they seek "to extend the knowledge and possession of nature," which translates into "the promotion of scientific discoveries and industrial development"; (3) they maintain a "renovating project" that is expressed in a secularization of life; and (4) in a "democratizing project," they trust in the democratizing and liberating power of "education, the diffusion of art, and specialized knowledge to achieve rational and moral evolution" (*Hybrid Cultures: Strategies for Entering and Leaving Modernity*, trans. Christopher L. Chiappari and Silvia L. López [Minneapolis, 1995], 12–13).

In this essay, I will use as synonyms "premodernity/premodern," on the one hand, and "countermodernity/countermodern," on the other. With that usage I wish to imply, as García-Canclini suggests, that due to the "multitemporal heterogeneity" of the countries of Latin America, premodernity is not necessarily a historical stage *preceding* modernity. Premodernity and modernity are, on the contrary, cultural expressions coexisting, in conflict but intertwined, in the same society and "epoch."

27. The passage cited, which refers to Eduardo Galeano, is from Juan Duchesne-Winter, *Narraciones de testimonio en América Latina: Cinco estudios* (Río Piedras, P.R., 1992), 35.

28. Walter J. Ong, *Orality and Literacy: The Technologizing of the Word* (New York, 2002). On the orality/writing problem, see also Jacques Le Goff, *El orden de la memoria: El tiempo como imaginario* (Barcelona, 1991), 131–83, and Michel de Certeau, *The Writing of History*, trans. Tom Conley (New York, 1988), 209–283.

29. Jack Goody, *The Domestication of the Savage Mind* (New York, 1977).

30. Patrick H. Hutton, *History as an Art of Memory* (Hanover, N.H., 1993), esp. xi–xxv, 27–51, 73–90, 124–53. See also de Certeau, *The Writing of History*, 1–113.

31. Hutton, *History*, 37–39. According to Hutton, Giambattista Vico analyzed ancient texts for the purpose of disentangling their "hidden meanings" about oral traditions. Hutton's chapters about the sociologist Maurice Halbwachs and the historian Philippe Ariès also have a bearing on this theme. The notion of authors and texts in which orality and literacy "intersect" is also found in Lienhard, *La voz y su huella*.

32. Rama, *Lettered City*, 63.

33. See García-Cuevas, *Juan Bosch*, 123–24.

34. "Entrevista," 228, 239–40. Among the narrations that he heard as a child were many myths of indigenous origin. It is interesting to note that one of Bosch's first books was a collection of narrations, traditions, and "histories" inspired by the island's native inhabitants (*Indios: Apuntes históricos y leyendas* [1935] [3rd ed.; Santo Domingo, 1992]). Río Verde is a rural sector of La Vega where Bosch lived in childhood.

35. Rosario-Candelier, *La narrativa*, 94.

36. Stories of the first classification include "El resguardo," "La pájara," "La sangre," "Lucero," and "San Andrés"; of the second, "La verdad," "El cobarde," "Chucho," "La pulpería," "Revolución," "Sombras," "El alzado," "Cundito," and "Lo mejor." All of these stories appear in Juan Bosch, *Cuentos escritos antes del exilio* (Stories Written before the Exile) (7th ed.; Santo Domingo, 1987) (cited hereinafter as *Cuentos*, followed by the corresponding page number[s]).

37. García-Cuevas points out that Bosch's novel *La mañosa* also begins with a direct reference to orality (*Juan Bosch*, 95). For this period, the turn of

the twentieth century, Ramos alludes to the new modes of transportation and communication—the railroad, the telegraph, the steamboat, the newspaper—as emblems par excellence of modernity (*Divergent Modernities*).

38. García-Cuevas, *Juan Bosch*, 169.

39. On the elements in his narrations that evoke personal testimony, see "Entrevista," 228–29, and García-Cuevas, *Juan Bosch*, 168–78. Duchesne-Winter dubs as "testimonial narrative" those accounts in which (1) "an authentic witness (or witnesses)" is presented; (2) "the declarations of the witnesses are the principal matter of the story"; and (3) "the account attempts to confine itself strictly to the factuality of the event, in accordance with the models of factuality that have been adopted or presented" (*Narraciones de testimonio*, 5).

40. The idea of a "crossing" of "positions in conflict" is employed by Ramos in his analysis of the works of Martí (*Divergent Modernities*, 62–71). The epistemological and theoretical problems of the "encounter" between orality and literacy constitute an important field of thought within current ethnography. See James Clifford and George E. Marcus (eds.), *Writing Culture: The Poetics and Politics of Ethnography* (Berkeley, 1986), and Clifford Geertz, *Works and Lives: The Anthropologist as Author* (Stanford, 1991).

41. Juan Bosch, *La mañosa* [1936] (21st ed.; Santo Domingo, 1994). For more on this work, consult Franco, *Historia de las ideas políticas*, 256–59; Rosario-Candelier, *La narrativa*, 163–96; and especially García-Cuevas, *Juan Bosch*. Several of his stories, particularly those from "before the exile," also deal with the subject of the "revolutions."

42. Hutton, *History*, 78. On history as "representation," see White, *Content of the Form*, esp. 1–25, and Roger Chartier, *El mundo como representación: Estudios sobre historia cultural* (2nd ed.; Barcelona, 1995), 45–62.

43. David K. Herzberger, *Narrating the Past: Fiction and Historiography in Postwar Spain* (Durham, N.C., 1995), 85.

44. Rosario-Candelier, *La narrativa*, 163–96, and García-Cuevas, *Juan Bosch*.

45. Said, *Orientalism*, and the excellent analysis of *Facundo* that Ramos gives in *Divergent Modernities*. The reference to the "Berber spirit" of the Dominican people is from a commentary on *La mañosa* published in 1936 and quoted by Rosario-Candelier, *La narrativa*, 177.

46. Juan Bosch, "Rosa," from *Más cuentos escritos en el exilio* (More Stories Written in Exile) (11th ed.; Santo Domingo, 1987), 260 (cited hereinafter as *Más Cuentos*, followed by the corresponding page number[s]).

47. Juan Bosch, "Un niño," in ibid., 54.

48. "Rosa," 284.

49. "Guaraguaos," in *Cuentos*, 193. On the notion of "wildness," see White, *Tropics of Discourse*, 150–82.

50. "Entrevista," 241.

51. Rosario-Candelier, *La narrativa*, 228.

52. "El socio," *Más cuentos*, 161–86. Bosch alleges that don Anselmo was based on the historical figure of "Mamón" Henríquez, a great landowner (*latifundista*) of the Cibao who "was said to be in league with the Devil" ("Entrevista," 229).

53. The relationship between the figure of the Devil, magic, and money is examined by Michael T. Taussig, *The Devil and Commodity Fetishism in South America* (Chapel Hill, N.C., 1983), and Lauren Derby, "Haitians, Magic, and Money: *Raza* and Society in the Haitian-Dominican Borderlands, 1900 to 1937," *Comparative Studies in Society and History* 36, no. 3 (1994): 488–526.

54. Juan Bosch, "Forzados," in *Camino real: Cuentos* [1933] (3rd. ed., facsimile; Santo Domingo, 1983), 47–52 (cited hereinafter as *Camino*, followed by the corresponding page number[s]). The concept of "moral outrage" is from Barrington Moore Jr., *Injustice: The Social Bases of Obedience and Revolt* (White Plains, N.Y., 1978). On forced labor, see Orlando Inoa, *Estado y campesinos al inicio de la Era de Trujillo* (Santo Domingo, 1994); Pedro L. San Miguel, "El Estado y el campesinado en la República Dominicana: El Valle del Cibao, 1900–1960," *Historia y Sociedad* 4 (1991): 42–74, and "Peasant Resistance to State Demands in the Cibao during the U.S. Occupation," trans. Phillip Berryman, *Latin American Perspectives* 22, no. 3 (1995): 41–62.

55. In his stories, the power of the State is represented systematically by its apparatus of repression: the army, the police, the courts. See "Luis Pie" and "La nochebuena de Encarnación Mendoza," both in *Cuentos escritos en el exilio* (Stories Written in Exile) (16th ed.; Santo Domingo, 1988), 51–76 (cited hereinafter as *Cuentos en exilio*, followed by the corresponding page number[s]), and "El muerto estaba vivo," in *Más cuentos*, 117–43. The political interpretation of these stories is also suggested in Bosch's brief essay "Un pueblo en un libro," prologue to the work by Juan Isidro Jimenes-Grullón, *La República Dominicana: Análisis de su pasado y su presente* [1940] (3rd ed.; Santo Domingo, 1974), in which Bosch sets forth the thesis of conflicts between the countryside and the city. I thank Eugenio García-Cuevas for making me aware of this crucial text, to which I will be referring again later.

56. *Camino*, 98–104; the quotation is from p. 102.

57. "El muerto estaba vivo," in *Más cuentos*, 117–43; the quotation is from

p. 142. García-Cuevas alludes to a passage in *La mañosa* that also presents "two opposing conceptions of the world" (*Juan Bosch*, 124).

58. See Goody, *Domestication*; Geertz, *Works and Lives*; and Clifford and Marcus, *Writing Culture*.

59. The first two stories appear in *Cuentos en exilio*, 61–87; the third in *Más cuentos*, 55–71; and the last in *Cuentos*, 15–30. For a classification of Bosch's stories based on the behaviors, values, and beliefs of the campesinos, see Rosario-Candelier, *La narrativa*.

60. García-Cuevas interprets this appropriation in terms of the way in which the "petite bourgeoisies"—at least its more radical sectors—expropriated "campesino voices" (*Juan Bosch*, 164).

61. "La verdad," in *Cuentos*, 31–50. According to the bibliography compiled by Piña-Contreras, this story was first published in Puerto Rico, in December 1938 (*Juan Bosch: Bibliografía*, 158). Given its inclusion in the collection of stories written "before the exile," however, it appears to have been written in the Dominican Republic circa 1937.

62. See Luis Manuel Patrocinio, *Enrique Blanco: El rebelde solitario* (Santo Domingo, 1971); Luis Arzeno-Rodríguez, *Enrique Blanco: ¿Héroe o forajido?* (Santo Domingo, 1980); and Emilio Acosta-Estrella, *Enrique Blanco: Su historia y dramáticas aventuras* (Santo Domingo, 1983). To date, academic historiography has ignored this legendary figure of humble extraction, similar to the "social bandit" of Eric Hobsbawm (*Bandits* [rev. ed.; New York, 2000]).

63. I borrow the term from Adolfo Gilly, "La historia como crítica o como discurso del poder," in *Historia, ¿para qué?* (Mexico City, 1980), 195–225. On the "representation" of "reality" as a political struggle, see White, *Content of the Form*.

64. García-Cuevas, *Juan Bosch*, 156–59, 163–64.

65. Raymundo González, *Bonó, un intelectual de los pobres* (Santo Domingo, 1994), esp. 39–83.

66. Rama, *Lettered City*, 65. Also relevant is the analysis by Ramos on Sarmiento in *Divergent Modernities*, 3–22.

67. Ramos, *Divergent Modernities*, 12.

68. For discussions on the problem of "representation" of subalterns, see Gayatri Chakravorty Spivak, "Can the Subaltern Speak?" in Patrick Williams and Laura Chrisman (eds.), *Colonial Discourse and Postcolonial Theory: A Reader* (New York, 1994), 66–111, and Florencia E. Mallon, "The Promise and Dilemma of Subaltern Studies: Perspectives from Latin American History," *American Historical Review* 99, no. 5 (1994): 1491–515.

69. "Camino real," in *Camino*, 121–52. This story also appears in *Cuentos*, 247–81, but the latter version differs in several passages from the original, from which I have taken my quotations.

70. "Camino real," 131.

71. On the problem of the "authority" of letters and, consequently, of men and women of letters, see Rama, *Lettered City*; Ramos, *Divergent Modernities*; Arcadio Díaz-Quiñones, "El enemigo íntimo: Cultura nacional y autoridad en Ramiro Guerra y Sánchez y Antonio S. Pedreira," *Op Cit.: Boletín del Centro de Investigaciones Históricas* 7 (1992): 9–65; and Juan Gelpí, *Literatura y paternalismo en Puerto Rico* (Río Piedras, P.R., 1993).

72. Rama, *Lettered City*, 112.

73. Ángel Rama, *La ciudad letrada* (Hanover, N.H., 1984), 154. [This phrase is omitted in the English translation of this book by John Charles Chasteen. Trans.]

74. This venerable "enlightened" myth can be found in every modern radical tradition from the Jacobins onward. See Georg Lukács, *History and Class Consciousness: Studies in Marxist Dialectics*, trans. Rodney Livingstone (Cambridge, Mass., 1971), esp. 83–221; E. P. Thompson, *The Making of the English Working Class* (New York, 1966), esp. 711–832; Eric J. Hobsbawm, *Workers: Worlds of Labor* (1st U.S. ed.; New York, 1984), esp. 11–73; and George Rudé, *Ideology and Popular Protest* (New York, 1980).

75. The quotation is from Julio Ramos, introduction to *Amor y anarquía: Los escritos de Luisa Capetillo* (Río Piedras, P.R., 1992), 14. This essay includes an excellent discussion of the appropriation by the subaltern sectors of the written word.

76. Céspedes, "El efecto Rodó"; Mateo, *Mito y cultura*; García-Cuevas, *Juan Bosch*; and Roberto Cassá, *Movimiento obrero y lucha socialista en la República Dominicana (Desde los orígenes hasta 1960)* (Santo Domingo, 1990), 242–56. Ramón Marrero-Aristy was one of the most outstanding promoters of social vindication to end up serving Trujillo.

77. Ramos, *Divergent Modernities*, 153 (emphasis in the original).

78. Carlos Fuentes, *Valiente mundo nuevo: Épica, utopía y mito en la novela hispanoamericana* (Mexico City, 1992), 28.

79. Bosch, "Un pueblo en un libro," in Jimenes-Grullón, *La República Dominicana*, 7–15. The Cassá reference is to his *Movimiento obrero*, 257–63, in which Cassá presents a critical evaluation of Jimenes-Grullón's book and of Bosch's prologue. See also Franco, *Historia de las ideas políticas*, 261–63.

80. Bosch, "Un pueblo en un libro," 7.

81. This argument owes much to the essay by Silvia Álvarez-Curbelo, "El discurso populista de Luis Muñoz Marín: Condiciones de posibilidad y mitos fundacionales en el período 1932–1936," in Silvia Álvarez-Curbelo and María Elena Rodríguez-Castro (eds.), *Del nacionalismo al populismo: Cultura y política en Puerto Rico* (Río Piedras, P.R., 1993), 13–35.

82. See Abelardo Villegas, *Reformismo y revolución en el pensamiento latino-americano* (Mexico City, 1972).

83. García-Cuevas, following Iván Salvá-Méndez, alludes to "the transition from the rural to the urban" that occurred in Bosch's fictional works during those years (*Juan Bosch*, 69).

84. These observations on the role of parties in the modernizing process follow Rama's arguments in *Lettered City*, esp. 105–12.

85. Bosch, "Un pueblo en un libro," 11, 14.

86. Ibid., 14.

87. "Camino real," 152.

88. Bosch, "Un pueblo en un libro," 13.

89. Unlike Bosch's fictional and political works, which have inspired a good number of critiques, commentaries, and studies, his historical texts have been largely ignored (see the meticulously documented work by Piña-Contreras, *Juan Bosch: Bibliografía*, 201–39). In this respect, Franco has been a precursor (*Historia de las ideas políticas*, 254–87).

90. This work should be read in conjunction with others that announce the emergence of modern social analysis in the Dominican Republic and that, in addition, spring from parallel political programs, in dialogue and debate. Among these are the work by Jimenes-Grullón, *La República Dominicana*, from 1940, and a later one by José R. Cordero-Michel, *Análisis de la Era de Trujillo (Informe sobre la República Dominicana, 1959)* (5th ed.; Santo Domingo, 1987). For a brief discussion, see Wilfredo Lozano and Ivette Sabbagh, "La sociología dominicana: Una evaluación," in *Ciencias Sociales en la República Dominicana: Evolución y bibliografía* (Santo Domingo, 1989), 22–23.

91. Bosch, *Trujillo*, 9.

92. For a recent example of this historiographic current, consult Luis Martínez-Fernández, *Torn between Empires: Economy, Society, and Patterns of Political Thought in the Hispanic Caribbean, 1840–1878* (Athens, Ga., 1994).

93. Bosch, *Trujillo*, 12–13, 19.

94. See my essays "Racial Discourse and National Identity," and "The Imagined Colony," in this volume; see also González, "Peña Batlle." On historical narration as a tragedy, see White, *Metahistory*, esp. 1–42, 191–229.

As examples of this type of narrative, see Manuel A. Peña-Batlle, *Ensayos históricos* (Santo Domingo, 1988), and Joaquín Balaguer, *La isla al revés: Haití y el destino dominicano* (5th ed.; Santo Domingo, 1989). Regarding myths about "golden ages" and "decadence," see Le Goff, *El orden de la memoria*, 11–45, 87–127.

95. Bosch, *Trujillo*, 33–43, and Franco, *Historia de las ideas políticas*, 263–66.

96. Bosch, *Trujillo*, 151, 179–88.

97. Bosch is given to elaborate, detailed psychological reconstructions, as can be seen in many of his stories and biographies (a genre very similar to the novel). For examples, see *Hostos; Judas Iscariote, el calumniado* [1955] (10th ed.; Santo Domingo, 1994); *David: Biografía de un rey* [1963] (9th ed.; Santo Domingo, 1990); and *Bolívar y la guerra social* [1966] (5th ed.; Santo Domingo, 1986). [At least one of these biographies has been translated into English; see *David, the Biography of a King*, trans. John Marks (New York, 1966). Trans.] Space does not permit a lengthy discussion of his biographies; I do, however, wish to highlight the importance of studying them as historical documents representing the varied circumstances of Bosch's own eventful political life. It may be hypothesized that, to Bosch, his biographies are a reflection of himself: Bosch is Hostos, the intellectual devoted to "the cause"; Judas, "slandered" by the intrigues of the correligionarios; David, ruler of a rural nation (an interpretation suggested by Bosch himself); and Bolívar, faced with the dilemma of a "social war" whose outcome was uncertain. [This argument is further elaborated in Pedro L. San Miguel, "Las biografías de Juan Bosch: La construcción de una *genealogía*," in San Miguel, *Los desvaríos de Ti Noel: Ensayos sobre la producción del saber en el Caribe* (San Juan, P.R., 2004). Trans.]

98. Bosch, *Trujillo*, 124. For an analysis of discursive practices that feminize "the masses," the "others," see Kelvin A. Santiago-Valles, *"Subject People" and Colonial Discourses: Economic Transformation and Social Disorder in Puerto Rico, 1898–1947* (New York, 1994), and David Spurr, *The Rhetoric of Empire: Colonial Discourse in Journalism, Travel Writing, and Imperial Administration* (Durham, N.C., 1993), 170–83.

99. Mateo, *Mito y cultura*, esp. 129–60; San Miguel, "Racial Discourse," in this volume; and Roberto Cassá, *Capitalismo y dictadura* (Santo Domingo, 1982), 751–79.

100. Bosch, *Trujillo*, 43–65, 101–11; this last quotation is from p. 111.

101. Ibid., 133–42.

102. On the relationship between biologism, racism, and conservative thought, see Said, *Orientalism*; Todorov, *On Human Diversity*, 90–170; Georg

Lukács, *The Destruction of Reason*, trans. Peter Palmer (Atlantic Highlands, N.J., 1981), 667–715; Hannah Arendt, *The Origins of Totalitarianism* (2nd ed.; Cleveland, 1958), 158–220; and Richard Graham (ed.), *The Idea of Race in Latin America, 1870–1940* (Austin, 1990). For the Dominican Republic in particular, see San Miguel, "Racial Discourse"; Meindert Fennema and Troetje Loewenthal, *La construcción de raza y nación en la República Dominicana* (Santo Domingo, 1987); Jesús Zaglul, "Una identificación nacional *defensiva*: El antihaitianismo nacionalista de Joaquín Balaguer. Una lectura de *La isla al revés*," *Estudios Sociales* 25, no. 87 (1992): 29–65; and Orlando Inoa's important compilation, *Bibliografía haitiana en la República Dominicana* (Río Piedras, P.R., 1994).

103. Bosch, *Trujillo*, 80, 86–87, 92–93, 95–100. In later works, Bosch would abandon, or modify substantially, these opinions, especially those that considered Haiti's influence on the "Dominican destiny" to be absolutely negative. Thus it would be inappropriate to characterize Bosch's thought as anti-Haitian, although this may be said of the greater part of traditional historiography, conditioned by the imprint of Trujillo and a socially conservative nationalism. In this sense, it may be held that Bosch's thought vis-à-vis Haiti is *not* essentialist, whereas essentialism *is* a defining feature of conservative Dominican tradition.

104. Ibid., 96.

105. Ibid., 152.

106. Ibid., 123–24.

107. Bosch, *Cuba*, 20.

108. Ibid., 97.

109. Ibid., 251–52.

110. Bosch, *Interpretación*, 21–22, 29, 36, 39–42, 53.

111. These observations owe much to Cassá, "Historiografía," 35–36. See also García-Cuevas, *Juan Bosch*.

112. Bosch, *Composición social*, 30, 40, 42 (emphasis mine).

113. Ibid., 48, 51. On the formation of the Dominican *campesinado*, or "peasantry," see Raymundo González, "Campesinos y sociedad colonial en el siglo XVIII dominicano," *Estudios Sociales* 25, no. 87 (1992): 15–28, and "Ideología del progreso y campesinado en el siglo XIX," *Ecos: Órgano del Instituto de Historia de la Universidad Autónoma de Santo Domingo* 1, no. 2 (1993): 25–43; Pedro L. San Miguel, "The Making of a Peasantry: Dominican Agrarian History from the Sixteenth to the Twentieth Century," *Punto y Coma: Revista Interdisciplinaria de la Universidad del Sagrado Corazón* 2, nos.

1–2 (1990): 143–62, and *Los campesinos del Cibao: Economía de mercado y transformación agraria en la República Dominicana, 1880–1960* (Río Piedras, P.R., 1997), chap. 1.

114. Bosch, *Composición social*, 96, 100, 111.

115. Bosch, *Interpretación*, 14–24; the quotation is from p. 22.

116. Bosch, *Composición social*, 130.

117. Ibid., 161.

118. Ibid., 222.

119. Ibid., 239.

120. Ibid., 250.

121. Ibid., 269.

122. See A. H. Alcántara-E. and I. R. Lawrence-Mazara, "La interpretación materialista de la historia y la sociedad dominicana en Juan Bosch" (thesis, Universidad Católica Madre y Maestra, 1984), and Anthony P. Maingot, "Politics and Populist Historiography in the Caribbean," in Alistair Hennessy (ed.), *Intellectuals in the Twentieth-Century Caribbean* (2 vols.; London, 1992), 2:145–74. For an analysis of Bosch's thinking during the 1970s, see Franco, *Historia de las ideas políticas*, 278–87, and the interview reproduced in Rosalba Campra, *América Latina: La identidad y la máscara* (Mexico City, 1987), 135–40.

123. See Joyce Appleby, Lynn Hunt, and Margaret Jacob, *Telling the Truth about History* (New York, 1994), 1–90.

124. This is patent in Bosch's more-recent works, in which the campesino is only a marginal actor, except for his participation in the "revolutions" of the early twentieth century. See, for example, *Clases sociales en la República Dominicana* [1982] (6th ed.; Santo Domingo, 1989), and *Las dictaduras dominicanas* (Santo Domingo, 1988). It is worthy of mention that in *La Guerra de la Restauración* [1982] (3rd ed.; Santo Domingo, 1984), Bosch highlights the active and decisive participation of the campesinos, especially those of the Cibao, in the War of Restoration, "the most notable page of Dominican history" (7).

INDEX

African culture: and natal alienation, 37; Haitian culture as extension of, 39; and Price-Mars, 68,
69, 70, 74, 78; and Haitian elite,
83

African population: and civilization, 23; as "other," 36; and identity, 37; and Bonó, 47; and Balaguer, 58–59, 61; and racial
composition, 78. *See also* Blacks;
Mulattoes; Race relations; Racial
composition; Racial mixing;
Slaves and slavery

Afro-Antillean culture, 68

Afro-Antillean population, 24

Afro-Dominican cultural elements,
10, 36, 37

Afro-Dominican population, 27,
43–44

Agriculture: and Sánchez-Valverde,
10, 12; and Bonó, 13, 14; and
Haiti, 40–41; and border zone,
92; and Cuba, 101; and civilization, 109–10; agrarian populism,
120

Alfau-Durán, Vetilio, 16

Álvarez-Curbelo, Silvia, 122

Amaru, Túpac, 83

Amparos Reales, 13

Anderson, Benedict, 63, 102

Annexationists, 46, 56–57, 84, 87,
88, 89

Anthropology: and Balaguer, 26,
58, 61–62

Antiannexation movement, 89

Anti-Trujillo movement, 27–28

Antoine, Jacques, 69

Báez, Buenaventura, 51, 88

Balaguer, Joaquín: and historiography, 9; and race relations, 26, 32,
53, 58, 140 (n. 73); and colonial
period, 26–27, 28, 60; on racial
composition, 26–27, 32, 58–62,
65; and tragic visions, 28, 31, 124;
and anti-Haitian discourse, 40,
53

Barbarism: and civilization, 22,
82–84, 104, 109–10, 114–15; and
Massacre of 1937, 91; and campesinos, 103–4; and Bosch, 109

Bellegarde, Dantès, 69

Berman, Marshall, 96, 102–3

Blacks: and identity, 36, 45–46, 94,
95, 96; and Cuban identity, 37;
and criollo societies, 38; Haitians
as, 39, 41; and Sánchez-Valverde,
41, 42, 43–44, 45; and Bonó, 48,
50; and Balaguer, 58–59, 61; and
economics, 63; and Dominican
national identity, 64, 65, 103; and
Price-Mars, 69, 70, 71–72, 73,
75, 82, 90, 92, 94, 96; and Peña-
Batlle, 75; and Boyer, 81; and bar-

barism, 82, 83; and race wars, 83–84; and Haiti/Dominican Republic relations, 87–88, 90; and Duvalier, 96. *See also* African population; Race relations; Racial composition; Racial mixing

Blanco, Tomás, 60, 95

Blue Party, 127

Bobadilla, Francisco de, 11, 18

Bolívar, Simón, 84

Bonó, Pedro Francisco: and historiography, 9; and saga of people, 12–15, 23; and economics, 13, 14, 15, 47, 137 (n. 33); and racial mixing, 14, 32; and race relations, 14, 49–51; and politics, 47, 50, 58, 85; and Haitian Domination, 47–48, 51, 52, 81; and Bosch, 115

Borges, Jorge Luis, 67, 71, 76, 81, 93, 97, 102

Bosch, Juan: and historiography, 9, 30–31, 99, 100, 102, 122–32, 176 (n. 89), 177 (n. 97); and García, 19; literary work of, 27, 99–100, 102, 104–18, 120, 121, 132, 171 (n. 34); in exile, 27, 100–101, 118, 119, 122; and tragic visions, 27–29, 31, 32, 124, 125, 129, 132; and modernization, 28, 30, 32, 100–101, 105, 106, 109, 110–11, 113, 114–18, 121, 122–23, 129, 131, 132, 167–68 (n. 8); and politics, 30, 99, 100, 101, 102, 104, 105, 108, 114, 115–20, 122–23, 173 (n. 55); and memory, 98–102, 105, 108, 113, 132; and peñas, 104, 170 (n. 22); and campesinos, 104–5, 107, 108, 110, 111, 113–18, 119, 120, 121, 122, 130,

132, 170 (n. 24), 179 (n. 124); and Price-Mars, 157 (n. 11)

Bourbon reforms, 127

Bovarism, 69, 87, 92

Boyer, Jean-Pierre, 46, 48, 50, 80–81, 83, 85

Braceros, 52–53, 64

Braudel, Fernand, 15

Brazil, 37

Buendía, Aureliano, 99

Calvino, Italo, 119

Campesinos: and Bonó, 14–15, 52, 115; and Balaguer, 26, 27, 61; myth of white campesinos, 26, 61, 95; and Santo Domingo, 39; and Boyer, 46; and Haitian rule, 51; and border zones, 53; resistance to U.S. occupation, 68–69; and identity, 69; exploitation of, 70; and Haitian elite, 83; and barbarism, 103–4; and Bosch, 104–5, 107, 108, 110, 111, 113–18, 119, 120, 121, 122, 130, 132, 170 (n. 24), 179 (n. 124); and State, 111; population of, 154 (n. 110). *See also* Rural masses

Caonabo, Cacique, 16

Capitalism: Peña-Batlle on, 24, 54; Bosch on, 28, 32, 105, 115, 127–28, 129, 130; and migration, 66

Caribbean: and race relations, 23, 82; and foreign occupations, 31; identity in, 35–38, 94–95; and racial composition, 49; Negritude movement in, 68; effect of Haitian Revolution, 75; political programs in, 120; Bosch on, 123

Carr, Edward Hallett, 3, 4

Cassá, Roberto, 15, 27, 57, 119, 138
(n. 62)
Caste system: Peña-Batlle on, 25;
Bosch on, 28–29, 124; Price-
Mars on, 70; and caste war, 83,
84. *See also* Social hierarchy
Catholic Church: García on, 19; and
Balaguer, 27; and Dominican
Republic, 39; and Boyer, 46;
Peña-Batlle on, 54
Cattle ranchers: and Bonó, 13; and
Santo Domingo, 39; and Boyer, 46
Caudillismo, 24, 46, 125
Cédulas, 13
Charles III (king of Spain), 21
Chevalier, Diyetta, 126
Christianity: and civilization, 60,
82–83. *See also* Catholic Church
Cimarronaje, 73, 157 (n. 25)
Civilization: and García, 17, 18, 19,
22; and Spain, 17, 56; and barba-
rism, 22, 82–84, 104, 109–10,
114–15; and nation-State, 23, 84;
and Haiti's population, 60; and
Price-Mars, 71; and whiteness,
82; and Haitian Revolution, 84;
and Duvalier, 96; of campesinos,
104; and oral tradition, 106; and
Bosch, 109, 114, 121, 130, 132;
and writing, 118; and power, 121;
and State, 121–22
Coiscou-Henríquez, Máximo, 158
(n. 28)
Colonial period: Sánchez-Valverde
on, 9–12; Bonó on, 12–15, 48–
49, 54; García on, 16, 22; and
identity, 21–22, 138–39 (n. 65);
Peña-Batlle on, 25, 26, 54–55;
Balaguer on, 26–27, 28, 60;

Bosch on, 28–29, 123, 126–27,
132; and Caribbean, 35; and slav-
ery, 38; and race relations, 49,
138 (n. 65); and
Haiti/Dominican Republic rela-
tions, 64, 126; Price-Mars on,
67–68, 72, 76–77
Columbus, Christopher, 17
Comegente, 83–84, 161 (n. 64)
Comte, Auguste, 2
Conchoprimismo, 103
Cordero-Michel, Emilio, 21, 138
(n. 62)
Costa Rica, 101, 127, 128, 129, 130
Criollo class: and Puerto Rico, 12,
70; and Cuba, 12, 127–28
Criollo identity: and Sánchez-
Valverde, 10, 12, 41
Criollo slaves: and identity, 36, 37
Criollo societies: reconceptualiza-
tion of, 37; inclusion of blacks
and mulattoes in, 38
Croce, Benedetto, 73
Cuba: and criollo class, 12, 127–28;
and identity, 37; fear of slave
insurrection in, 84; and slavery,
88; and Bosch, 101, 127–28, 129,
130; Dominican emigration to,
153 (n. 108)
Cuban Revolution, 30

De Certeau, Michel, 1, 2, 32, 119
Del Rosario-Pérez, Ángel, 93
Demography: and racial composition, 36, 60; and formation of
Dominican nation, 58, 60, 153–
54 (n. 108); and Haiti/Domini-
can Republic relations, 66, 72,
91, 92

Dépestre, René, 94, 95

Dessalines, Jean-Jacques, 21, 78–80

Devastations of 1605–6, 11, 12, 19–20, 38, 41

Díaz-Quiñones, Arcadio, 60, 95

Divine history, 2

Dominican culture: African influences on, 59; and indigenous population, 152 (n. 97). *See also* Spanish culture

Dominicanization, 57

Dominican pessimism, 23, 24, 103–4

Dominican Republic: historical narratives of, 1–2; and identity, 5, 38–40, 96–97; and tragic visions, 8–12; and saga of people, 12–15; U.S. occupation of, 24, 52, 104, 125, 131; national discourse of, 40; formation of, 46, 47–48, 56, 58, 86; and Bonó, 46, 48; as oldest Christian country in America, 56; and Peña-Batlle, 56, 58; underdevelopment of, 103. *See also* Haiti/Dominican Republic relations; Santo Domingo; Trujillo, Rafael L.

Dominican Revolutionary Party, 101, 119

Dorra, Raúl, 1, 5

Duarte, Juan Pablo, 87

Duchesne-Winter, Juan, 172 (n. 39)

Duvalier, Jean-Claude, 96, 166 (n. 114)

Eastern Europe, 66

Economics: and Sánchez-Valverde, 9, 10, 11, 40–45, 58; and Bonó, 13, 14, 15, 47, 137 (n. 33); and García, 18, 19, 20, 21; and State, 23; and Balaguer, 26, 59, 60; and tragic visions, 27; and Bosch, 29, 100, 101, 122, 128, 130–31; and slaves, 35, 36–37, 49, 130; and identity, 35–36; and Afro-American culture, 36; and Saint-Domingue, 39; and nation formation, 62–63; and Haiti/Dominican Republic relations, 66, 91, 92; exploitation of masses, 70; and Price-Mars, 70, 76; and recession in Dominican Republic, 98–99; and Haitian Domination, 160 (n. 53)

Education, 2, 71

Elite. *See* Haitian elite; Hispano-Dominican elite

Emigration: of Hispano-Dominican elite, 11, 26, 30, 31, 41, 44, 46, 60, 61, 126; from Europe, 23, 50; of Haiti's population, 39, 59, 60, 64, 65, 66, 91–92; Dominican emigration to Cuba, 153 (n. 108)

England, 38, 86

Enlightenment, 2, 13, 22

Enriquillo, Cacique, 17

Ethnology: and Price-Mars, 67, 68, 71, 76–78; and Bosch, 113, 114

Europe: and modernization, 28, 32, 94–95; and annexation, 46; and Dominican Republic's mulattoism, 50; national regeneration through contact with, 50, 149–50 (n. 61); fascism in, 57, 58, 64; and nation formation, 63; and "others," 66; and Haitian elite, 69; and whiteness, 82; and civilization, 83

Facts: and scientific method, 2; and historiography, 2, 3, 32, 33; and truth, 2, 114; and poetics of history, 4; analysis of, 6

Fanon, Frantz, 95

Fascism: in Europe, 57, 58, 64

Fatalism, 31

Female slaves, 42

Fennema, Meindert, 58

Ferrand (military officer), 21, 78–79

Fictional texts: and historiography, 5, 8, 32; and Price-Mars, 67; and literary work of Bosch, 99–100, 102, 104–18, 120, 121, 132, 171 (n. 34); and politics, 119

Flores-Galindo, Alberto, 32, 35

Folklore, 71

Foreign occupations: Bosch on, 28, 30, 31, 123–24, 125

Foucault, Michel, 118

France: and Spain, 20–21, 38, 77; and colonial period, 25, 38–39, 48; cession of Santo Domingo to, 26, 60, 61, 76; penetration of Hispaniola, 29, 53–54; Bosch on, 30; and Haiti/Dominican Republic relations, 38–39, 77, 86, 87, 130; Sánchez-Valverde on, 40–41, 45; Peña-Batlle on, 54; Haiti's independence from, 79, 80

Francoist Spain: literature of, 5

Freedmen/freedwomen: and power, 22; and identity, 36; Sánchez-Valverde on, 42; and Boyer's smallholdings distribution, 46; and Haiti, 51, 74; Peña-Batlle on, 55; and Haitian Domination, 63

Freyre, Gilberto, 68

Fuentes, Carlos, 119

García, José Gabriel: and historiography, 9; and Ranke, 15; and documentalist tradition, 15–16; moral judgments of, 16–20; and civilization, 17, 18, 19, 22; and Spanish Conquest, 17–18, 31; on Haitian Revolution, 21, 76, 83, 138 (n. 62)

García-Canclini, Néstor, 170 (n. 26)

García-Cuevas, Eugenio de J., 115, 171–72 (n. 37)

Geertz, Clifford, 7

Geffrard, Nicholas Fabre, 88, 89, 90

Gelpí, Juan, 33

Geographic factors: Sánchez-Valverde on, 41; and colonial period, 76–77; and Haiti/Dominican Republic relations, 90

Gold: and colonial period, 77

González, Raymundo, 32, 85

Governing classes: and Bosch, 30, 31

Gramsci, Antonio, 65

Guacanagarí, Cacique, 17

Guerra, Ramiro, 95

Haiti: and identity, 5, 96–97; García on, 17, 21; anti-Haitian discourse, 23–24, 27, 38, 39–40, 51, 53, 57, 64–65, 93, 125; Peña-Batlle on, 24, 25, 29, 55, 56; Balaguer on, 26–27; Bosch on, 29, 126, 130, 178 (n. 103); and slavery, 37, 38, 39, 73–74, 88; as "other," 38–40, 45, 65, 66, 84; and racial composition, 48, 58–

59; Bonó on, 49–51, 64; and Price-Mars, 68, 71, 72, 90; independence of, 75, 78, 79; and era of questions of limits, 90–92. *See also* Haiti/Dominican Republic relations; Saint-Domingue

Haitian culture: as extension of African culture, 39; Peña-Batlle on, 55; Balaguer on, 58–59, 60; Price-Mars on, 68

Haitian Domination: Peña-Batlle on, 25, 54, 56; as occupation, 46; and Bonó, 47–48, 51, 52, 81; and Dominican population, 60, 63, 154 (n. 110); and Boyer, 80–81; and Price-Mars, 80–82, 85–86; and Bosch, 125, 126, 130

Haitian elite: and race relations, 22; and Price-Mars, 69, 70–71, 80; and African culture, 83

Haitian Revolution: García on, 21, 76, 83, 138 (n. 62); and race relations, 22, 45–46, 139 (n. 66); Peña-Batlle on, 25, 55, 56, 74–75; Bosch on, 30, 31, 126, 130; and Haiti/Dominican Republic relations, 39, 76; and Dominican demography, 60, 153 (n. 108); Price-Mars on, 74–79

Haitians: blacks as, 39, 41; migration to Dominican Republic, 39, 59, 60, 64, 65, 66, 91–92; as labor sector in Dominican sugar industry, 52–53, 59, 64, 65, 91–92; and masks, 52–53, 66; as primitive, 53, 59, 60, 63; massacre of, 57, 65, 91–92, 164 (n. 92); as "other," 63, 64

Haiti/Dominican Republic relations: and border issues, 21, 39, 53, 54, 57, 59, 64, 65, 77, 90–92; Bosch on, 30; and France, 38–39, 77, 86, 87, 130; and Haitian Revolution, 39, 76; and formation of Dominican Republic, 46–47, 48; and indivisibility of island, 48, 53, 72, 79, 81, 85–90; Bonó on, 49–51; and nationalism, 53, 57–58, 64, 65, 178 (n. 103); and Spanish culture, 54, 56, 59; and Trujillo, 57; and colonial period, 64, 126; and demography, 66, 72, 91, 92; and Price-Mars, 69, 71, 76, 85–93, 97; and Bovarism, 69, 87, 92; and human freedom, 73, 78–80, 88; and racial composition, 76–78, 82; and Haitian Domination, 80–82; and civilization vs. barbarism, 82–83; and race relations, 87–88; and War of Restoration, 89–90; and identity, 96–97. *See also* Haitian Domination

Hegel, Georg W. F., 2

Henríquez-Ureña, Pedro, 94

Herzberger, David K., 5, 98, 108–9

Heureaux, Ulises (Lilís), 127, 131

Hispanicism, 82, 93, 94, 95

Hispaniola: historiography of, 5; and Spanish Conquest, 10; García on, 17, 20; and France, 38–39; and slavery, 49; identity in, 65; unification of, 72; Price-Mars on, 76, 79, 85, 86, 89; and gold, 77. *See also* Dominican Republic; Haiti

Hispano-Dominican elite:
impoverishment of, 11, 12, 42;
emigration of, 11, 26, 30, 31, 41,
44, 46, 60, 61, 126; Sánchez-
Valverde on, 11, 41–42, 44, 45;
and racial mixing, 12, 44, 45; and
civilization, 23; and Dominican
pessimism, 24; Balaguer on, 26–
27, 60–61; Bosch on, 29; and
identity, 35; mulattoization of,
44; and Haitian Domination, 46;
and national identity, 65
Hispanophilia, 57
Historical interpretation, 3, 4
Historical narratives: as canon, 1–
2, 32, 33; and poetics of history,
4–7; analysis of facts in, 6; errors
in, 6; and politics, 7; and Bosch,
102
Historiography: and religious discourse, 2; and facts, 2, 3, 32, 33;
and power, 3–4, 6, 32, 33; and fictional texts, 5, 8, 32; and Bosch,
9, 30–31, 99, 100, 102, 122–32,
176 (n. 89), 177 (n. 97); and real/
discourse relationship, 32; and
totems, 33; and utopias, 33–34;
and poetics of time, 67; and
Price-Mars, 67, 68, 72–73, 76,
87, 162 (n. 74)
Hostos, Eugenio María de, 101, 127,
168 (n. 10)
Humanism: and Price-Mars, 73
Hurbon, Laënnec, 22, 83, 96
Hutton, Patrick H., 6, 106, 108, 171
(n. 31)

Identity: and power, 5, 97; and historical narratives, 6; criollo iden-

tity, 10, 12, 41; Haitian Revolution's effect on, 21–22, 138–39
(n. 65); Peña-Batlle on, 25; and
historiography, 33; and Hispano-
Dominican elite, 35; of slaves, 35,
36, 37, 74; in Caribbean, 35–38,
94–95; and Bonó, 52; in Hispaniola, 65; and "others," 66,
94–95; and campesinos, 69; and
Price-Mars, 70, 73, 93–94; and
Haiti/Dominican Republic relations, 90; and exclusivism, 94.
See also National identity
Imagined communities: and historiography, 33; and Haitians, 52,
91; nation-States as, 63, 70, 103–
4; and slaves, 73; and racial composition, 78; and race wars, 84;
and Bosch, 102
Imperialism: of Haiti, 27, 59, 60,
85; Bosch on, 31, 131; Price-Mars
on, 72; and Haiti/Dominican
Republic relations, 90
Indigenism, 18, 43, 68, 95–96
Indigenous population: decline in,
11, 12, 13, 20, 26, 41, 60; García
on, 16–17, 18, 19, 20; and civilization, 23; Sánchez-Valverde on,
43, 44, 152 (n. 97); Bonó on, 47;
contributions of, 68; and Dominican culture, 152 (n. 97)
Individualism, 24
Irizarri, Pedro, 37–38

Jamaica, 52
Jimenes-Grullón, Juan Isidro, 27–
28, 119, 121

Kahler, Erich, 72

Latin America: and race relations, 23, 82, 84; and identity, 94–95; political programs in, 120; national regeneration through contact with Europe, 149–50 (n. 61)

Le Goff, Jacques, 11

Letrados: and Haitian Revolution, 22; and tragic vision, 23, 24; and utopias, 24; and Bonó, 51–52, 115; and rural masses, 65, 120–21; and subaltern sectors, 68; and African culture, 69; and civilization, 82, 84–85; and Dominican pessimism, 103–4; and politics, 117; and modernization, 120

Liberalism: and García, 16, 17, 18, 19, 20; and Bonó, 47, 52

Lienhard, Martin, 64

Literature. *See* Fictional texts

Loewenthal, Troetje, 58

Macandal, François, 83

Margins: and barbarism, 22; and utopias, 33; and alternative views of world, 64; and identity, 95

Mariátegui, José Carlos, 68, 94

Maroons, 37, 73

Martí, José, 38, 85

Martínez-Fernández, Luis, 161

Marx, Karl, 2, 75, 96

Marxism: and Bosch, 30; and nation formation, 62–63

Masks: and Haitians, 52–53, 66

Massacre of 1937, 57, 65, 91–92, 164 (n. 92)

Mateo, Andrés L., 3, 8, 23, 93, 96

Meanings: and process of symbolization, 4; of fiction compared

with historiography, 5; reading's role in, 6–7; and archetypes of fiction, 8

Memory: and power, 3; and politics of representation, 6, 108–9; and Balaguer, 27; and Price-Mars, 73–74; and Bosch, 98–102, 105, 108, 113, 132; and orality and writing, 106

Mestizaje: complexity of, 36; and indigenous population, 43; and Bonó, 52; and Balaguer, 61; Price-Mars on, 72, 77

Mexico: colonial history of, 12

Michelet, Jules, 13, 15

Migration from Europe: and whitening of population, 23, 50

Mintz, Sidney, 39

Modernization: and tragic visions, 27; and Bosch, 28, 30, 32, 100–101, 105, 109, 110–11, 113, 114–17, 121, 122–23, 129, 131, 132, 167–68 (n. 8); and Europe, 28, 32, 94–95; and Bonó, 50, 115; and race relations, 84; and Berman, 102–3; and writing, 104; and rural masses, 106; and power, 110–12; and letrados, 120; definition of, 170 (n. 26)

Monte y Tejada, Antonio del, 138 (n. 62)

Moore, Barrington, 75

Moral judgments: of Bonó, 14, 48, 49; of García, 16–20; of Sánchez-Valverde, 42, 45; of Price-Mars, 70–71

Mörner, Magnus, 83

Mulattoes: and identity, 36; and criollo societies, 38; and

nationality, 38; and Sánchez-
Valverde, 42, 43, 44; Dominican
Republic compared with Haiti,
49; and Bonó, 49, 50; and Gallo-
Latin cultural tradition, 69; and
Price-Mars, 74; and Dominican
national identity, 103
Mulattoism, 50

National discourse, 40
National identity: and García, 22;
and Balaguer, 26, 61–62; and
Dominican whiteness, 39, 48,
60–61, 77–78, 87, 90; and
Spanish culture, 39, 64, 65, 82,
96, 125; and Bonó, 47; and Price-
Mars, 68; and power, 97
Nationalism: and García, 16–17, 18,
20, 22; and Peña-Batlle, 25, 53,
56, 57, 58, 65; and Balaguer, 26,
53, 58, 59, 65; and tragic visions,
27; and historiography, 33; and
Bonó, 47, 50, 66; and Haiti/
Dominican Republic relations,
53, 57–58, 64, 65, 178 (n. 103);
elements of, 62; and Price-Mars,
69–70, 72, 73; and Duarte, 87;
and Bosch, 102, 120, 126; in
Cuba, 127
National liberation movement,
31
National sovereignty, 23, 46
Nation-State: and progress, 2; and
historiography, 3, 5; and Bonó,
13; and García, 16; and civilization, 23, 84; and tragic visions,
27; elements for emergence of,
62; and "other," 63, 64; as imaginary community, 63, 70, 103–4;

and Price-Mars, 72; and Bosch,
102, 122. *See also* State
Natural sciences, 2
Negritude, 68, 93–96
Nolasco, Sócrates, 93

Ogé, Vincent, 74
Ong, Walter, 105
Orality: and Price-Mars, 73; and
writing, 105–6, 108, 115, 171
(n. 31), 172 (n. 40); and rural
masses, 106, 115; and Bosch,
106–8, 113, 114, 171–72 (n. 37)
Ortiz, Fernando, 68
Ovando, Nicolás de, 11, 18–19

Peaceful invasion theory, 64
Pedreira, Antonio S., 95
Peña-Batlle, Manuel Arturo: and
historiography, 9; on Haiti, 24,
25, 29, 55, 56; and race relations,
24, 32, 53, 58; and tragic vision,
24–25, 28, 31, 124; on slavery, 25,
54, 74; on Haitian Revolution,
25, 55, 56, 74–75; and anti-
Haitian discourse, 40, 53, 73, 158
(n. 28); and voodoo, 82
Pérez-Memén, Fernando, 160
(n. 54)
Peru: colonial history of, 12
Pezuela, Juan de la, 38
Piracy, 20
Politics: and writing, 4, 5, 106; and
historical narratives, 7; García
on, 18, 20; Balaguer on, 26; and
Bosch, 30, 99, 100, 101, 102,
104, 105, 108, 114, 115–20, 122–
23, 173 (n. 55); and Bonó, 47, 50,
58, 85; and Price-Mars, 70–71,

86–87, 90; and race relations, 84; and fictional texts, 119

Politics of representation: and memory, 6, 108–9

Popular culture, 64, 68, 71, 84

Population decline: and indigenous population, 11, 12, 13, 20, 26, 41, 60; and Hispano-Dominican elite, 11, 26, 30, 31, 41, 44, 46, 61, 126; Balaguer on, 26, 60; Bosch on, 29, 30; and Devastations of 1605–6, 41; Price-Mars on, 77

Positive spirit, 2

Power: of State, 3, 112, 114, 131, 173 (n. 55); and historiography, 3–4, 6, 32, 33; and identity, 5, 97; and writing, 5, 117–18; and García, 18; and freedmen, 22; and Dominican pessimism, 24; and Dominican rebels, 46; and masks of Haitians, 53; and Haitian government leaders, 96; and modernization, 110–12; and Bosch, 115–18, 119, 121; and letrados, 120, 121; and civilization, 121

Premodernity, 100, 103, 105, 109, 110, 114, 170–71 (n. 26)

Price-Mars, Jean: and historiography, 67, 68, 72–73, 76, 87, 162 (n. 74); on colonial period, 67–68, 72, 76–77; and African culture, 68, 69, 70, 74, 78; and Haiti/Dominican Republic relations, 69, 71, 76, 85–93, 97; and nation-State, 72; on Haitian Revolution, 74–79; on Hispaniola, 76, 79, 85, 86, 89; and Haitian Domination, 80–82, 85–86; Dominican critics of, 93–94; and

Duvalier, 96, 166 (n. 114); and Bosch, 157 (n. 11)

Process of symbolization: and meanings, 4

Profane history, 2

Progress: and historiography, 2; García's belief in, 17; and civilization, 23, 84

Progressive romanticism: and Bonó, 12–13

Protestant Reformation, 24, 54

Psychologism: and Bosch, 124–25

Puerto Rico: and criollo class, 12, 70; and slavery, 37–38, 88; and Dominican sugar industry, 52; myth of white campesino, 61; Dominican migration to, 66; and white campesino, 95

Race relations: and Bonó, 14, 49–51; and Haitian Revolution, 22, 45–46, 139 (n. 66); and civilization, 23, 84; and anti-Haitian discourse, 23–24; and Peña-Batlle, 24, 32, 53, 58; and Balaguer, 26, 32, 53, 58, 140 (n. 73); and Toussaint L'Ouverture, 38; and colonial period, 49, 138 (n. 65); and Price-Mars, 70; and Haiti/Dominican Republic relations, 87–88

Racial composition: and civilization, 23; Peña-Batlle on, 24, 32; Balaguer on, 26–27, 32, 58–62, 65; Bonó on, 32, 47, 48; Sánchez-Valverde on, 43, 47; and Haiti, 48, 58–59; of Haitian elite, 70; and Haiti/Dominican Republic relations, 76–78, 82

Racial mixing: and Sánchez-
Valverde, 12, 43–44; and Bonó,
14, 32; and Balaguer, 26, 61; and
Bosch, 29, 32; and social hier-
archy, 36. *See also* Mestizaje
Rama, Ángel, 69, 106, 115
Ramírez y Fuenleal, Sebastián, 19
Ramos, Julio, 84–85, 115, 118
Ranke, Leopold von, 2, 16–17
Reading: and meanings, 6–7
Religious discourse: and histo-
riography, 2
Repartimientos, 11
Rhetorical functions: and facts, 6
Rice, Anne, 8, 62
Rights of man: and Bonó, 48
Rodríguez-Demorizi, Emilio, 16,
93, 165 (n. 101)
Rosario-Candelier, Bruno, 107
Rural masses: domestication of, 23;
insurrectionary proclivities of,
24; and letrados, 65, 120–21; as
basis for New World societies,
69–70; and Hispanicism, 95;
and Dominican pessimism, 103;
as internal "others," 103–4, 109,
169 (n. 19); and oral traditions,
106, 115; potential violence of,
112; and civilization, 121. *See also*
Campesinos
Russia, 103

Sabana Larga, battle of, 88
Saco, José Antonio, 37
Saga of the people: and Bonó, 12–
15, 23
Said, Edward W., 109
Saint-Domingue: slavery compared
with Santo Domingo, 9–10, 11,

12, 13–14, 48, 76–77; Sánchez-
Valverde on, 9–10, 11, 12, 40,
41–42, 45; Bonó on, 13; García
on, 20; Peña-Batlle on, 24–25;
Bosch on, 29–30; and eco-
nomics, 39; Price-Mars on, 92–
93. *See also* Haiti
Sánchez-Valverde, Antonio: and
economics, 9, 10, 11, 40–45, 58;
on Saint-Domingue, 9–10, 11,
12, 40, 41–42, 45; on Santo
Domingo, 9–11, 23, 42–43, 135
(n. 5); on indigenous population,
43, 44, 152 (n. 97); and Dominican sugar industry, 52
Santana, Pedro, 46, 51, 88
Santo Domingo: Spain's neglect of,
9, 11, 12, 29, 41, 42, 61, 126; slavery compared with Saint-
Domingue, 9–10, 11, 12, 13–14,
48, 76–77; Sánchez-Valverde on,
9–11, 23, 42–43, 135 (n. 5); Bonó
on, 13–14; García on, 20–21; Balaguer on, 26, 60, 61; cession to
France, 26, 60, 61, 76; Bosch on,
28–29, 126–27, 130; and economics, 39; occupation by Haitian armies, 46; annexation to
Spain, 46, 51, 57, 88, 125; Peña-
Batlle on, 54; Spain's influence
on, 55; independence of, 56, 86,
87; Price-Mars on, 77–78. *See
also* Dominican Republic
Savagery, 82
Scientific paradigm, 2
Secularization of learning, 2
Skin color: and identity, 35–36, 95
Slave revolt refugees, 25
Slaves and slavery: comparison of

Saint-Domingue and Santo
Domingo, 9–10, 11, 12, 13–14,
48, 76–77; Bonó on, 13, 15, 48,
52; Tannenbaum's theories on,
14; Peña-Batlle on, 25, 54, 74;
and identity, 35, 36, 37, 74; and
economics, 35, 36–37, 49, 130;
and Haiti, 37, 38, 39, 73–74, 88;
Sánchez-Valverde on, 41, 42, 45;
and slave insurrection, 45, 83–
84; abolition of slavery, 46, 48,
52, 75, 81, 88; Balaguer on, 61;
Price-Mars on, 72, 73–74, 81, 86,
90. See also Haitian Revolution
Slave trade: Balaguer on, 26; and
Afro-American culture, 36; and
colonial system, 37; eradication
movements, 38; Peña-Batlle on,
55; and Dominican population,
61
Smallholdings, 46, 52
Smuggling: Sánchez-Valverde on,
11; García on, 19, 21; Peña-Batlle
on, 24, 29; Bosch on, 29
Social authority: and Bosch, 30, 31,
129–30, 131
Social hierarchy: and Peña-Batlle,
25, 54, 56; and Bosch, 29, 122–
23, 124, 129, 130–31, 132; and
economics, 35; and racial mixing,
36; of Haiti, 39; of Santo
Domingo, 39; and Sánchez-
Valverde, 47; of plantation economy, 49; and Balaguer, 59; and
identity, 94; of political parties,
120
Social sedimentation, 15
Sociology, 13, 28, 47, 67, 71, 123
Solano, José: García on, 21

Soviet Union, former, 66
Spain: Francoist Spain, 5; neglect of
Santo Domingo, 9, 11, 12, 29, 41,
42, 61, 126; Sánchez-Valverde
on, 9–10, 40, 41; Bonó on, 14,
47; and García, 16, 19, 20–21;
and France, 20–21, 38, 77; Peña-
Batlle on, 25; Bosch on, 28, 29,
31–32, 130; Santo Domingo
annexed to, 46, 51, 57, 88, 125;
influence on Santo Domingo, 55;
Balaguer on, 61; and gold, 77;
and Haiti/Dominican Republic
relations, 86. See also Colonial
period
Spanish Civil War, 57
Spanish Conquest: Sánchez-
Valverde on, 10; Taínos'
resistance to, 16; García on, 17–
18, 31; Bosch on, 28, 31, 124;
Bonó on, 47
Spanish culture: and Balaguer, 27,
58, 59, 62, 65; and national identity, 39, 64, 65, 82, 96, 125; and
Peña-Batlle, 54, 55–57, 58, 65
State: power of, 3, 112, 114, 131, 173
(n. 55); and identity, 5; García on,
22; and national sovereignty, 23;
and historiography, 33; centralization of, 105; and modernization, 111–12, 129; and civilization, 121–22. See also Nation-
State
Statistical language: and Balaguer,
60
Subaltern sectors: and Bonó, 13, 47;
and utopias, 33; and nationalism,
63; and Price-Mars, 68; and
Haitian Revolution, 75; and iden-

tity, 95; of Dominican Republic, 103. *See also* Rural masses

Subjectivity: of reading, 6, 7

Sugar industry, 49, 52, 59, 64, 65, 128, 129, 130, 131

Symbolization: process of, 4

Symbols: historical narratives as, 6

Taínos: resistance to Conquest, 16

Tannenbaum, Frank, 14

Testimonial narratives, 108, 172 (n. 39)

Time: and historiography, 67

Tobacco, 14, 52, 130

Todorov, Tzvetan, 63, 66

Tortuga: García on, 20; Peña-Batlle on, 29; Bosch on, 29, 142 (n. 101)

Toussaint L'Ouverture, François Dominique: and Dominican support, 21; and race relations, 38; and freedom of Haitian masses, 46; and indivisibility of island, 53; Peña-Batlle on, 74; Price-Mars on, 79; García on, 138 (n. 62)

Trade: García on, 20, 21; Bosch on, 30; and France, 38; and Haiti, 40. *See also* Slave trade

Tragic visions: and historiography, 8–9, 23, 126; and Sánchez-Valverde, 9–12, 23, 44; and Peña-Batlle, 24–25, 28, 31, 124; and reactionary authors, 27; and democratic authors, 27, 141 (n. 89); and Bosch, 27–29, 31, 32, 124, 125, 129, 132; and Balaguer, 28, 31, 124; and utopias, 33–34

Treaty of Basilea (1795), 54, 56, 76

Trujillo, Rafael L.: and historiography and power, 3–4, 5; Peña-Batlle on, 25, 57, 58, 125; and tragic visions, 27; Bosch on, 28, 29, 31, 101, 114, 115, 118, 120, 123–26, 131–32; and anti-Haitian discourse, 40, 53, 57, 64–65, 93, 125; and border issues, 90–92; and Massacre of 1937, 91–92; ideology of, 93; and identity, 96

Truth: and facts, 2, 114; by assertion, 4; and poetics of history, 4; and fiction, 5; and historiography, 32, 33; definition of, 112; and orality, 114

United States: occupation of Dominican Republic, 24, 52, 104, 125, 131; anti-imperialist defiance of, 30; and annexation, 46, 87, 88; Dominican migration to, 66; and "others," 66; occupation of Haiti, 68, 69; and Haiti/Dominican Republic relations, 86; and slavery, 88

Utopias: and identity, 5, 66; and letrados, 24; and historiography, 33–34; and tragic visions, 33–34; and Sánchez-Valverde, 42, 45; and Balaguer, 65; and Haiti/Dominican Republic relations, 92, 93; and Bosch, 101, 102, 132; of campesinos, 104, 117

Venezuela, 128, 130

Vietnam: and United States, 30

Vincent, Sténio, 90

Voodoo: and anti-Haitian discourse, 39, 55; and Balaguer, 58–

59; as religion, 68, 73; as barbarism, 82

War of Restoration, 46, 47, 89, 179 (n. 124)
White, Hayden, 4, 8, 9, 82, 102, 118, 168 (n. 13)
Whiteness: Balaguer on, 26, 60–61; and identity, 36; and Dominican national identity, 39, 48, 60–61, 77–78, 87, 90; and Sánchez-Valverde, 44; Bonó on, 50; and oppressive slave system, 78; and Dessalines, 80; and civilization, 82. *See also* Hispano-Dominican elite; Race relations; Racial composition; Racial mixing

Whitening of population: and migration from Europe, 23, 50; and civilization, 82
Working classes: and Bonó, 14–15
Writing: and politics, 4, 5, 106; and power, 5, 117–18; and modernization, 104; and orality, 105–6, 108, 115, 171 (n. 31), 172 (n. 40); and civilization, 118; and past, 119

Yunén, Rafael E., 62

Zaglul, Jesús M., 64, 93